T0318295

'A timely well-researched contribution on the Indian pharmaceutical industry. Policymakers should take note of the concerns raised in respect of the impact of reforms on industrial development, innovation and access to medicines.'

Dinesh Abrol, Institute for Studies in
Industrial Development, New Delhi

'India's pharmaceutical industry is widely acknowledged as a success story but a major weakness is the import dependence on one country, China. Attracting our attention to this aspect which has important policy implications is one of the important merits of the book.'

Sudip Chaudhuri, Indian Institute
of Management Calcutta

# Pharmaceutical Industry and Public Policy in Post-Reform India

This book examines the impact of economic reforms in India on the pharmaceutical industry and access to medicines. It traces the changing production and trade pattern of the industry, research and development (R&D) preferences and strategies of Indian pharmaceutical firms, the patent system, pricing policy measures and their shortcomings. It also analyses the public health financing system in India driven largely by out-of-pocket expenditure – about 60 per cent – and characterised by a very high share of medicines in total health expenditure.

A masterful insight into a topical area, the work will be indispensable to those working in the pharmaceutical industry and on public policy. It will be of interest to researchers, scholars, students, and policy-makers of economics, industrial policy, public policy, intellectual property rights and health financing.

**Reji K. Joseph** is Assistant Professor at the Centre for International Politics, Central University of Gujarat, India.

# Critical Political Economy of South Asia
Series editors: C. P. Chandrasekhar and Jayati Ghosh,
both at the *Centre for Economic Studies and Planning,
Jawaharlal Nehru University, New Delhi, India*

At a time when countries of the South Asian region are in a state of flux, reflected in far-reaching economic, political and social changes, this series aims to showcase critical analyses of some of the central questions relating to the direction and implications of those changes. Volumes in the series focus on economic issues and integrate these with incisive insights into historical, political and social contexts. Drawing on work by established scholars as well as younger researchers, they examine different aspects of political economy that are essential for understanding the present and have an important bearing on the future. The series will provide fresh analytical perspectives and empirical assessments that will be useful for students, researchers, policy makers and concerned citizens.

The first books in the series cover themes such as the economic impact of new regimes of intellectual property rights, the trajectory of financial development in India, changing patterns of consumption expenditure and trends in poverty, health and human development in India, and land relations. Future volumes will deal with varying facets of economic processes and their consequences for the countries of South Asia.

## Pharmaceutical Industry and Public Policy
## in Post-Reform India
*Reji K. Joseph*

# Pharmaceutical Industry and Public Policy in Post-Reform India

Reji K. Joseph

Routledge
Taylor & Francis Group

LONDON AND NEW YORK

First published 2016 by Routledge

2 Park Square, Milton Park, Abingdon, Oxfordshire OX14 4RN
711 Third Avenue, New York, NY 10017

*Routledge is an imprint of the Taylor & Francis Group, an informa business*

First issued in paperback 2017

*British Library Cataloguing-in-Publication Data*
A catalogue record for this book is available from the British Library

*Library of Congress Cataloging-in-Publication Data*
A catalog record has been requested for this book

ISBN: 978-1-138-89842-4 (hbk)
ISBN: 978-0-8153-7599-9 (pbk)

Typeset in Galliard
by Apex CoVantage, LLC

# Contents

# Figures

# Tables

# Foreword

The Indian pharmaceutical industry has made such tremendous strides since the early 1990s that it has acquired the epithet 'the pharmacy of the world'. Not only has the industry thrown a lifeline to millions of suffering people in the developing world, but patients in developed countries are also being offered the option of affordable medicines. The contribution that Indian companies have made towards mitigating the scourge of pandemics like HIV/AIDS, tuberculosis and malaria in several countries in Africa and Asia has been immense. Needless to say, the pharmaceutical industry is among the very few industries in India that have successfully overcome the challenges posed by the globalisation of the Indian economy.

This success story of the Indian pharmaceutical industry has not yet been narrated in a cogent manner. It is for this reason that Dr Reji K. Joseph deserves to be commended. Dr Joseph systematically analyses the developments in the Indian pharmaceutical industry, particularly the multifarious challenges it has had to encounter. The factors that resulted in the strengthening of the industry, especially the policy framework which was made available to it, is dealt with in a very systematic manner in this book.

One of the most salient features of this study is that it sheds light on a hitherto less discussed aspect of the pharmaceutical industry, namely, its engagement in the global markets. The period Dr Joseph has chosen for his study is precisely the one in which the industry started going beyond Indian shores. Over time, the industry has not only increased its exports covering almost all the major therapeutic groups, it has discovered a number of new markets. The changing dynamics of the industry's global engagement has many useful lessons.

The most attractive feature of this book is that it discusses a rather complex set of issues in extremely readable style. I am sure that students of the subject as well as policy makers will benefit greatly from the insights that Dr Joseph presents in his study.

**Biswajit Dhar**
Professor, Centre for Economic Studies and
Planning, Jawaharlal Nehru University

# Acknowledgements

This book is the revised and updated version of a doctoral thesis submitted to Jawaharlal Nehru University (JNU), New Delhi. It was a great privilege for me to pursue my doctoral work at the Centre for Economic Studies and Planning, JNU. I was fortunate to have Professor Jayati Ghosh as my supervisor at the Centre. Her invaluable guidance and support made this work presentable. I am especially grateful to Professor Ghosh for her constructive criticisms and relentless prodding, which allowed me to sharpen my ideas. Despite her busy schedule, she never kept me waiting for her comments. I remember with admiration the comments and edits on the final draft that she offered while she was in Geneva to receive the International Labour Organization's Decent Work Research Prize.

Professor Biswajit Dhar, contributed substantially to my thesis and to this book. He has been contributing to my academic growth since 2007, when I joined the WTO Centre of the Indian Institute of Foreign Trade. I gratefully acknowledge his guidance in overcoming the data problems I faced in studying pharmaceutical exports and imports. My discussions and arguments with him on various issues related to the pharmaceutical industry helped me sharpen the arguments in my thesis. I am thankful to him for introducing me to individuals and groups working on the pharmaceutical industry.

I gratefully remember the late Professor Arjun Sengupta, who encouraged me to join the JNU PhD programme. I was fortunate to work with him at the Centre for Development and Human Rights and at the National Commission for Enterprises in the Unorganised Sector, and to receive his overall guidance as Chairman at the Research and Information System for Developing Countries (RIS, New Delhi).

This work would not have been possible without the support of my wife Smitha Jose. She was very understanding and cooperated unconditionally with me in my struggle to complete this work. She made many sacrifices, especially during the last few years, in order to support our family. I thank her sincerely. I fondly remember the moments when our daughter, Sandra, played with her colour pencils on the draft of my chapters. I thank my parents and siblings for all their support throughout my life, especially during the last phase of my doctoral thesis.

I gratefully acknowledge the guidance of Professor Mohanan Pillai and Professor Indrani Chakraborty, my MPhil supervisors at the Centre for Development Studies (CDS), Thiruvananthapuram, where I conducted research in pharmaceutical industry issues.

I am grateful to Dr Pronab Sen, Country Director of International Growth Centre (IGC) India Central and former Chief Statistician of India, and Dr Vishan Dass, Department of Pharmaceuticals, for their clarifications and guidance relating to data issues, especially in the pharmaceuticals trade.

The encouragement and support extended to me by the academic community at various places was crucial to the completion of this work. I am thankful to Professor Sudip Chaudhuri, Indian Institute of Management Calcutta; Professor Chalapathi Rao, Institute for Studies in Industrial Development (ISID); Professor K. N. Harilal (CDS), Professor Sachin Chaturvedi, RIS; Dr Moushumi Basu, Centre for International Politics, Organization and Disarmament, JNU; Professor Dinesh Abrol, ISID; Dr Santhosh M. R., Tata Institute of Social Sciences; Dr Ravinder Jha, Delhi University; Mr Gopakumar K. M., Third World Network; Dr Ravi Srinivas, RIS; and Dr Priyadarshi Dash, RIS. I thank Mr T. C. James, NIPO/RIS, for taking the trouble of reading my draft and giving his suggestions.

I am grateful to my friends and relatives who encouraged me at different stages of my study. I am thankful to Dr Amit Sengupta, People's Health Movement; Dr Sebastian N., Sikkim University, Gangtok; Dr Salvin Paul (Sikkim University); Dr Sobin George, Institute for Social and Economic Change, Bengaluru; Mr V. K. George, Naandi Foundation; Dr Kishore Jose, Central University of Gujarat; Dr Sony Kunjappan (Central University of Gujarat); Ms Jainy Anish; Dr Poornima Varma, Indian Institute of Management, Ahmedabad; Dr Vinayaraj V. K., Centre for Education and Communication, New Delhi; Dr Uma Purushothaman, Observer Research Foundation; and Mr Tinu Joseph, Centre for the Study of Regional Development, JNU. I am very grateful to all my colleagues and friends at the Central University of Gujarat who have always supported me in my academic endeavours.

I also acknowledge that there are many others who directly or indirectly helped me complete this work. I am thankful to all of them.

# Abbreviations

| | |
|---|---|
| ACTA | Anti-Counterfeiting Trade Agreement |
| ANDA | Abbreviated New Drug Application |
| API | active pharmaceutical ingredient |
| ASEAN | Association of Southeast Asian Nations |
| BCPW | Bengal Chemical and Pharmaceutical Works Ltd |
| BDMA | Bulk Drug Manufacturers' Association (India) |
| BIMSTEC | Bay of Bengal Initiative for Multi-Sectoral Technical and Economic Cooperation |
| BoT | balance of trade |
| BRICS | Brazil, Russia, India, China, and South Africa |
| CAGR | compound annual growth rate |
| CDRI | Central Drug Research Institute |
| CEWG | Consultative Expert Working Group |
| CIPR | Commission on Intellectual Property Rights |
| CIS | Commonwealth of Independent States |
| CL | compulsory licence |
| CMIE | Centre for Monitoring Indian Economy |
| CNS | central nervous system |
| CRAMS | contract research and manufacturing services |
| CRO | contract research organisation |
| CRP | collaborative research project |
| CSIR | Council of Scientific and Industrial Research |
| DCGI | Drug Controller General of India |
| DDPF | Drug Development Promotion Foundation |
| DGCI&S | Directorate General of Commercial Intelligence and Statistics |
| DGEHS | Delhi Government Employee Health Scheme |
| DIPP | Department of Industrial Promotion and Policy |
| DMF | drug master files |

| | |
|---|---|
| DNDi | Drugs for Neglected Diseases Initiative |
| DP | Drug Policy |
| DPCO | Drug Price Control Order |
| DPRP | Drugs and Pharmaceuticals Research Programme |
| DRDO | Defence Research and Development Organisation |
| DSIR | Department of Scientific and Industrial Research |
| DST | Department of Science and Technology |
| EDL | Essential Drug List |
| EMA | European Medicines Agency |
| FDI | foreign direct investment |
| FERA | Foreign Exchange Regulation Act |
| FFS | form-fill-seal |
| FICCI | Federation of Indian Chambers of Commerce and Industry |
| FTA | free trade agreement |
| GATT | General Agreement on Tariffs and Trade |
| GMP | good manufacturing practices |
| GoI | Government of India |
| GoM | Group of Ministers |
| GSK | GlaxoSmithKline |
| GSPA-PHI | Global Strategy and Plan of Action on Public Health, Innovation and Intellectual Property |
| HAL | Hindustan Antibiotics Ltd |
| HLEG | High-Level Expert Group |
| HS | harmonised system |
| IBEF | India Brand Equity Foundation |
| IBSA | India, Brazil and South Africa |
| ICAR | Indian Council for Agricultural Research |
| ICMR | Indian Council of Medical Research |
| IDMA | Indian Drug Manufacturers' Association |
| IDPL | Indian Drugs and Pharmaceuticals Ltd |
| IICT | Indian Institute of Chemical Technology |
| IIFT | Indian Institute of Foreign Trade |
| IIS | Indian Institute of Science |
| IIT | Indian Institute of Technology |
| IP | intellectual property |
| IPAB | Intellectual Property Appellate Board |
| IPR | intellectual property right |
| ISID | Institute for Studies in Industrial Development |
| KAPL | Karnataka Antibiotics and Pharmaceuticals Ltd |
| MAT | moving annual turnover |

| MHRA | Medicines and Healthcare Products Regulatory Agency |
|------|------|
| MMV | Medicines for Malaria Venture |
| MNC | multinational corporation |
| MRP | maximum retail price |
| MRTP | Monopolies and Restrictive Trade Practices |
| NCE | new chemical entity |
| NCL | National Chemical Laboratory |
| NDA | National Drug Authority |
| NDDS | novel drug delivery system |
| NLEM | National List of Essential Medicines |
| NME | new medical entity |
| NMITLI | New Millennium Indian Technology Leadership Initiative |
| NPPA | National Pharmaceutical Pricing Authority |
| NPPP | National Pharmaceutical Pricing Policy |
| NRI | non-resident Indian |
| NSS | National Sample Survey |
| NSTMIS | National Science and Technology Management Information System |
| NWGPL | National Working Group on Patent Laws |
| OECD | Organisation for Economic Co-operation and Development |
| OGL | open general licence |
| OSDD | Open Source Drug Discovery |
| PHFI | Public Health Foundation of India |
| PhRMA | Pharmaceutical Research and Manufacturers of America |
| PPP | public–private partnership |
| PRDSF | Pharmaceutical Research and Development Support Fund |
| PSU | public sector unit |
| R&D | research and development |
| RCA | revealed comparative advantage |
| RDPL | Rajasthan Drugs and Pharmaceuticals Ltd |
| RRL | Regional Research Laboratory |
| S&T | science and technology |
| SAARC | South Asian Association for Regional Cooperation |
| SBIRI | Small Business Innovation Research Initiative |
| SITC | Standard International Trade Classification |
| SLP | special leave petition |
| SME | small and medium enterprises |
| SPIC | SME Pharma Industries Confederation |

| | |
|---|---|
| STG | standard treatment guidelines |
| TB | tuberculosis |
| TNMSC | Tamil Nadu Medical Service Corporation |
| TRIPS | Trade Related Aspects of Intellectual Property Rights |
| UGC | University Grants Commission |
| UN | United Nations |
| UNAIDS | Joint United Nations Programme on HIV/AIDS |
| UNCTAD | United Nations Conference on Trade and Development |
| UNDP | United Nations Development Programme |
| UNICEF | United Nations International Children's Emergency Fund |
| UPA | United Progressive Alliance |
| USFDA | United States Food and Drug Administration |
| USGAO | United States Government Accountability Office |
| USTR | United States Trade Representative |
| WAP | weighted average price |
| WHO | World Health Organization |
| WPI | wholesale price index |
| WTO | World Trade Organization |

# Introduction

## Policy reforms in India's pharmaceuticals sector

The pharmaceutical industry in independent India has received disproportionate attention in academic research as well as in public discourse. The sector has witnessed calibrated government interventions towards building up a successful knowledge-based industry. In the span of three decades from the 1950s through the 1970s, the Indian pharmaceutical industry has grown from its formerly meagre existence, with a low production base, heavy dependence on imports, domination by foreign firms and high prices of drugs, to being one of the largest pharmaceutical industries in the world. Today, the pharmaceutical sector in India ranks 11th in terms of global exports, and its prices are among the lowest in the world.[1] Globally, the industry is the third largest producer of medicines in terms of volume and ranks 14th in the world in terms of value (GoI 2012a).

The direction of growth of the industry has been guided by policy interventions in various spheres. The industrial licensing policy was an instrument for directing the industry towards the production of essential drugs. The public sector and the indigenous private sector were given preference so as to keep the foreign sector at bay. The requirement of the Foreign Exchange Regulation Act (FERA) that foreign equity shares be kept below 40 per cent reduced the control of foreign firms over the Indian pharmaceutical sector. The Patents Act, 1970, eliminated product patents in pharmaceuticals, and also substantially reduced the period of protection compared to the Indian Patents and Design Act, 1911, that enabled Indian companies to engage in reverse engineering. The Monopolies and Restrictive Trade Practices (MRTP) Act, 1969, checked the anti-competitive practices of not only foreign firms but also large Indian firms. The drug policies were geared to balancing the needs of controlling prices and providing sufficient profits to manufacturers so as to maintain their interest in production. Linking the production of formulations to the indigenous production of bulk drugs from the basic stage (ratio parameter)[2] forced Indian firms to acquire technology for indigenous production. The Council of Scientific and Industrial Research (CSIR) set up by the Government of India played an important role in developing the technologies needed for the industry. Indigenous research and development (R&D) efforts have been promoted by providing exemptions from price control for a limited period.

These policy interventions have resulted in the Indian pharmaceutical industry becoming self-reliant in the production of the entire range of formulations and about 70 per cent of bulk drugs.[3] Its products are now priced among the lowest in the world. Hence, the industry plays an important role in the health care systems of a number of countries, especially the developing and least developed countries. When Cipla introduced the triple cocktail of antiretroviral drugs (stavudine + lamivudine + nevirapine) in 2000 at US$350 per person per year, the originator company's price for the drug in developing countries fell from US$10,000 to US$727 (Chaudhuri 2005a). The originator's price came down further as more Indian generic companies began to produce the triple cocktail drug. By the early 1990s, the industry had begun entering the regulated markets of the United States and the European Union through the export of good-quality and low-cost generic drugs.

When the industry reached the threshold level of growth, there came a package of reforms induced by both exogenous and endogenous compulsions. These reforms aimed at the liberalisation of restrictions on the industry as well as the incentivisation of pharmaceutical firms. The Modifications in Drug Policy, 1986, incorporated in 1994, brought the liberalisation measures set forth in the Statement on Industrial Policy, 1991, into the pharmaceutical sector. The Statement on Industrial Policy, issued on 24 July 1991, heralded the era of economic liberalisation of the Indian economy. Sweeping reforms in the pharmaceuticals sector included the liberalisation of restrictions on foreign direct investment (FDI), technology collaborations involving foreign companies, the complete elimination of restrictions on imports, and the abolition of the ratio parameter linking the production of formulations to the indigenous production of bulk drugs. The liberalisation package also contained provisions for the initial relaxation and subsequent elimination of reservations for the public sector industry.

The mid-1990s also witnessed India entering into commitments under the Trade-Related Aspects of Intellectual Property Rights (TRIPS) of the World Trade Organization (WTO) to bring product patents back into the pharmaceuticals sector. India and other developing countries were forced to accept the TRIPS Agreement as part of the single under-taking requirement[4] in the Final Act of the Uruguay Round of trade negotiations. This pact did not allow any country to opt out of agree-ments not suitable to its development requirements. India, like many other developing countries, found itself vulnerable during negotiations under the threat of the Special 301 provisions of the US 1988 Omnibus Trade and Competitiveness Act (Chimni 2010). India was not prepared to change its patent law, but the reform was forced upon the country by external compulsions.

The main economic rationale for granting patents is the incentivisa-tion of innovation. It is argued that, without patent protection, oth-ers may imitate new products without incurring any R&D investment costs, thereby limiting the chances of the innovator recouping his or her investment. Levin *et al.* (1987) show that patents are the most effec-tive means of protecting process and product innovations in the drug industry.[5] They find that process patents are 40 per cent and product patents 51 per cent more effective as a means of protecting returns from industrial innovations in pharmaceuticals as compared to industries as a whole. Product patents were found to be highly effective as a means of preventing duplication only in 5 out of 130 narrowly defined lines of business, and pharmaceuticals were at the top among these 5.[6] Mansfield (1986) finds that around 65 per cent of pharmaceuticals innovations would not have taken place if patent protection were not available.

Historically, however, it has been proved that product patents can benefit a country in terms of innovation only when its industrial capabili-ties have reached a certain level. If product patents alone could result in greater innovation, the Indian pharmaceuticals market would have been flooded with innovations after 1911, which is not the case. Japan, a lead-ing industrialised country, introduced product patents in pharmaceuti-cals only in 1976 (Aoki, Kubo and Yamane 2006). The Netherlands, another advanced country, abolished its 1817 patent law in 1869 in an attempt to industrialise the country (Chang 2003). The desirability of product patents in developing countries was not properly evaluated before the TRIPS Agreement was signed (Chaudhuri 2005b).

India's decision to become a signatory to the TRIPS Agreement resulted in many studies and discussions being conducted on the impact of TRIPS on the Indian pharmaceutical industry. The prime concern was the price of medicines. With product patents in place, patent monop-oly would lead to very high prices of patented medicines, making these medicines unaffordable for a vast majority of the population. Moreover, Indian firms would not be able to produce generics as they had been doing by using alternative processes. As many developing countries were dependent on cheap generics from India to sustain their public health programmes, they too were very concerned about what was likely to happen to the Indian pharmaceuticals industry.[7] The other concern was the impact of TRIPS on R&D in the Indian pharmaceutical sector. A number of studies expressed concern that product patents were not sufficient to incentivise firms to invest in R&D to generate drugs for diseases which are mostly prevalent in developing countries. They pointed out that R&D decisions are made on the basis of commercial considerations, and developing country diseases did not offer an attractive market for pharmaceutical majors (Attaran and Gillespie 2001; CIPR 2002; Dhar and Rao 1993; Keayla 1994).

The introduction of reforms in the pharmaceuticals sector and the signing of the TRIPS Agreement both occurred in the mid-1990s. Both events were expected to have significant impacts on the pharmaceutical industry, yet most of the studies and debates were focused on the latter. There was no adequate discussion of the impacts of abolition of import restrictions on the Indian pharmaceutical industry. Would it adversely impact the balance of trade (BoT)? How would the abandonment of the ratio parameter affect the production of drugs in India? What impact would the liberalisation of foreign investment have on the pharmaceutical industry? This book aims to fill this gap in the literature. Chapter 1 provides an overview of the evolution of the Indian pharmaceutical industry since 1947. It offers detailed information on the scenario that existed in the Indian pharmaceuticals market in 1947, the policy interventions after 1947 that led to the emergence of the pharmaceutical industry in India, and the outcomes of those policy initiatives. The chapter also provides a description of the policy reforms introduced in the pharmaceuticals sector from 1994. A brief analysis of the current scenario of the Indian pharmaceutical industry is also offered.

A few studies have focused on the trade aspect of the Indian pharmaceuticals industry. Chaudhuri (2005b: Chapter 6) studies the prospects and challenges facing the Indian pharmaceuticals sector in the realm of exports. The study covers formulations and bulk drugs separately. But the period of Chaudhuri's study is limited mainly to two years: 1999–2000 and 2001–02. Further, it offers no discussion of imports. Dhar and Gopakumar (2008) conducted an analysis of the performance of the Indian pharmaceutical industry. This study analyses the sector's export performance over a period of 10 years. However, the analysis is confined to selected firms, and no analysis of imports is included. The study by Jha (2007) covers both exports and imports, among other variables, examining both formulations and bulk drugs over a period of 10 years. However, this study too focuses on select firms. Chapter 2 of this volume provides an analysis of exports and imports of pharmaceutical products. It contains a detailed discussion of the various sources of trade data for pharmaceutical products and describes the challenges of obtaining time series trade data for the Indian pharmaceutical industry. The chapter provides an analysis of emerging patterns of trade, as well as discussing how the changing trade pattern is affecting the production structure of the Indian pharmaceutical industry. This chapter also analyses the impact of import liberalisation and the abolition of the ratio parameter on the bulk drug industry in India.

A number of studies have been conducted on R&D in the Indian pharmaceutical industry in the context of the TRIPS Agreement (Abrol, Prajapathi and Singh 2011; Chaudhuri 2005b: Chapter 5, 2007, 2010; Dhar and Gopakumar 2008). The studies by Chaudhuri (2005b, 2007, 2010) and by Dhar and Gopakumar (2008) go into the details of R&D undertaken by Indian firms – new chemical entities, modifications in current molecules, new drug delivery systems, and so on. Chaudhuri also conducts a firm-wise analysis of the R&D pipeline, and finds that R&D efforts are concentrated on global diseases like cancer and cardiovascular diseases. Chaudhuri (2007) analyses the preparedness of the Indian pharmaceutical industry for developing a new chemical entity in-house, revealing the limitations faced by the industry in this regard. Abrol, Prajapathi and Singh (2011) find that R&D investment by foreign firms is concentrated mostly in clinical trials. Chapter 3 of the present book examines the overall R&D trends in the pharmaceutical industry. A firm-wise analysis is offered to explain the changes in these trends. The chapter also covers the limitations of the Indian pharmaceutical industry in developing new chemical entities. It describes the strategies adopted by firms at different levels to overcome these limitations by collaborating with multinational corporations (MNCs), leading to the globalisation of Indian pharmaceutical firms.

Chapter 4 focuses on intellectual property rights (IPRs) and access to medicines. Various other studies have focused on these themes (see Chaudhuri 2005b: Chapters 7 and 8; Dhar and Gopakumar 2008; Gopakumar 2010; Hoen 2009; James 2009; Khor 2012; Love 2007; Watal 2000). Chaudhuri (2005b) and Watal (2000) view the drug price control system in India as a mechanism that might check the rise in drug prices as an outcome of the introduction of product patents in the pharmaceuticals sector. Others explore the access to medicines scenario in the context of the incorporation of TRIPS flexibilities in patents law in

India. Chapter 4 of this book brings out the importance of the price of medicines in the Indian health care system. It analyses important TRIPS flexibilities existing in the Patents Act of India, and examines their outcomes in terms of ensuring competition, thus reducing the price of medicines. The chapter also looks into some of the challenges of exercising TRIPS flexibilities, such as compulsory licensing, due to the increasing collaboration of Indian firms with MNCs.

Any discussion of access to medicines in India cannot be complete without touching upon the drug price control mechanism in the country. The reforms introduced in the pharmaceuticals sector did not directly require liberalising the drug price control system. Yet, the price control system witnessed liberalisation in the form of the adoption of a market-based approach to drug pricing. Selvaraj (2001) and Sengupta *et al.* (2008) have conducted detailed analyses of the effectiveness of the drug price control system in India in checking the rise in drug prices. A new market-based system of price control was introduced in recent years through the National Pharmaceutical Pricing Policy (NPPP) 2012 and the Drug (Price Control) Order (DPCO), 2013. One empirical study on the impact of the new mechanisms exists (ISID-PHFI 2014). No other empirical study on the new system has been conducted, primarily on account of the huge expenses involved in obtaining the market data based on which the new drug price control system operates. Chapter 5 in this volume provides a review of the new drug price control system in India. It offers an analysis of the improvements in the new system over previous drug price control mechanisms. It also provides a critical analysis of the shortcomings of the new system, especially those relating to the transparency and fairness of the ceiling prices arrived at by the National Pharmaceutical Pricing Authority (NPPA), the question of bringing in price competition into the pharmaceutical market, and the limitations of IMS Health's market data, which is used by NPPA for arriving at ceiling prices.

Finally, the Conclusion summarises the major findings of the book and offers the relevant recommendations to policy makers. The bulk drug segment, the backbone of the Indian pharmaceutical industry, is in crisis due to the inflow of cheap bulk drugs and other raw materials from China. Additionally, the bulk drug segment faces severe regulatory hurdles, as it is one of the highly polluting industries. Revival of the bulk drug sector is crucial for sustaining the vibrancy of the Indian pharmaceutical industry in the long run. This calls not only for new technologies that would reduce the number of chemical processes involved in the manufacture of bulk drugs, but also a policy framework that is friendlier towards the small and medium enterprises (SME) sector, which is the major producer of bulk drugs in India. Although the Patents Act of India has incorporated a number of flexibilities provided in the TRIPS Agreement, such as compulsory licensing for the promotion of public health, the private sector pharmaceutical industry has not been forthcoming in exercising these flexibilities. The reluctance of the private sector is not surprising, as its emerging business model includes multinational companies as an integral part of R&D, production and marketing.

Therefore, the public sector pharmaceutical industry in India will have to play an important role in the promotion of public health through the exercise of TRIPS flexibilities. The role of the public sector is also crucial in evolving strategies for the development of new drugs for the treatment of neglected diseases, an area where the private sector lacks interest. In the new scenario, the public sector pharmaceutical industry is becoming an essential component of the strategy to promote public health, and hence its revival has become imperative. While it may be admitted that the drug price control mechanism in India has been quite successful in ensuring reasonable price of medicines, the mechanism contains serious deficiencies. Questions have been raised regarding transparency in the methods used for calculating ceiling prices, and the accuracy of the ceiling prices arrived at. The drug price control system in India needs to facilitate public scrutiny of the effectiveness of the mechanism by making relevant data available to the public.

## Notes

1   Ranking in exports of pharmaceutical products based on the Standard International Trade Classification. Data accessed from United Nations Commodity Trade Statistics Database (UN COMTRADE, Rev. 3), www.comtrade.un.org.
2   The ratio parameter linked the production of finished goods directly with the indigenous production of raw materials. This was required to check the tendency among companies to import raw materials (intermediates and bulk drugs), rather than producing them within India, and process them into finished goods (formulations). The 1978 Drug Policy restricted the value of formulations to five times the value of production of all bulk drugs and intermediates (for details, see M. Pillai 1984).
3   Statistics obtained from Government of India (GoI), Department of Pharmaceuticals, http://pharmaceuticals.gov.in/aboutus.htm (accessed on 1 October 2014).
4   The single undertaking requirement of the Marrakesh Agreement, which established the WTO, meant that membership to WTO is subject to countries accepting all the multilateral agreements of the WTO in a single step. In order to become members of the WTO, developing

countries had no other option but to accept the TRIPS Agreement along with other agreements.

5  The index of effectiveness of patents in the study is based on a seven-point scale, industries where patents are most effective in protecting innovation ranking highest. Industries that scored higher than five points in the index were treated as industries where patents were highly effective. The pharmaceuticals industry ranked highest in terms of the effectiveness of both product and process patents: process patents, 4.9 points; and product patents, 6.5 points.

6  The five industries where product patents were found to be highly effective were: pharmaceuticals, organic chemicals, plastic materials, inorganic chemicals, and steel mill products.

7  Important studies on the impact of TRIPS on the Indian pharmaceutical industry include: Chaudhuri (2005a, 2005b); Dhar and Gopakumar (2003); Lalitha (2002); Scherer and Watal (2001); Sengupta (1998); and Watal (2000).

# Chapter 1

# An overview of the Indian pharmaceutical industry

The history of medical science in India can be traced back to the period of the Vedas. Ayurveda, an indigenous form of medical science practice, has its roots in the *Atharvaveda* (*c.* 1200–1000 BC). The medical classics *Charaka Samhita* and *Sushruta Samhita* (AD 500–600) are both said to derive from the Vedic period (Thakar 2010). Ayurveda faced a setback with the growing prevalence of the Unani system, which was introduced in India by the Muslim rulers. In turn, the Unani system witnessed a decline when the British introduced the allopathic system of medicine in the subcontinent.

The modern pharmaceutical industry in India was pioneered by eminent Indians like P.C. Roy, T.K. Gajjar and Rajmitra B.D. Amin. P.C. Roy established the first Indian-owned drug firm, Bengal Chemicals and Pharmaceutical Works, in 1901 at Calcutta (now Kolkata). T.K. Gajjar and Rajmitra B.D. Amin started Alembic Chemical Works in Baroda (now Vadodara) in 1907. These firms not only faced severe competition from overseas producers, they also had to cope with the prejudice among local people. Smith, Stainstreet & Co. Ltd, one of the earliest pharmaceutical companies to be established with foreign capital in India, started manufacturing drugs in 1918 (Borkar 1983). Most other foreign pharmaceutical firms at that time imported readymade preparations and sold them in the Indian market (GoI 1975; Raman 1989).

In the early stages of the development of the pharmaceutical industry in India, a number of advances in medical treatment occurred around the globe. Louis Pasteur's discovery of pathogenic bacteria as the cause of several infectious diseases led to British scientists travelling to India to study tropical infectious diseases. Such epidemics had been taking a heavy toll of men in the British army. As a result of this interest, four government-sponsored pharmaceutical research institutes were set up: the Haffkine Institute in Bombay (now Mumbai) (established in 1899), the King Institute of Preventive Medicine in Madras (now Chennai) (established 1904), the Central Drug Research Institute at Kasauli (established 1905), and the Pasteur Institute at Coonoor (established 1907).

The pharmaceutical industry in India received a further fillip with the beginning of the First World War. Imports were almost completely cut off during the war period. Hence, the demand for allopathic drugs shot up, facilitating the recognition that indigenous development of the industry was inevitable. Local R&D initiatives were encouraged. As a result, Indian firms were successful in discovering a few drugs that were in high demand at that time. The new compound urea stibamine, synthesised by U. N. Brahmachari, was developed through local R&D. It was highly effective in treating kala-azar, a scourge during those days. The most remarkable success was achieved in the manufacture of vaccines in the following years (GoI 1975). Bengal Immunity was set up in 1919 by leading physicians and scientists of Bengal, including Nilratan Sirkar, K. K. Bose and P. C. Roy. This unit undertook the manufacture of sera and other biological products for the first time in India. However, the industry again faced hurdles after the war.

The resumption of imports after the end of the war affected the growth of the local industry. Yet even in this adverse situation, the industry continued to grow, albeit very slowly until 1939. It began to produce biologicals like sera and vaccines, anaesthetics, and a few simple drugs based on coal-tar distillation such as naphthalene and cresol. The domestic industry contributed as little as 13 per cent of the country's medical requirements in 1939. The Second World War, however, once again placed the domestic pharmaceutical industry in an important position. By 1943, the industry met as much as 70 per cent of domestic medical requirements (GoI 1954).

The Second World War came as a blessing in disguise to the domestic pharmaceutical industry, which began to manufacture a number of drugs based on indigenous raw materials. These were mainly drugs in the category of phytochemicals. Progress was also made in the manufacture of synthetic drugs and biological products. Some units took up the production of synthetic anti-dysentery drugs, anti-leprosy drugs and arsenicals. Formulation activity increased considerably based on imported bulk drugs (GoI 1954).[1]

The post-war period did not see any decline in the demand for drugs. The industry achieved self-sufficiency in the production of sera and vaccines. After the war, the pharmaceuticals sector in the West witnessed rapid technological breakthroughs. The period between 1940 and 1955, particularly, saw a remarkable number of discoveries in the pharmaceutical sciences. The age of 'wonder drugs' was inaugurated with the introduction of a number of new drugs such as sulphonamides, penicillin, streptomycin, tetracycline, and corticosteroids. These advances led to changes in the structure and operation of pharmaceutical firms. Earlier, firms had produced the entire range of medicines required by physicians. But with the emergence of new technologies, they began to specialise in particular product lines, marketing the finished products under brand names. The introduction of new technologies and the emergence of new production systems in the West adversely impacted the situation of Indian firms. The introduction of new chemotherapeutic products and antibiotics led to most products manufactured by Indian firms becoming obsolete (Bagath 1982).

At the time of India's independence, the global pharmaceutical industry was undergoing major transformations in terms of its technology landscape and production systems. The participation of Indian pharmaceutical firms in the development and production of new drugs required not only upgrading their technology capabilities, but also reforming the patent system. The product patent system that existed at the time of independence had become a stumbling block for the development of the indigenous pharmaceutical industry in India. The monopoly rights under the product patent system not only allowed technologically advanced foreign firms to engage in imports rather than producing within India, but also prevented Indian firms from manufacturing patented medicines (GoI 1975). The patents regime existing in India at that time, namely, the Patents and Designs Act, 1911, provided for patent rights for inventions for a period of 14 years (this was increased to 16 years in 1930). The act provided that a person who introduced any manner of new manufacture (Section 1.8) would have exclusive rights to make, sell and use the invention in the country (Section 12.1). The development of an indigenous drug industry in the post-independence period required strong government interventions and support.[2]

## The Indian pharmaceutical industry in the post-independence period

At the time of independence in 1947, the Indian pharmaceutical market was dominated by western MNCs, which controlled 80–90 per cent of the market.[3] These companies also held about 99 per cent of the patents granted for pharmaceutical products in the country. They engaged primarily in imports rather than production within the country for the supply of medicines in India (Greene 2007). The indigenous production of drugs was worth only Rs 100 million in 1947 (Narayana 1984). The exclusive privileges granted to patentees resulted in the lack of availability of medicines in India and exorbitant prices for medicines that were supplied.

A number of cases demonstrate that MNCs were unwilling to supply their patented medicines in India; neither did they allow Indian firms to market these drugs domestically. Beecham introduced ampicillin, a semi-synthetic penicillin, in Europe in the early 1960s. But it was unwilling to supply the drug in India 'except on terms and conditions which were totally unacceptable' (Hamied 1988). A similar case involved propranolol, a cardiac drug, which was developed by Imperial Chemical Industries (ICI) in the mid-1960s (*ibid.*). Many other cases may be cited where MNCs took a long time to launch new drugs in India. Keayla (1994) points out that many life-saving drugs took more than 15 years to reach India, after their introduction in the international market. Those drugs which were made available domestically were priced at abysmally high levels. The report of the US Senate Committee on the Judiciary on administered prices in the drug industry observed:

> India which does grant patents on drugs provides an interesting case example. The prices in India for the broad spectrum antibiotics, aureomycin and achromycin, are among the highest in the world. As a matter of fact, in drugs generally, India ranks among the highest priced nations of the world – a case of an inverse relationship between per capita income and the level of drug prices.
>
> (US Senate 1961: 112)

The government of independent India faced the twin challenges of ensuring the availability as well as affordability of drugs. The strategy adopted in the initial years was to address these challenges with the help of MNCs.

## Initiatives in the initial years after independence

In the initial years of the post-independence period, the policy of industrialisation by way of import substitution was not made applicable to the pharmaceutical industry. Foreign capital was encouraged, because no other alternative to the drug technology held by foreign companies was available (Narayana 1984; S. Singh 1985). The 1948 Industrial Policy Resolution had viewed foreign knowledge and technology as important instruments for the industrialisation of the country. According to the resolution, 'It should be recognised that participation of foreign capital and enterprise, particularly as regards industrial technique and knowledge, will be of value to the rapid industrialisation of the country' (GoI 1948: para. 10). Pharmaceuticals and drugs formed one of the 18 industries recognised by the resolution as industries requiring 'investment of a high degree of technical skill'.

This liberal approach resulted in many foreign pharmaceutical companies forming subsidiaries in India. Most foreign firms established themselves merely as trading concerns, importing finished drugs from abroad and selling them domestically, without establishing manufacturing units in India. The indigenous sector at the time was engaged mainly in the processing and formulation of medicines based on imported fine chemicals and bulk drugs. The indigenous production of several new drugs had not yet commenced (GoI 1975). Realising that the mere encouragement of MNCs would not help address the challenges the country was facing, the government appointed three major committees to study and offer recommendations on the reform of the patent system, reducing import dependence, and building up a strong indigenous industry.

A Pharmaceutical Enquiry Committee headed by General Bhatia (the Bhatia Committee) was appointed in 1954 to study India's increasing dependence on foreign countries for chemicals and bulk drugs needed for the manufacture of essential drugs. The committee found that Indian companies were not engaging in the production of advanced drugs, like chemotherapeutic drugs and antibiotics, but rather were concentrating on galenicals. Even in the production of galenicals, it was observed that Indian firms had been undermining quality standards in an attempt to be competitive. The committee recommended that no more new licences be issued for the production of galenicals. It also suggested the withdrawal of licences from undertakings that did not meet the required standards in terms of staff and equipment.

Further, the committee recommended that: (*a*) indigenous production of drugs be encouraged from the basic stage of drug manufacture; (*b*) no new foreign companies be allowed to set up factories unless they manufactured products that were not produced by others, starting from basic chemicals or intermediaries; (*c*) agreements that forbade the sale of bulk drugs to other processors be discouraged in order to promote the processing capability of the indigenous sector; and (*d*) an organisation be established for the monitoring of drugs prices. The government, however, found itself unable to pursue policies based on the recommendations made by the Bhatia Committee, due to its heavy dependence on foreign capital. India's reliance on foreign firms increased further in 1957–58, when there was a severe foreign exchange crisis (Narayana 1984).

The Committee on the Revision of Patents Law was constituted in April 1957, with Justice N. Rajagopala Ayyangar as its chairman. The committee submitted its report, popularly known as the Ayyangar Committee Report, in 1959. The report viewed patents as an essential mechanism for encouraging innovation and as a vital instrument for industrialisation. Exclusive rights to the exploitation of an invention for a specific period of time, as enshrined in the patent system, provided an assurance to the inventor that his/her invention would be rewarded with financial returns. The report pointed out that the Soviet Union, which followed a socialist economic structure, had a patent system in place. However, the committee recognised that the benefits accruing to a country from the patent system depended on the technological capability of that country to maintain the rate of innovation and the working of patents within the country (GoI 1959).

At the same time, patent rights could be abused to create protected foreign markets in which others could neither produce nor sell the patented invention without the patentee's permission, thus hampering the welfare of people and the industrialisation process in developing countries (GoI 1959). The Ayyangar Committee Report cited the example of the German chemical industry, which had maintained the US as a protected market using this system. During the First World War, the US confiscated all German patents and licensed them to its own manufacturers, paving the way for the emergence of the US chemical industry. The committee cautioned that developing countries like India should not blindly imitate the patent system in industrialised countries. The patent system had to be designed 'with special reference to the economic conditions of the country, the state of its scientific and technological advance, its future needs and other relevant factors' (*ibid.*: para. 44). The committee noted that ensuring the availability of food and medicines to everyone at reasonable prices was of vital concern to India. Keeping in view the concerns regarding the availability and affordability of food and medicines and the industrialisation of the country, the committee recommended sweeping reforms in Indian patent law.

The major recommendations of the Ayyangar Committee included allowing only process patents in chemicals, drugs and food, and no patents for products in these sectors. It also suggested empowering the government with the authority to grant compulsory licences (CLs) in cases where patents were not working locally, or if patentees refused to license their rights. The recommendations of the committee formed the basis for the Patents Bill, which was introduced in the Lok Sabha in 1965; however, this bill lapsed. In 1967, an amended bill was introduced, which was finally passed in 1970 as the Patents Act, 1970. This act replaced the 1911 act as far as patents were concerned. It came into force in 1972 with the publication of the Patent Rules. India's patent policy relied heavily on the Ayyangar Committee recommendations until the country joined the WTO in 1994 (Ragavan 2006).

In 1974, the Government of India appointed a committee headed by Jaisuklal Hathi (the Hathi Committee). This committee was tasked with looking into various facets of the drug industry in India and recommending measures for the rapid growth of the industry, particularly the small-scale sector, while ensuring that the public sector attained a leadership role in production as well as R&D. It was also to make recommendations on how to ensure a high quality of drugs, reduce the prices of drugs, and ensure equitable distribution of basic drugs and raw materials especially to the small-scale sector.

The Hathi Committee submitted its report in 1975 (GoI 1975). The report was an extensive, comprehensive study of the Indian pharmaceutical market. The committee found that domestic firms had been engaging in the production of low-quality drugs, while MNCs had been selling their parent firms' products without investing in production in India. Expenditure on R&D in the Indian pharmaceutical industry was as low as 1 per cent of the turnover, compared to 12–15 per cent in advanced countries. The organised sector, which was dominated by foreign firms, accounted for 80 per cent of the market. The committee observed that ensuring the availability of medicines (prophylactics and curatives) should constitute an important social responsibility of the state, on par with the provision of food and shelter, and recommended that the pharmaceutical industry be divorced from the normally accepted norms of trade for profits. The committee recommended: (*a*) the creation of a National Drug Authority (NDA) for regulating the prices of medicines and coordinating policies pertaining to the drugs sector; (*b*) assigning a leading role to the public sector in the production of technology and capital-intensive bulk drugs, and in R&D; (*c*) the introduction of production controls so as to meet production targets; (*d*) favourable discrimination towards Indian companies to facilitate them in the production of bulk drugs and formulations; (*e*) the requirement that companies producing bulk drugs share 50 per cent of the production with non-associated formulators; and (*f*) monitoring by the NDA of the prices of imported bulk drugs and raw materials.

The recommendations of these committees led to major reforms in patent law, industrial policy and drug policy (DP) in India. Apart from the Patents Act, 1970, FERA was introduced in 1973 to regulate MNCs. A new DP was introduced in 1978, which aimed at ensuring the availability as well as affordability of medicines. However, it must be remembered that the Government of India had adopted various initiatives at the beginning of the 1950s to ensure that the domestic pharmaceutical industry grew in the desired direction. The industry was brought under the purview of the Industries (Development and Regulations) Act, 1951, which aimed at the development and regulation of certain industries. A calibrated approach to the building of indigenous R&D capabilities was adopted from the early 1950s. Jawaharlal Nehru, the then prime minister, believed that technology capability, if built up in partnership with foreign commercial firms, would lead to a commercial approach to scientific problems. This was not considered desirable given the prevailing social conditions in India. Nehru insisted that the Indian drug industry, like other manufacturing industries, not be developed under the aegis of foreign firms; instead, he assigned a major role to the public sector in the development of the pharmaceuticals industry:

> We have built up a considerable number of laboratories and I have specially laid stress on research and the scientific approach, rather than the commercial approach to scientific problems. The commercial approach can pay dividends in a country like the US where the whole basis of the social structure is commercial and individual profit making. We cannot emulate the US in this and have to find a different way, a way in which the State takes a large hand and science has free play. To some extent, this free play of science is limited by the buying up of talent by commercial firms for their own advantage. We become parties to this latter process, if we try to develop under the aegis of a big foreign commercial firm.[4]

But Nehru was not totally set against the participation of foreign firms, and had clear ideas about when to collaborate with foreign capital and in which sectors:

> I am anxious and eager to help Indian firms and Indian engineers and technicians and not to have foreign firms undertaking major works in India where they can be dispensed with. But I am quite clear in my mind that the most important test is the experience of the firm and their technical competence. In relatively small projects

special experience might not be needed, but in a large project that experience is of the first importance. If it is clear that the foreign firm has this experience and technical competence then I would choose that firm almost regardless of other factors.[5]

The implementation of the 'penicillin project' in the second half of the 1950s in India demonstrates Nehru's approach. Despite the eagerness of the industry ministry to collaborate with Glaxo or Pfizer or Merck for the penicillin project, Nehru persuaded the ministry to forge an alliance with the World Health Organization (WHO) (Tyabji 2004). N.L. Macpherson of WHO, who was familiar with the penicillin production process, was the key resource person. The experts also identified a non-infringing process for the production of penicillin. The project came into force in 1951 and by 1955 the original production target (400,000 mega units a month) had been exceeded by a considerable extent. Production reached 750,000 mega units in January 1956, and 890,000 mega units in February. This project was instrumental in helping policy makers understand the difficulties in building technology capabilities under the existing IPR regime.

## Policy initiatives in the 1970s

Increasingly, it was realised that the support extended to MNCs was not resulting in the desired outcomes. The government then decided to regulate the industry stringently. The recommendations made by various committees provided the necessary inputs. The most important policy reform that was instrumental in giving the Indian pharmaceutical industry global recognition was the Patents Act, 1970. The act allowed only process patents in drugs and pharmaceuticals, as recommended by the Ayyangar Committee. The period of protection was reduced from 14 to 7 years (or 5 years from the date of sealing the patent, whichever was earlier). The local production of patented subject matter was made mandatory. Indian pharmaceutical firms were able to produce patented drugs using alternative processes. An important outcome of the act was that the interval between the launch of a drug in developed country markets and its launch in India was reduced considerably to four or five years, in contrast to much longer periods in the past (Table 1.1).

Indian manufacturers, as just mentioned, were able to produce patented drugs using alternative processes. This led to the flourishing of the indigenous segment of the Indian pharmaceutical industry. For instance, cefaclor is a drug used in the treatment of bacterial infections such as

*Table 1.1*  Interval before the introduction of new medicines in India after 1970

| Drug | Year of launch | |
|---|---|---|
| | World | India |
| Ranitidine (anti-ulcer) | 1983 | 1985 |
| Cimetidine (anti-ulcer) | 1976 | 1981 |
| Norfloxacin (antibacterial) | 1984 | 1988 |
| Astemizole (non-sedating antihistamine) | 1986 | 1988 |
| Acyclovir (antiviral) | 1985 | 1988 |
| Salbutamol (bronchodilator) | 1973 | 1976 |
| Mebendazole (antihelmintic) | 1974 | 1978 |
| Ibuprofen (anti-inflammatory) | 1967 | 1973 |
| Lorazepam (anxiolytic) | 1977 | 1978 |

*Source:* Hamied (1988: n.p.).

pneumonia. The molecule had been owned by the drug manufacturer Eli Lilly since 1979. Eli Lilly had patented more than 70 processes for the manufacture of the molecule to prevent others from manufacturing the drug. But the Indian firm Ranbaxy managed to develop a non-infringing process in 1991, after three years in R&D efforts costing US$2 million. Ranbaxy's process was superior to the processes used by Eli Lilly. This forced Eli Lilly to enter into a joint venture with Ranbaxy for the production of cefaclor (Athreye and Kale 2006).

The flourishing generics industry in India not only allowed the fast introduction of new drugs in the country, but also enabled those drugs to be priced at very low levels (Abrol and Jayaraj 1988).[6] Table 1.2 shows the prices of certain medicines in India in 1998 in comparison to their prices in other countries. The originator of ranitidine (Glaxo) was one among the 20 suppliers of the drug in India (Hamied 1988), but its local price was just 2 per cent of that in the UK. Had there been product patents in India, the monopoly power of Glaxo would have impacted the availability as well as the price of the drug in India.

*Table 1.2* Comparative drug prices in 1998 (in Indian rupees)

| Drug/Brand | Company | India | Pakistan | Indonesia | UK | US |
|---|---|---|---|---|---|---|
| Ranitidine (Zantac) 150 mg x 10 s | Glaxo | 7.16 | 122.16 | 658.85 | 320.85 | 739.60 |
| Times costlier | | | 17 | 92 | 45 | 103.3 |
| Diclofenac sodium (Voveran) 50 mg x 10 s | Ciba-Geigy | 5.64 | 56.74 | 177.18 | 125.88 | 505.68 |
| Times costlier | | | 10 | 31 | 22 | 90 |
| Piroxicam (Dolonex/Feldene) 20 mg x 10 s | Pfizer | 24.64 | 78.3 | 218.45 | 240.12 | 1210.88 |
| Times costlier | | | 3 | 9 | 10 | 49 |

*Source:* Ghosh and Keayla (1998: 17).

Before the Patents Act, 1970, the MRTP Act, 1969, was enacted to curb the expansionist tendencies of big companies. The threshold limit for describing a unit as monopolistically large was fixed at Rs 200 million. The prior approval of the central government became mandatory for the establishment of new undertakings, expansion of new undertakings, mergers, amalgamations and takeovers, and the appointment of directors in certain cases.

In 1973, the most important of all regulations to contain the expansion of the foreign sector, FERA, was adopted. This act made it mandatory for all subsidiaries of foreign firms operating in India to bring down their equity shares to a maximum of 40 per cent. Exceptions were allowed in cases where foreign firms could prove themselves to be particularly useful to the country in terms of the technology they employed, or in terms of exports.[7] The act had a profound impact on the pattern of equity holding. The number of foreign subsidiaries in the pharmaceutical industry came down from 10 to 2 between 1973 and 1985. The number of firms holding more than 50 per cent equity declined from 21 to 14 during the same period (Panikar, Pillai and Sundari 1992; Pillai 1984).

Measures were also taken to regulate the prices of essential medicines in India. The Drugs (Control of Prices) Order, 1963, issued under the Defence of India Act, 1915, required freezing prices as of 1 April 1963. The Drugs Prices (Display and Control) Order, 1966, allowed for markups over ex-factory costs not exceeding 150 per cent. A drawback of the 1966 order was that the government was not empowered to reduce the prices of drugs where prevailing markups were over 150 per cent.

The drug price control measures that followed the 1966 order were issued under the Essential Commodities Act, 1955.

The DPCO of 1970 was promulgated under Section 3 of the Essential Commodities Act, with the objective of bringing down the prices of essential drugs by curbing excessive profits. The order stipulated that a company's pre-tax profit from its pharma business should not exceed 15 per cent of its pharma sales (net of excise duty and sales tax). In case profits exceeded this sum, the surplus was to be deposited with the government. Product-wise margins were kept flexible, as long as the overall margin did not exceed the stipulated norm. However, the order brought under its purview only 18 bulk drugs and their formulations. The prices of other bulk drugs were frozen, and manufacturers were asked to declare the prices of the remaining bulk drugs and not to increase prices without the approval of the government. In the case of formulations, the selling price was fixed on the criteria that the markup on material cost, conversion cost and packing charges would be 75 per cent. The markup could be increased to 100 per cent in the case of new combinations of existing drugs and 150 per cent for new drugs, that is, drugs containing new chemical entities. Manufacturers were given the option of adopting an alternative pricing scheme. They were free to fix prices within the ceiling of a 75 per cent markup for 18 essential drugs and 150 per cent for others, subject to the condition that the gross profit before tax did not exceed 15 per cent of sales.

A major drawback of the 1970 DPCO was that it had no mechanism to check overpricing based on inflated costs. In 1971, Hoechst (now part of Aventis) reported to the government a price of Rs 24,735 per kilogram for the bulk drug Baralgan Ketone, and used it as a base for its formulation. Under the 1979 DPCO, Baralgan Ketone was included in the list of bulk drugs for which the government was to fix the maximum selling price on the basis of a return of 12–14 per cent on net worth. Interestingly, the same company applied for a price of Rs 3,500 per kilogram for the drug[8] (Chaudhuri 2005b).

Modifications to the DPCO of 1970 became imminent, especially in the context of the Hathi Committee recommendations. An immediate outcome of these recommendations was the promulgation of the first DP of India in March 1978. Since 1978, the DP became the major policy instrument governing the direction of the pharmaceutical industry. The major objectives of the 1978 DP were:

- to develop self-reliance in drug technology,
- to provide a leadership role to the public sector,

- to foster and encourage the growth of the Indian pharmaceutical sector,
- to make drugs available at reasonable prices, and
- to reduce dependence on imports.

The 1978 DP divided drugs into three groups for the purpose of reserving items for production by various sectors in the industry. The first group consisted of items that could be produced only by the public sector. Twenty-five drugs were reserved for production by the public sector. The second group was reserved for production by the Indian/domestic sector. This group contained 16 drugs. The third group was open to all sectors, including the foreign sector. In considering industrial licence applications, preference was to be given to Indian companies over MRTP units and foreign companies. The public sector was assigned a leading role in the production and distribution of drugs and pharmaceuticals, and adequate outlays were provided for this.

Another important feature of the 1978 DP was its emphasis on the consumption of indigenously produced bulk drugs. It made it mandatory for all firms producing formulations based on imported bulk drugs, or bulk drugs manufactured from the penultimate stage, that they would produce the bulk drug concerned from the basic stage indigenously within a period of two years. These firms were also required to supply 50 per cent of the total production of bulk drugs to non-associate formulators. The DP further restricted the value of a firm's formulation production to five times the value of its total bulk drug production. All these measures made for a situation in which any significant increase in the production of formulations essentially depended on an increase in the indigenous production of bulk drugs.

Furthermore, the practice of loan licensing, i.e. firms getting products manufactured by other firms and selling them under their own name, was also prohibited under the 1978 DP. The DP also required foreign firms operating in India with a turnover in drugs exceeding Rs 50 million per year to establish R&D facilities in India. They were required to spend at least 4 per cent of their turnover as recurring expenditure on R&D. The policy also liberalised licences for production meant for exports. A company could produce any amount for export and had flexibility in the use of foreign exchange. The policy also proposed the abolition of brand names, starting with five drugs, and extending to all single-ingredient dosage forms.[9] The 1978 DP was a milestone in the subsequent development of the drug industry in India. All these policy measures had a profound impact on the indigenous sector. The share of the domestic sector in total pharmaceutical production in India increased from 27 per cent in 1975–76 to 52 per cent in 1980–81 (Narayana 1984).

The 1978 DP was followed by a new DPCO issued in the following year. The 1979 DPCO, unlike previous orders, adopted a selective approach. Bulk drugs and formulations were divided into the 'scheduled' group and the group of 'others'. The retail prices of scheduled formulations were to be calculated on the basis of markups over materials and other costs. The maximum selling prices of scheduled bulk drugs were fixed taking into consideration specified rates of return on net worth/capital employed. The 1979 DPCO categorised drugs into four groups (Table 1.3). The first three categories came under the scheduled group.

The philosophy behind this graded system of pricing was to make essential drugs cheaper. Categories I and II together came to be known as the essential and life-saving drugs categories. On the whole, the DPCO of 1979 brought 347 bulk drugs and 4,000 formulations, accounting for 90 per cent of the market share, under its purview (Sengupta *et al.* 2008). In order to incentivise indigenous R&D, the order provided exemption from price control for a period of five years for new drugs introduced in India that had not been patented elsewhere.

The 1978 DP and the 1979 DPCO had several drawbacks. A major lacuna was the lack of production control measures. The 1978 policy contained no clause to compel manufacturers to produce essential drugs. This, when coupled with the graded pricing structure of the 1979 DPCO, proved disastrous. Pharmaceutical companies reduced their production of drug categories that had lower permitted markups. The study by Narayana (1984) shows that the share of sales value of categories I and II (essential and life-saving) formulations fell from 21 per cent in 1978 to 16.8 per cent in 1980. In contrast, the sales value of category III and decontrolled formulations increased commensurately. The study suggests that the lower markups permitted in categories I and II led to a decline in the availability of those medicines. It should be

*Table 1.3* Price structure under DPCO, 1979

| Category | Ceiling in markups (%) |
| --- | --- |
| Category I: Life-saving | 40 |
| Category II: Essential | 55 |
| Category III: Less essential | 100 |
| Category IV: Non-essential | No price control |

*Note:* DPCO 1979 does not explicitly mention the term 'category IV'.
*Source:* Compiled by the author from DPCO 1979.

noted that the DPCO of 1970 had assumed that the lower profitability of category I and II drugs would be adequately compensated by higher markups in the remaining categories.

Learning from the drawbacks of the 1978 DP and 1979 DPCO, the government announced a new DP in 1986 with the objectives of ensuring rationalisation, quality control and growth of the drugs and pharmaceuticals industry in India. The salient features of the 1986 DP were as follows:

- Scheduled drugs were grouped into two categories instead of three as in the previous DP.
- The maximum retail price (MRP) of domestically produced scheduled formulations was not to exceed 75 per cent of the ex-factory cost for category I (drugs required for national health programmes), and 100 per cent for category II (other essential drugs) formulations.[10]
- The manufacturers of scheduled bulk drugs were given three options to fix their prices: (*a*) 14 per cent post-tax return on net worth; (*b*) 22 per cent return on capital employed; or (*c*) long-term marginal costing with 12 per cent internal rate of return in the case of new plants.
- For imported formulations, selling and distribution expenses, including interest and importers' margin, were fixed at a maximum of 50 per cent of the landed cost.
- The number of drugs reserved for the public sector was reduced to 15.
- In order to encourage higher production of bulk drugs in the country, the ratio parameter between the ex-factory value of bulk drug production to that of formulations was revised. The ratio parameter was settled at 1 : 4 for FERA companies. For non-FERA companies, the ratio parameter would be related to the size of the company: companies with production up to Rs 100 million, between Rs 100 million and Rs 250 million, and in excess of Rs 250 million, were given ratios of 1 : 10, 1 : 7 and 1 : 5, respectively.

The DPCO following the 1986 DP was announced after the list of drugs in each category was finalised. The DPCO, which was promulgated on 16 August 1987, reduced the number of drugs under price control from 347 to 142, an estimated decrease from 90 per cent of the market to 70 per cent of the market (Sengupta *et al.* 2008).

It was argued in the early 1980s that India had become one of the cheapest drug makers in the world. And the rate of increase of drug prices was slower than that of the general price level. Panikar, Pillai and Sundari (1992) observe that the rate of increase in the wholesale prices of drugs was less than one-third that of all commodities taken together – around

35 per cent and 118 per cent, respectively, during the 1970s. The differential rate of increase further widened during the 1980s. This observation strengthens the claim that the price control order put in place in the 1970s had a remarkable effect on the prices of drugs and medicines in the country.

The impact of policy reforms in the 1970s on the Indian pharma industry was huge. The share of the domestic sector in total pharmaceutical production in India increased from 27 per cent in 1975–76 to 52 per cent in 1980–81 (Narayana 1984). The indigenous production of drugs grew from Rs 100 million in 1947 to Rs 1,680 million in 1965–66, and further to Rs 94,530 million in 1994–95 (*ibid.*; IDMA 2004). Significant progress was made towards self-reliance and self-sufficiency, employing appropriate technology, based essentially on the use of indigenous raw materials. In the production of bulk drugs, the share of the domestic sector had reached 82 per cent in 1987 (Hamied 1988). By the end of the 1980s, Indian generic firms had come to be known the world over for their competence.[11] One of Ranbaxy's active pharmaceutical ingredient (API) manufacturing plants received the approval of the US Food and Drug Administration (USFDA) in 1988 (Athreye and Kale 2006).[12]

The beginning of the 1990s witnessed the liberalisation of economic policies in India. The process of economic liberalisation reversed many of the earlier regulations aimed at guiding the economy in a desired direction. The Statement on Industrial Policy of 24 July 1991 formally launched a new era in the Indian economy.

## Liberalisation measures in the 1990s

The new industrial policy announced in July 1991 bore witness to the change in the approach of the government. It proposed that 'the role played by the government [was] to be changed from that of exercising control to one of providing help and guidance by making essential procedures fully transparent and eliminating delays' (GoI 1991: para. 2). The statement outlined the basic framework of the reforms that were to be initiated in the economy. The three major features of the framework relevant to the pharmaceutical sector are as follows:

1   Industrial licensing was abolished for all industries. However, in the case of drugs and pharmaceuticals, the implementation of this measure would depend on the DP.
2   There was recognition of the requirement of foreign investment and technology collaboration for technology transfer, marketing

expertise, the introduction of modern managerial techniques, and the exploration of new possibilities for promotion of exports. In order to invite foreign investment into high-priority industries requiring large investments and advanced technology, it was decided that:

- automatic approval would be given for direct foreign investment up to 51 per cent foreign equity in high-priority industries; and
- automatic permission would be given for foreign technology agreements in high-priority industries.

    Drugs and pharmaceuticals fell in the list of high-priority industries. But the implementation of the policy was made subject to the provisions of the DP.

3    The Statement on Industrial Policy recognised the need for a complete revision of the MRTP Act. It was decided that:

- The pre-entry scrutiny of investment decisions by MRTP companies was no longer required.
- The MRTP Act was to be amended to remove the threshold limits of assets in respect of MRTP companies and dominant undertakings. The thrust of policy would be on controlling unfair or restrictive business practices.
- The provisions relating to mergers, amalgamations and take-overs were also to be repealed. Similarly, the provisions regarding restrictions on acquisition of and transfer of shares would also be appropriately incorporated in the Companies Act.

The Foreign Exchange Regulation Act was amended in 1993, and then was abolished completely in 1999. After the 1993 amendment of FERA, all companies incorporated in India were treated as Indian companies even if they were fully owned by foreign nationals or companies. Similarly the MRTP Act was amended in 1991 and was then replaced by the Competition Act, 2002. The need for a review of the 1986 DP became evident after 1991, as the implementation of the liberalisation policies in the pharmaceutical sector necessitated a new DP.

## Liberalisation measures in the drugs and pharmaceuticals sector

The economic reforms of 1991 trickled down to the pharmaceutical sector from September 1994 with the announcement of the Modifications in Drug Policy, 1986. The modified DP, together with subsequent economic policies, substantially liberalised the licensing and other regulations in the pharmaceutical sector. Thus, the liberalisation measures announced in the industrial policy statement of 1991 took effect in the pharmaceutical sector only in 1994. The major liberalisation measures introduced in the pharmaceutical sector through the new DP were as follows:

1   Industrial licensing was abolished for all bulk drugs and their intermediaries, except the five identified bulk drugs that continued to be reserved exclusively for the public sector,[13] bulk drugs produced by the use of recombinant DNA technology, and bulk drugs requiring *in vivo* use of nucleic acids as the active principles. Reservation of drugs for the public sector was abolished entirely in 1999. Licensing was also abolished for all formulations, except specific cell/tissue targeted formulations.

2   In order to achieve the objective of production from basic stages, the tariff mechanism was to be resorted to instead of industrial licensing.

3   The ratio parameters linking bulk drug and formulation production were abolished. The mandatory requirement that a percentage of bulk drug production be supplied to non-associate formulators was also abolished.

4   The restrictions imposed on the use of imported bulk drugs were abolished. Imports of drugs and pharmaceuticals are regulated through the export-import (EXIM) policy now in force. All items except those requiring clearance under the Narcotics and Psychotropic Substances Act, 1985, are allowed under open general licences (OGL).

5   Automatic approval of foreign technology agreements in drugs and pharmaceuticals was permitted, except for those drugs produced by the use of recombinant DNA technology.

6   Foreign investment up to 51 per cent of equity was permitted under the automatic approval route. Investment above 51 per cent would be considered on a case-by-case basis. The FDI cap was raised to 74 per cent in 2000 (GoI 2000) and to 100 per cent in 2003 (RBI 2003).

7   As a measure for incentivising R&D, new drugs that had not been produced elsewhere, if developed through indigenous R&D, were placed outside the price control system for a period of 10 years.

8   The drug price control system was completely revised. The new mechanism proposed in the 1994 DP would operate through a single list of scheduled bulk drugs and formulations based thereon,

with uniform maximum allowable post-manufacturing expenses (MAPE) of 100 per cent.

9    For the first time in India, the criteria of 'market competition' and 'annual turnover' were introduced in identifying drugs to be brought under price control. The criteria used for keeping drugs under price control were: (*a*) annual turnover of Rs 40 million or more; or (*b*) annual turnover of Rs 10 million or more where a single formulator held 90 per cent or more of the market share in the retail market; whereas (*c*) drugs with sufficient market competition, i.e., those that had at least five bulk drug producers and at least 10 formulators with none having more than a 40 per cent market share in the retail market, were kept outside of price control.

The new DPCO was announced in 1995. Based on the criteria of market competition and annual turnover, 74 bulk drugs were identified, the prices of which were controlled under the DPCO of 1995. These drugs were listed in the first schedule annexed to the order. Formulations containing any of the scheduled bulk drugs fell under the purview of the DPCO. The maximum sale price of a scheduled bulk drug was calculated as follows:

1    Post-tax return of 14 per cent on net worth.[14] In case production was from the basic stage, an additional 4 per cent return was considered.

2    Post-tax return of 22 per cent on capital employed.[15] In case production was from the basic stage, an additional 4 per cent return was considered.

3    In the case of a new plant, an internal rate of return of 12 per cent based on long-term marginal costing, depending on the option for any of the specified rates of return that might be exercised by the manufacturer of a bulk drug.

The retail prices of formulations were fixed if they contained any of the scheduled bulk drugs as an ingredient. The formula for the pricing of formulations containing scheduled bulk drugs was as follows:

$$R.P. = (M.C. + C.C. + P.M. + P.C.) \times (1 + MAPE/100) + ED$$

where
R.P. is the retail price
M.C. refers to material cost. It includes the cost of drugs and other pharmaceutical aids used, including overages,[16] if any, plus process

loss thereon specified as a norm from time to time by notification in the official *Gazette*.

C.C. refers to the conversion cost worked out in accordance with established procedures of costing. It is fixed as a norm every year by notification in the official *Gazette*.

P.M. refers to the cost of the packing material used in the packaging of the concerned formulation, including process loss, and is fixed as a norm every year by notification in the official *Gazette*.

P.C. refers to packing charges worked out in accordance with established procedures of costing, and is fixed as a norm every year by notification in the official *Gazette*.

MAPE includes all costs incurred by a manufacturer from the stage of ex-factory cost to retailing. It also includes the trade margin and the margin for the manufacturer. It should not exceed 100 per cent for indigenously manufactured scheduled formulations.

E.D. refers to excise duty.

For imported bulk drugs and formulations, the landed cost, including customs duty and clearing charges, was the benchmark for fixing prices. The margin allowed to the importer was such that selling and distribution expenses including interest and profit were covered. However, the margin allowed could not exceed 50 per cent of the landed cost.

The DPCO of 1995 provided that any increase in the price of formulations, once fixed by the government, required the prior approval of the government. Manufacturers and importers intending to market new dosage forms or new pack sizes of scheduled formulations were required to obtain prior approval of the prices of these products from the government. The manufacturers of non-scheduled drugs (i.e. drugs not under direct price control) were not required to obtain price approvals from the NPPA. However, the NPPA monitors the prices of such drugs to ensure that the annual increase is not more than 10 per cent. The annual cap on price increase for the non-scheduled category of drugs was reduced from 20 per cent to 10 per cent in April 2007.

The new criteria for identification of drugs to be brought under the price control system brought down the number of drugs under price control from 142 to 74. A major drawback of the price control mechanism under the modified DP, however, was that it did not link health needs to price control. Further, it has been found that in the pharma market, competition has no direct effect on prices; in many cases, the market leader is also the price leader, or its price is among the highest in therapeutic markets. For example, in the atorvastatin (10 mg, pack size 10) market, which had 58 sellers in 2008, Ranbaxy was the price leader (Rs 68) as well as the market leader, whereas the least expensive drug by Hetero was priced at Rs 9.10. Similarly, in the cetirizine (10 mg, pack size 10) market that had 80 sellers in 2008, GlaxoSmithKline (GSK) was the market leader, charging Rs 27.8. On the other hand, the most expensive cetirizine product by Bactolac cost Rs 35.8, and the least expensive by Khandelwal cost Rs 0.98 (Selvaraj and Farooqui 2012).[17]

The DPCO of 1995 remained in force until May 2013, when a new DPCO was notified. A few important studies on the impact of DPCO 1995 on drug prices should be noted here. Selvaraj (2001) offers a comparative analysis of the pre- and post-DPCO 1995 price trends of major essential drugs. He analyses the prices of 71 essential drugs between 1994 and 2000. Of these, 37 were taken off the DPCO 1995 list, while 34 were included in DPCO 1995. The 37 drugs not included in DPCO 1995 had been under the purview of previous DPCOs, and were subsequently decontrolled. Selvaraj's analysis shows that the prices of drugs that remained under price control tended to be either stable or showed a downward movement, whereas the prices of drugs formerly under DPCO but later decontrolled exhibited an upward movement. The hike was most pronounced in the anti-allergic category (418.13 per cent). The rise in the prices of other categories of drugs was as follows: anti-infectives (129 per cent), mydriatics and cycloplegics (327 per cent), cardiac disorders (197 per cent), peripheral vasodilators (146 per cent), antidiuretics (265 per cent), drugs acting on the uterus (184 per cent), anti-tuberculosis (129 per cent) and antileprotics (148 per cent). Gentamycin in the antibiotics category was the only exception, demonstrating a downward trend (8 per cent). Selvaraj's study clearly shows that if drugs are moved out of price control, their prices increase.

Chaudhuri (2005b) analyses the prices of the 50 largest brands as reported by ORG-MARG in 2002. These brands accounted for 15 per cent of the retail formulation market. Chaudhuri considers 118 different dosage forms and pack sizes for all 50 brands for which price data were available for 1995 and 2003 from CIMS. The results show that products whose prices increased substantially between 1995 and 2003 were the not-controlled drugs, and products whose prices declined or increased only marginally were generally those under price control. Eleven dosage forms showed price increases of more than 100 per cent, of which 10 were in the not-controlled category. Of the 32 dosage forms that saw price rises of 25–100 per cent, 26 were in the not-controlled category. Of the 40 dosage forms whose prices remained the same or decreased between 1995 and 2003, 34 were under price control and only 6 were not controlled.

## Drug policy, 2002

The Government of India attempted to further liberalise control over drugs prices through the DP of 2002. The new criteria brought a bulk drug under the price control net if the moving annual turnover (MAT) was more than Rs 250 million and if any of its formulators had a market share of more than 50 per cent, or if a bulk drug had a MAT of less than Rs 250 million but above Rs 100 million and the market share of any one of its formulators was greater than 90 per cent. For a scheduled bulk drug, the rate of return in the case of basic manufacture would be higher by 4 per cent over the existing rates of 14 per cent return on net worth or 22 per cent return on capital employed. All formulations containing a bulk drug as identified by these criteria, either individually or in combination with other bulk drugs, including those not identified for price control as bulk drugs, would be placed under price control. The DP of 2002 was expected to bring down further the number of drugs under price control to between 20 and 25.

The DP of 2002 also included certain provisions for further incentivising R&D in the pharmaceuticals sector. A manufacturer producing a new drug patented under the Indian Patent Act, 1970, and not produced elsewhere, if developed through indigenous R&D, would be eligible for exemption from price control in respect of that drug for a period of 15 years from the date of the commencement of its commercial production in the country.

However, before the policy could be implemented, it was stayed by the Karnataka High Court. A special leave petition was filed in the Supreme Court against the order of the Karnataka High Court. The Supreme Court *vide* its interim order of 10 March 2003 stayed the order of the Karnataka High Court. However, it also directed that 'the petitioner shall consider and formulate appropriate criteria for ensuring essential and life-saving drugs not to fall out of price control and to review the drugs which are essential and life-saving in nature till 2nd May, 2003' (GoI 2011a: 4). Accordingly, the central government reviewed the National Essential Drug List, 1996, and brought out a new list called the National List of Essential Medicines (NLEM), 2003, which was made available to the Supreme Court. Under the new list, 354 drugs were recognised as essential medicines. The NLEM was revised in 2011, and the revised list contains 348 essential drugs.

## Pharmaceutical policy, 2006

Meanwhile, the Government of India constituted a task force under the chairmanship of Pronab Sen to 'explore options other than price controls to make available life-saving drugs at reasonable prices' (GoI 2005a: 2). The task force submitted its report in 2005. It recommended that price controls should be based on the essentiality of the medicines and not on turnover. It also recommended that the prices of formulations be regulated. To start the process, it suggested that the government announce ceiling prices for the drugs contained in the NLEM on the basis of weighted average prices (WAP) of the top three brands by value of single-ingredient formulations prevailing in the market. In cases where fewer than three brands existed, the WAP of all existing brands would be considered (*ibid.*).

The Government of India also constituted a committee in August 2004 under the chairmanship of the joint secretary of the Department of Chemicals and Petrochemicals. The mandate of this committee was to examine the span of price control (including trade margin) in the light of the National Common Minimum Programme of the United Progressive Alliance (UPA) government (GoI 2005b). The interim report of the committee recommended that drugs in the NLEM form the basket of drugs that needed to be subjected to some kind of price management. For price control, a more effective system of monitoring needed to be introduced. In this system, drugs should be classified into two groups. 'Category A' would consist of drugs considered essential but not falling in the price control list. This category would be subjected to intensive monitoring with a lower price movement cap, which could be between 10 and 15 per cent per year. 'Category B' would consist of all other drugs outside Category A and price-controlled drugs. This category would be subjected to normal monitoring. The report also recommended that generic medicines without brand names needed to be promoted.

Based on these recommendations, the Ministry of Chemicals and Fertilisers prepared the 'Draft Pharmaceutical Policy 2006'. However, this policy was not notified. While the policy was still pending the approval of the Group of Ministers (GoM), a new draft policy dealing with drug price regulation – the Pharmaceutical Pricing Policy, 2011 – was released for public comments in October 2011. The policy proposed a market-based approach to price ceilings for essential drugs: the WAP of the top-selling three brands by value (of a single-ingredient formulation) would form the ceiling mark (GoI 2011a). This criterion was heavily criticised, given that market leaders in the pharmaceutical sector in India were also price leaders, i.e. their prices tended to be among the highest. Taking into consideration the comments and criticisms received on the draft policy, a GoM finalised the new pricing policy in 2012.

## National pharmaceutical pricing policy, 2012

The NPPP of 2012 was announced on 7 December 2012. The objective of the policy is to

> put in place a regulatory framework for pricing of drugs so as to ensure availability of required medicines – essential medicines – at reasonable prices even while providing sufficient opportunity for innovation and competition to support the growth of industry, thereby meeting the goals of employment and shared economic well-being for all.
>
> (GoI 2012a: Section 2)

In addition to the emphasis on reasonable prices for essential medicines, the policy also emphasises a market-based pricing mechanism and the regulation of prices of formulations only. The new policy proposes to regulate the prices of all drugs listed in the NLEM of 2011. The NLEM was prepared by an expert committee in the Ministry of Health and Family Welfare, drawing from the WHO Model List of Essential Medicines, the Essential Drug List (EDL) existing in different states in India, and medicines used in various National Health Programmes and emergency care. The NLEM also specifies the dosage forms of essential drugs. The NPPP proposes to regulate the prices of dosage forms listed in the NLEM. Unlike earlier pricing regimes, the NPPP will not regulate the prices of bulk drugs.

A new DPCO was issued in 2013. It adopts a market-based approach to the regulation of drug prices, as against the cost-based system that had existed previously. A detailed review of DPCO 2013 is provided in Chapter 5 of this book.

### Changes in the patents regime

The most important pharmaceutical policy reform in the post-1994 period consists of the modifications introduced in the patents regime on account of India's obligations under the TRIPS Agreement. The process patent regime in drugs and pharmaceuticals under the Patents Act, 1970, which had paved the way for making the Indian pharmaceutical industry globally competitive, was replaced by a product patent regime through amendments in the Patents Act. At the ministerial conference held at Marrakesh in 1994, the Government of India ratified the Final Act of the 1986–94 Uruguay Round of trade negotiations establishing the WTO; thereafter, it became obligatory for India to make its IPR regime compliant with the TRIPS requirements. Though the provisions of the TRIPS Agreement were expected to be in force by 1 January 1996, developing countries were allowed an additional four years, i.e. until 2000, to amend their laws and make them TRIPS-compliant.[18] Developing countries that had process patent regimes in place prior to 1995 were given until 2005 to introduce product patents in areas covered by process patents.[19] Thus, India had until 1 January 2005 to introduce product patents in pharmaceuticals. However, the agreement required members availing of this transition facility to make provisions for receiving patent applications.[20]

India met its obligations under the TRIPS Agreement in three steps. The first step was the introduction of the Patents (Amendment) Act, 1999, which provided for receiving patent applications (mailbox applications) and for exclusive marketing rights.[21] Second, the Patents (Amendment) Act, 2002, introduced comprehensive amendments to bring various provisions of the Patents Act, 1970, into conformity with the TRIPS Agreement.[22] The third and most important step, the introduction of the Patents (Amendment) Act, 2005, provided for product patent rights along with the already existing process patent rights. This act was passed by Parliament in April 2005 and came into force with retrospective effect from 1 January 2005.

Four major concerns have been raised in the context of India signing the TRIPS Agreement. The question whether the introduction of product patents in developing countries like India would incentivise R&D for the development of new drugs was debated intensively, both nationally and internationally. The report of the Commission on Intellectual Property Rights (CIPR 2002) established by the British government expresses serious doubts about the probability of developing countries benefiting from R&D for new drugs, especially for the treatment of diseases more prevalent in these countries. The report points out that the R&D strategies of pharma majors are focused on the development of a few 'blockbusters', and therefore these firms would be unwilling to invest in R&D for the development of drugs to treat tropical diseases which do not constitute a big market, like cardiovascular or cancer diseases.[23] Lanjouw (1998) argues that the low per capita spending on health in developing countries as compared to advanced countries constitutes a disincentive for pharma majors to invest in R&D. She points out that of the 775 new drugs introduced in developed country markets between 1975 and 1989, only 8 were for tropical diseases. Two of these eight were developed in the US military laboratory. Similar concerns have been expressed within the country regarding the possibility of India benefiting from R&D under the new patent regime (Dhar and Rao 1993; Keayla 1994).

The second concern is that the introduction of product patents may lead to a rise in drug prices. As we have seen, India had already experienced very high drug prices under the 1911 patent regime. Some scholars have projected the likely rise in prices. Watal (2000) projects a 242 per cent rise in medicine prices in India. The issue of prices of medicines was intensely debated in Parliament when the bill amending the Patents Act, 1970, was introduced in 2005. One member of Parliament asked whether we would be

> able to meet our own requirements at a cheaper rate after adopting this product regime? Can it be assured that we would be able to meet the requirements of medicine of our people? Because, that was not our experience in the past.
>
> (Supreme Court of India 2013: para. 81)

The third concern relates to exports and imports. There have been apprehensions that exports of generic drugs may be restricted as a result of product patents being introduced in all countries, and imports may rise due to patent monopoly (Grace 2004; Lanjouw 1998). Such a situation would lead to a negative trade balance, with the country becoming import-dependent for medicines – a situation that existed at the time of independence, and which was overcome through calibrated policy interventions over a period of many decades.

The fourth concern, deriving from those described previously, and perhaps the most serious in the context of the new patent regime, is the very existence of the Indian generic industry. This concern is shared not only by the industry but also by parliamentarians, civil society groups, international organisations, academics, and foreign governments, especially in developing countries. Parvinder Singh, vice-chairman and managing director of Ranbaxy, the leading Indian pharma firm, explains the different dimensions of the impact of product patents on the Indian pharma industry. According to him, a change in the Patents Act, 1970,

> [would be] disastrous for the Indian economy in terms of (i) our current research activity . . . (ii) no new products would be introduced by Indian companies as is happening at present . . . (iii) the country will become entirely dependent on imports (of not only raw materials but also finished products) and at exorbitant prices,

(iv) export activity would receive major setback, substantially worsening the balance of payment position further, (v) monopolistic regimes will get established and competitive forces would get totally eliminated

(P. Singh 1988).

Similar concerns expressed by various constituencies led to the formation of the National Working Group on Patent Laws (NWGPL) in 1988, an informal public interest expert group. The NWGPL has established People's Commissions, members of which include eminent personalities from diverse fields in the country, like the bureaucracy, academia, industry, and law, to study various facets of the new patent regime and to publish reports. The Fourth People's Commission was established in 2003 to study the provisions of the Patents Amendment Bill, 2003. The commission was chaired by I. K. Gujral, former prime minister of India, and its members included Yash Pal, former chairman of the University Grants Commission, Muchkund Dubey, former foreign secretary, B. L. Das, India's former ambassador to the General Agreement on Tariffs and Trade (GATT) forum, Yusuf Hamied, chairman and managing director of Cipla, S. P. Shukla, former member of the Planning Commission, Prabhat Patnaik, former professor of economics at Jawaharlal Nehru University, Rajeev Dhavan, senior advocate of the Supreme Court of India, and Ashok Parthasarathi, former secretary to the Government of India. B. K. Keayla, former commissioner of payments, was its convener.

The commission's report systematically documents the various challenges faced by the Indian pharma industry.[24] The report cautions that 'a sound and balanced national patent system is of crucial importance for the autonomous development of any economy and for meeting public demand for drugs, pharmaceuticals and other essential commodities' (NWGPL 2004: 6). The findings and recommendations of the report became the basis for protests from various quarters when the UPA government attempted to introduce the Patents Amendment Bill in December 2004. Interestingly, concerns were also expressed by foreign countries regarding the challenges faced by the Indian pharma industry. Many developing countries, such as Ghana, Malawi, Lesotho, Cambodia, Indonesia, and Thailand, were concerned about the future of the Indian pharma industry, as their own antiretroviral programmes were dependent on affordable drugs supplied by India. Given this context, representatives of WHO and the Joint United Nations Programme on HIV/AIDS (UNAIDS) wrote to the health minister and the commerce and industry minister of India, respectively, urging that India should make use of the flexibilities provided in the TRIPS Agreement to the fullest extent possible, so that it could continue to produce and export generic drugs (Supreme Court of India 2013).

A detailed analysis of the extent to which these concerns were justified, and how they were addressed, is provided in the ensuing chapters. The following section offers an overview of the current state of play in the Indian pharmaceutical industry.

## The Indian pharmaceutical industry: its current state of play

The Indian pharmaceutical industry was estimated at US$18 billion, and the domestic pharmaceutical market was US$10.76 billion, in 2008 (GoI 2008a). By 2020, the industry is expected to reach US$91.45 billion (*Times of Oman* 2013). A large number of firms are engaged in the manufacture of drugs and pharmaceuticals: more than 250 large firms, and about 8,000 small-scale units (GoI 2008a).

### Sales

The sales turnover of the pharmaceutical industry has shown impressive growth since the mid-1990s. Table 1.4 provides the annual sales turnover figures since 1994–95. As seen from the table, the sales turnover, at current prices, has increased from Rs 119,482 million in 1994–95 to Rs 1,045,894 million in 2011–12. The data was obtained from the Prowess

*Table 1.4* Sales turnover in the Indian pharmaceutical industry (at current prices, in Rs million)

| | | | |
|---|---|---|---|
| 1994–95 | 119,482 | 2003–04 | 419,167 |
| 1995–96 | 141,294 | 2004–05 | 438,819 |
| 1996–97 | 154,433 | 2005–06 | 519,853 |
| 1997–98 | 173,689 | 2006–07 | 644,488 |
| 1998–99 | 217,718 | 2007–08 | 749,211 |
| 1999–2000 | 243,943 | 2008–09 | 872,573 |
| 2000–01 | 260,139 | 2009–10 | 927,110 |
| 2001–02 | 295,894 | 2010–11 | 1,014,409 |
| 2002–03 | 340,269 | 2011–12 | 1,045,894 |

*Source:* Prowess, Version 4.13, CMIE.

database of the Centre for Monitoring Indian Economy (CMIE). The database covers companies registered under the Companies Act, 1956, across industries; the list includes 653 pharmaceutical firms. The Prowess database provides an electronic compilation of data released by companies, often published in their annual reports.

However, the share of the domestic market (total sales *less* exports) in sales turnover has been on the decline. Its share declined from 82 per cent in 1994–95 to 56 per cent in 2011–12 (Prowess, Version 4.13, CMIE). This is due to the more rapid growth of exports, and not because of a decline in the domestic market as such. Exports of Indian pharmaceutical products are analysed in greater detail in Chapter 2.

## Production

The production of drugs showed impressive growth, from Rs 82,200 million in 1993–94 to Rs 1,528,920 million in 2012–13 (Figure 1.1).

## Market concentration

The domestic pharmaceutical market is a highly concentrated market, with the top five firms accounting for more than one-fifth of the market share. The top 10 firms accounted for 36 per cent of the market in 2011–12. The top 5 and top 10 firms' share of the market, as compared to 1994–95, have shown an increase (Table 1.5).

Market concentration appears to be even higher in therapeutic sub-markets. It is estimated that the top four firms accounted for 61 per cent in cephalosporins, 99 per cent in streptomycin and 93 per cent in chloramphenicol. In the streptomycin and chloramphenicol markets, respectively, a single firm held a market share of 89 per cent and 53 per cent (Mishra 2010).

## Foreign investment

It was expected that, with the liberalisation of foreign investment in pharmaceuticals, investments by MNCs in production, exports and R&D would increase. The Statement on Industrial Policy, 1991, declared that 'foreign investment and technology collaboration will be welcomed to obtain higher technology, to increase exports and to expand the production base' (GoI 1991: para. 13). However, these expectations did not materialise, and MNCs utilised the liberalised

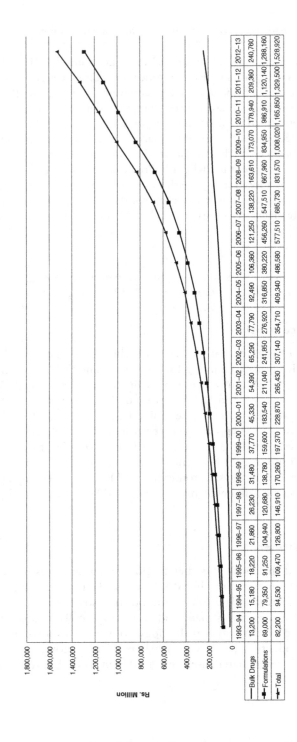

*Figure 1.1* Production of pharmaceuticals

*Source:* IDMA (2004) for data up to 2002–03; IDMA (2014) for data from 2003–04 to 2012–13.

| | 1993–94 | 1994–95 | 1995–96 | 1996–97 | 1997–98 | 1998–99 | 1999–00 | 2000–01 | 2001–02 | 2002–03 | 2003–04 | 2004–05 | 2005–06 | 2006–07 | 2007–08 | 2008–09 | 2009–10 | 2010–11 | 2011–12 | 2012–13 |
|---|---|---|---|---|---|---|---|---|---|---|---|---|---|---|---|---|---|---|---|---|
| Bulk Drugs | 13,200 | 15,180 | 18,220 | 21,860 | 26,230 | 31,480 | 37,770 | 45,330 | 54,390 | 65,290 | 77,790 | 92,490 | 106,360 | 121,250 | 138,220 | 163,610 | 173,070 | 178,940 | 209,360 | 240,760 |
| Formulations | 69,000 | 79,350 | 91,250 | 104,940 | 120,680 | 138,780 | 159,600 | 183,540 | 211,040 | 241,850 | 276,920 | 316,850 | 380,220 | 456,260 | 547,510 | 667,960 | 834,950 | 986,910 | 1,120,140 | 1,288,160 |
| Total | 82,200 | 94,530 | 109,470 | 126,800 | 146,910 | 170,260 | 197,370 | 228,870 | 265,430 | 307,140 | 354,710 | 409,340 | 486,580 | 577,510 | 685,730 | 831,570 | 1,008,020 | 1,165,850 | 1,329,500 | 1,528,920 |

Rs. Million

Table 1.5 Top 10 players in the domestic market (sales less exports)

| 2011–12 | | | 1994–95 | | |
|---|---|---|---|---|---|
| Company | Rs million | Market share (%) | Company | Rs million | Market share (%) |
| Cipla | 33,855 | 5.8 | GSK | 7,687 | 7.5 |
| Intas Pharmaceuticals | 26,345 | 4.5 (10.4) | Novartis | 4,304 | 4.2 (11.7) |
| GSK | 24,322 | 4.2 (14.6) | Ranbaxy Laboratories | 4,176 | 4.1 (15.7) |
| Lupin | 23,776 | 4.1 (18.7) | Lupin Laboratories | 3,108 | 3.0 (18.7) |
| Ranbaxy Laboratories | 22,647 | 3.9 (22.6) | Aventis Pharma | 2,712 | 2.6 (21.4) |
| Dr. Reddy's Laboratories | 19,397 | 3.3 (25.9) | Cipla | 2,678 | 2.6 (24.0) |
| Abbott India | 14,976 | 2.6 (28.5) | Pfizer | 2,399 | 2.3 (26.3) |
| Aurobindo Pharma | 14,547 | 2.5 (31.0) | Ambalal Sarabhai | 2,381 | 2.3 (28.6) |
| Jubilant Life Sciences | 13,756 | 2.4 (33.3) | Torrent Pharmaceuticals | 2,320 | 2.3 (30.9) |
| Wockhardt | 13,569 | 2.3 (35.7) | Abbott | 2,299 | 2.2 (33.1) |

Note: Figures in brackets indicate the cumulative market share.
Source: Computed by the author based on data from Prowess, Version 4.13, CMIE.

foreign investment policy to acquire leading Indian firms, rather than undertaking greenfield investments, so as to make their entry into the generics business easier. As of March 2010, MNC subsidiaries in India[25] as a whole had invested Rs 9,310 million in completed greenfield projects, which constituted only 7 per cent of the total investment on completed greenfield projects in the pharma sector.[26] The entire greenfield investment by all MNC subsidiaries taken together over a period of years constituted only a fraction of the investment that a single MNC had incurred in taking over Ranbaxy, a leading pharma firm in India. Daiichi acquired the majority stake in Ranbaxy in 2008 for Rs 211,230 million. Table 1.6 provides the takeover details of some leading Indian pharma firms. We may also note that only a few MNCs are engaged in greenfield investments in India. Of the top three profitable MNCs in India,[27] only one (GSK) had engaged in greenfield projects in India.[28]

Multinational pharma majors have been struggling in recent years to come up with new chemical entities. They are also faced with the expiry

*Table 1.6* Acquisition of leading Indian pharmaceutical firms

| Year of acquisition | Acquired Indian company | Acquiring foreign company | Acquisition value ($ million) | Acquisition value (Rs million)* |
|---|---|---|---|---|
| Aug 2006 | Matrix | Mylan | 736 | 33,330 |
| April 2008 | Dabur | Fresenius Kabi | 219 | 10,060 |
| June 2008 | Ranbaxy | Daiichi Sankyo | 4,600 | 211,230 |
| July 2008 | Shantha Biotech | Sanofi Aventis | 783 | 35,960 |
| Dec 2009 | Orchid (injectables business) | Hospira | 400 | 18,970 |
| May 2010 | Piramal Healthcare | Abbott | 3,720 | 169,520 |
| Dec 2010 | Paras | Reckitt Benckiser | 726 | 33,030 |

*Note:* *US$ million converted into Rs million by using the exchange rate given by the Reserve Bank of India.

*Source:* DIPP (2010: 8); Erman and Chatterjee (2010) for information in the last row of the table.

of blockbuster patents. For example, industry estimates indicate that 68 per cent of the sales of market leader Pfizer and 66 per cent of the sales of Eli Lilly in 2010 would have gone off patent in the subsequent three years (Dhar 2011). Hence, these companies have been forced to enter the generics business. The acquisition of firms with established networks gives them easy entry to the generics trade.

### Research and development

The pharmaceuticals industry is the most R&D-intensive industry in India. In this sector, R&D intensity (i.e. R&D as a percentage of sales) grew from 1 per cent in 1994–95 to 5 per cent in 2009–10.[29] Compared to other major sectors such as chemicals (including drugs and pharmaceuticals) and transport, this growth is phenomenal. Figure 1.2 shows R&D intensity in five major sectors in India.

### Advertising and marketing

The Indian pharmaceutical industry spends more on promotional activities (advertising and marketing) than it spends on R&D. It spent

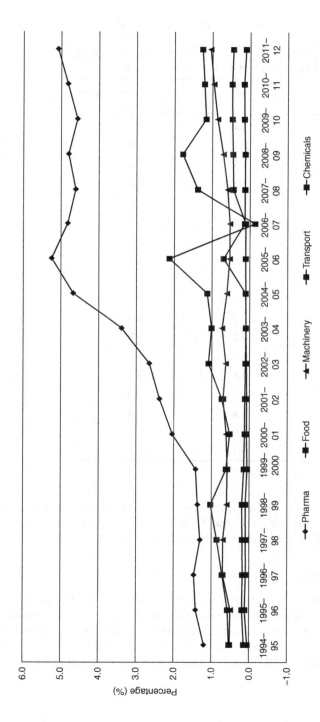

*Figure 1.2* R&D as percentage of sales in important sectors

*Source:* Prowess, Version 4.13, CMIE.

*Table 1.7* Investment of Indian pharmaceutical industry in R&D and advertising and marketing (% of sales turnover)

|  | *R&D* | *Advertising and marketing* |
|---|---|---|
| 1994–95 | 1.2 | 5.5 |
| 1995–96 | 1.4 | 5.0 |
| 1996–97 | 1.5 | 5.2 |
| 1997–98 | 1.3 | 5.8 |
| 1998–99 | 1.4 | 5.1 |
| 1999–2000 | 1.4 | 5.8 |
| 2000–01 | 2.0 | 5.9 |
| 2001–02 | 2.4 | 5.8 |
| 2002–03 | 2.7 | 6.2 |
| 2003–04 | 3.4 | 6.2 |
| 2004–05 | 4.7 | 6.2 |
| 2000–06 | 5.2 | 5.8 |
| 2006–07 | 4.8 | 5.6 |
| 2007–08 | 4.6 | 5.5 |
| 2008–09 | 4.8 | 6.0 |
| 2009–10 | 4.6 | 5.4 |
| 2010–11 | 4.8 | 5.4 |
| 2011–12 | 5.1 | 6.7 |

*Source:* Prowess, Version 4.13, CMIE.

6.7 per cent of total sales turnover on promotional activities in 2011–12, whereas investment in R&D was 5.1 per cent. The gap was greater in 1994–95, when investment in R&D was very low (Table 1.7).

## Conclusion

The growth of the Indian pharmaceutical industry testifies to the success of the calibrated policy interventions initiated by the Government of India in this sector. Once the industry had grown sufficiently to stand on its own feet, reforms were introduced so as to enable it to compete with the global majors. Revolutionary reforms were instituted in

areas such as industrial licensing, production controls, foreign investment and technology collaborations, import restrictions, and IP protection. Modifications to the IPR regime were later introduced, primarily
out of compulsion because of the commitments entered into under the
TRIPS Agreement, and not out of the felt need for such modifications.
Under the new liberalised policy regime, the pharmaceutical industry
has thrived in terms of growth in production, sales, exports, and R&D
investments. Yet, despite having a thriving drug industry, one that has
come to be known as the pharmacy of the world, one-third of the population of India still does not have access to essential medicines. This
is a major concern. In countries like India, expenditure on medicines
constitutes a significant share of the total expenditure on health care.
Therefore, medicines play a crucial role in the public health care system
in India. With the introduction of product patent rights in pharmaceuticals in India, what needs to be seen is whether Indian firms are in a
position to take advantage of the patents system.

## Notes

1  Bulk drugs or active pharmaceutical ingredients are the basic chemicals
   and ingredients necessary for the production of medicines. When active
   ingredients are put into dosage forms, they become formulations ready
   for use by patients.
2  The terms 'pharmaceutical industry' and 'drug industry' are used inter-
   changeably in the text.
3  In patent filings, the share of MNCs ranged between 78 and 90 per
   cent. Their share was 80 per cent in 1949, 87 per cent in 1955,
   85 per cent in 1965, and 78 per cent in 1970. For details, see Dhavan
   (1988).
4  Nehru to Deshmukh, 12 February 1951, Nehru Papers, first instalment,
   file no. 73, pp. 58–60, cited in Tyabji (2004).
5  Prime Minister's Office, note no. 310-PMO/54, 5 July 1954, Nehru
   Papers, first instalment, file no. 266, p. 51, cited in Tyabji (2004).
6  Drug price control orders also played a major role in reducing the
   domestic prices of drugs.
7  Those firms which exported a minimum of 60 per cent of their production were allowed to keep equity levels of up to 74 per cent. Those that
   exported 100 per cent of their production were permitted to maintain
   100 per cent equity.
8  The government fixed the price of Baralgan Ketone at Rs 1,810 per kilogram. The company obtained a stay order from the Delhi High Court
   and continued to charge the old price, i.e., Rs 24,735 per kilogram.
9  This recommendation could not be implemented due to legal loopholes
   (Sengupta et al. 2008).

10  This is exclusive of excise duties and local taxes.

11  Generic firms are firms manufacturing generic drugs. 'Generic drugs' are marketed under their chemical names, e.g., paracetamol that is marketed only as paracetamol. Outside India, in countries with a history of product patents in pharmaceuticals, companies other than the innovator have to market their drugs as generic preparations. In these countries, 'generic drug' refers to drugs produced by companies other than the patent holder. Generic drugs tend to be supplied at a lower cost. In India, generic drugs are marketed under brand names; e.g., paracetamol is marketed under such brand names as Crocin, Calpol, etc. These drugs are called 'branded generics'. 'Generic generics', on the other hand, refers to drugs that are marketed under their chemical names. The terms 'branded generic' and 'generic generics' are relevant only in the Indian context.

12  'Active pharmaceutical ingredient' or API is another term for bulk drugs.

13  The drugs reserved for the public sector were later reduced from 15 to 5 (vitamin B1, vitamin B2, folic acid, tetracycline, and oxytetracycline).

14  This is the paid-up share capital of a company plus free reserve, if any, and surpluses excluding outside investments which are not readily available for operational activity.

15  Net fixed assets plus the working capital of a manufacturer.

16  An overage is a fixed amount of the drug substance added in excess of the label claim in the formulation. Overage is permitted to compensate for the expected and documented manufacturing losses. However, the use of any overages has to be justified considering the safety and efficacy of the product. For details visit http://www.fda.gov/ohrms/dockets/dockets/05d0021/05d-0021-c000003–01-vol1.pdf (accessed on 6 October 2014).

17  In their study, the authors used IMS Health's market data for India in 2008.

18  Article 65.2 of the TRIPS Agreement.

19  Article 65.4 of the TRIPS Agreement.

20  Article 70.8 of the TRIPS Agreement.

21  Exclusive marketing rights entail a five-year patent-like monopoly for products covered by product patent applications made under the mailbox system. A company securing an exclusive marketing right has the exclusive right to sell or distribute in the country the article or substance covered in the patent application.

22  This act introduced 64 amendments (Basheer 2005).

23  According to the report, a drug is considered to be a blockbuster if its annual turnover is above $1 billion.

24  In 2003, the National Democratic Alliance government led by the Bharatiya Janata Party introduced the draft bill amending the Patents Act, 1970, so as to meet the deadline of 1 January 2005. The bill lapsed with the dissolution of the 13th Lok Sabha. The next year, in December 2004, the UPA government introduced the same bill in Parliament for the amendment of the Patents Act, 1970.

25  Investments by Indian firms that were taken over by MNCs (see Table 1.6) are not included in this category.
26  Based on Prowess CapEx data.
27  GlaxoSmithKline, Pfizer and Biddle Sawyer.
28  SK invested Rs 1,160 million in greenfield projects, of which 69 per cent was spent on its vaccine project, 20 per cent on a bulk drug project and 11 per cent on a drug plant project.
29  Expenditure on R&D is the total of R&D capital and current expenditures.

# Chapter 2

# Patterns of trade in the Indian pharmaceutical industry

The debate regarding the implications of liberalisation of import restrictions and production controls for the trade in pharmaceutical products gathered momentum with the decision to implement product patent rights in India. The removal of regulations insisting upon local production, the placing of pharmaceuticals in the OGL category, and the abolition of restrictions on foreign firms were all expected to encourage imports of pharmaceutical products into India. The introduction of the new patent regime raised apprehensions that growth in exports would be affected by the restrictions on generics producers' scope of operations, particularly their ability to export to preferred destinations. On the other hand, it was felt that imports would get a fillip because of the restricted scope of operation of domestic producers with regard to patented medicines. This would cause the balance of trade (BoT) to deteriorate.

Maskus and Penubarti (1995) analyse the data on exports from member countries of the Organisation for Economic Co-operation and Development (OECD) to 25 developing countries in 28 manufacturing sectors in 1984. They find that exporting firms discriminated in their sales decisions, taking account of local patent laws. Hence, exports to countries with stronger patent laws were larger in volume. Based on more disaggregated industry-wise data, P. J. Smith (1999) confirms the view that the export decisions of firms are influenced by the strength of patent rights in the importing countries. Smith's study is based on the US's exports (of all manufacturing industries at the two-digit level) to 92 countries in 1992. She finds that US exports were significantly influenced by patent rights in the importing countries. However, the direction of the relationship, i.e. market expansion and market power effects, depended on the threat of imitation.[1] Smith's study classifies countries into four groups depending on the strength of their patent rights and imitative capabilities:[2] (*a*) countries with weak patent rights and weak imitative abilities; (*b*) countries with strong patent rights and weak imitative abilities; (*c*) countries with weak patent rights and strong imitative abilities; and (*d*) countries with strong patent rights and strong imitative abilities. The author observes that the strengthening of patent rights in countries posing a strong threat of imitation encourages the expansion of exports, whereas strong patent rights enhance market power in countries where the threat of imitation is weak.

India was classified in the category of countries with weak patent rights and strong imitative abilities. Hence, a market expansion effect was expected to occur with the strengthening of patent rights. Following this reasoning, it was expected that imports to India, a country with a credible threat of imitation, would expand with the implementation of product patent rights. Pharmaceutical Research and Manufacturers of America (PhRMA), the most powerful association of innovator pharmaceutical firms in the world, estimated an annual loss of approximately US$500 million on account of deficiencies in the Indian patent regime (KEI 2000). At the same time, the Indian pharmaceutical industry would no longer be able to export generics of patented drugs, which had been a thriving trade in the past. This would leave the BoT in bad shape (P. Singh 1988).

Some scholars have attempted to assess the likely impact of the strengthening of patent laws on India's trade in pharmaceuticals. Lanjouw (1998) argues that imports of formulations would increase, but the BoT would not be affected adversely because of the export potential in the bulk drugs category. Her interviews with MNCs reveal that they would be interested in importing into India rather than producing in India, for two reasons. First, the transfer pricing loophole would give the patent-owning MNC an incentive to produce drugs elsewhere and then import them into India. Second, unlike generic drugs, manufacturing costs are a small component of the price of patented drugs. Therefore, India's advantages as a low-cost manufacturer would not be particularly useful in attracting investment in local production facilities. However, Lanjouw does not see an imminent threat to the BoT, as the likely surge in imports of formulations would be offset by exports of bulk drugs.

A study by Grace (2004) claims that there would be no decline in exports, as Indian firms are in a position to take advantage of the expiry of blockbuster patents. There exists a latent trade opportunity in pharmaceutical products for India. Better compliance with good manufacturing practices (GMP), low-cost production, and the expertise derived from more than three decades of reverse engineering of on-patent medicines, would allow Indian firms to explore exports opportunities in 'low volume–high priced' regulated markets, while retaining their traditional 'low priced–high volume' markets in Asia, Africa and Latin America.[3] Grace points out that Indian companies that hitherto focused on the domestic generics market would have to look beyond for sustaining their sales. Grace also suggests that the fast-growing bio-pharma sector in India would further boost exports.

The study by Chaudhuri (2005b) reveals a remarkable growth in pharmaceutical exports, particularly after 2000. The growth in exports to regulated markets, especially the US, is the major reason for this spurt; exports to regulated markets accounted for 39 per cent of exports in 2001–02. Dhar and Gopakumar (2008) also arrive at similar conclusions. Chaudhuri (2005b) further points out that in 2001–02, 52 per cent of the exports consisted of formulations, while the remaining were bulk drugs.[4] However, no major studies exist that provide detailed analysis of imports of pharmaceuticals into India. The present chapter attempts to fill this gap in the literature.

## Estimating exports and imports

Data on exports and imports of pharmaceutical products in India are available from government as well as industry sources. However, significant disparities exist among the data provided by the different sources, which makes it difficult to analyse the industry over a period of time. The annual report (2006–07) of the Department of Chemicals and Petrochemicals (GoI 2007a: 56) estimated imports of Rs 11,500 million in 2004–05, whereas the Bulk Drug Manufacturers' Association (India) (BDMA) reported a figure of Rs 56,300 million.[5] There have been instances of contradictions in the data provided by a single industry association. For example, the 42nd *Annual Publication* of the Indian Drug Manufacturers' Association (IDMA) (IDMA 2004) gives a detailed list of exports and imports of 'bulk drugs, intermediates, formulations, etc.', at the eight-digit level for 2002–03. It also provides aggregate export and import figures for the same year separately.[6] When we add up the data at the eight-digit level, exports amount to Rs 97,144.1 million, and imports to Rs 88,461 million. However, the aggregate data provided on a separate page of the report show exports of Rs 119,250 million and imports of Rs 11,025 million.[7] Those using the aggregate data would see a trade surplus of Rs 108,225 million, whereas those using the eight-digit-level data would conclude that the trade surplus was only Rs 8,633 million.

The disparity in the data provided by government sources is even more confusing: while the annual report of the Department of Chemicals and Petrochemicals (GoI 2007a: 56) quoted an exports figure of Rs 108,210 million in 2005–06, its website displayed a figure of Rs 221,160 million for the same year.[8] Data provided by two sources of the same ministry thus show a difference of more than 100 per cent. However, with the establishment of a dedicated department for pharmaceuticals (the Department of Pharmaceuticals) within the Ministry of Chemicals and Fertilizers in July 2008, attempts have been made to coordinate the data reported by different government sources. The disparities existed till very recently even in official estimates, which has made it difficult to use these data for any analysis of past trends.

In its attempts to address the anomalies in the data in government sources, the Department of Pharmaceuticals in early 2010 revised the list of pharmaceutical products that have been exported and imported. Subsequently, it re-estimated the exports and imports data for the preceding five years. The revised data, which I have accessed from the Department of Pharmaceuticals, refer to 456 products for exports and 434 products for imports at the eight-digit level of the harmonised system (HS) classification.[9] The exports estimates changed marginally, while a significant scaling up of imports estimates of up to 93 per cent occurred with the revision.[10] The Department of Pharmaceuticals' estimates of exports and imports before and after the revision are shown in Table 2.1. However, the revised imports estimates have not yet been made public,[11] whereas the revised exports estimates have been provided in the department's annual reports since 2010–11.

*Table 2.1* Exports and imports estimates by the Department of Pharmaceuticals before and after the revision of 2010 (in US$ million)

|  | Exports | | Imports | |
|---|---|---|---|---|
|  | Before revision | After revision | Before revision | After revision |
| 2004–05 | 3,972.6 (178,570) | 3,832.8 (172,280) | 698.3 (31,390) | 1,345.2 (60,470) |
| 2005–06 | 5,017.2 (222,160) | 4,794.5 (212,300) | 1,019.6 (45,150) | 1,824.6 (80,790) |
| 2006–07 | 5,939.7 (268,950) | 5,668.2 (256,660) | 1,295.7 (58,670) | 2,256.8 (102,190) |
| 2007–08 | 7,643.9 (307,590) | 7,294.7 (293,540) | 1,673.5 (67,340) | 2,940.1 (118,310) |
| 2008–09 | 8,369.6 (384,330) | 8,671.8 (398,210) | 1,862.4 (85,520) | 3,362.4 (154,400) |

*Note:* Figures in brackets indicate the estimates in Rs million. The Department of Pharmaceuticals made available the data in Rs crores. Exchange rates provided by the Reserve Bank of India for different years have been used to arrive at the figures in US$ million.

*Source:* Prepared by the author based on data made available to him by the Department of Pharmaceuticals.

The other limitation in relying on the data on exports and imports collected by the Department of Pharmaceuticals for the purpose of time series analysis is that data are available only from 2002–03. For the analysis of patterns of trade in the Indian pharmaceuticals sector after 1994, we would have to use data provided by different agencies. This is not desirable given the wide discrepancies among their data. Therefore, the only alternative is to compile trade statistics using HS codes for the period of our analysis based on a classification of pharmaceutical products. The Standard International Trade Classification (SITC) of the United Nations (UN) provides a classification of pharmaceutical products. The UN's Statistics Division offers export and import statistics based on the SITC in electronic format, known as COMTRADE. The WTO uses the SITC to identify leading exporters and importers in different sectors and also relies on COMTRADE for its annual publication, *International Trade Statistics.*[12]

As the Department of Pharmaceuticals uses its own classification of pharmaceutical products, the export and import statistics it provides are different from statistics based on SITC. *International Trade Statistics* (WTO 2009: 74, Table II.39) reports exports of US$5.8 billion in pharmaceutical products by India in 2008. The exports figures provided by the Department of Pharmaceuticals were US$7.3 billion and US$8.7 billion for 2007–08 and 2008–09, respectively. Similarly, COMTRADE reports pharmaceutical imports of US$3.4 billion by India in 2008, whereas the Department of Pharmaceuticals estimates imports of US$1.6 billion and US$1.9 billion for 2007–08 and 2008–09, respectively. Though the two series of estimates adopt different year-endings, differences of more than 80 per cent indicate that the Department of Pharmaceuticals follows a different classification of pharmaceutical products. A comparison of product coverage by SITC and the Department of Pharmaceuticals, respectively, explains the difference in the data provided by the two. Table 2.2 explains these differences in terms of the coverage and classification of pharmaceutical products.

The Department of Pharmaceuticals uses a different methodology for classifying pharmaceutical products. This classification cannot be used for making cross-country comparisons, as it is not based on the internationally accepted classification. Our analysis involves cross-country comparisons; therefore, COMTRADE is the ideal source of data for the purposes of this chapter.

Pharmaceutical products are classified into formulations (dosage forms) and bulk drugs. The US regulation on food and drugs defines a finished dosage form as a 'tablet, capsule or solution that contains a drug

*Table 2.2* Coverage of pharmaceutical products

|  | Department of pharmaceuticals | SITC |
|---|---|---|
| Coverage of HS at two digits | 15, 17, 28, 29, 30, 35, 38, 56, and 96 | 29 and 30 |
| Coverage of HS at six digits | 131 | 75 |
| Classification of bulk drugs and formulations | Bulk drugs: selected products from HS 15, 17, 28, and 29 | Bulk drugs: HS 30.01, 30.02, 30.05, and 30.06 and selected products from HS 29 |
|  | Formulations: HS 30 and selected products from HS 35, 38, 56, and 96 | Formulations: HS 30.03 and 30.04 |

*Source:* Compiled by the author using Conversion Table HS 2007 to SITC, Rev. 3, available at UN Statistics Division, http://unstats.un.org/unsd/trade/conversions/HS%20Correlation %20and%20Conversion%20tables.htm (accessed on 23 June 2010). The UN Statistics Division provides conversion and correspondence data between different HS classifications, SITC revisions and between HS and SITC.

substance, generally, but not necessarily, in association with one or more other ingredients'.[13] The European Medicines Agency (EMA) provides more detailed information on what a dosage form or formulation is. According to EMA, a dosage form is the form in which a pharmaceutical substance (API) is presented in the medicinal product package. The defining characteristics of dosage forms are determined by the state of the matter, delivery method, release characteristics, and the body part for which the product is formulated (EMA 2005). The USFDA defines an API as

> any substance or mixture of substances intended to be used in the manufacture of a drug (medicinal) and that, when used in the production of a drug, becomes an active ingredient of the drug product. Such substances are intended to furnish pharmacological activity or other direct effect in the diagnosis, cure, mitigation, treatment, or prevention of disease or to affect the structure and function of the body.
>
> (USFDA 2001: 47)

In India, these terms are defined only in the DPCO, which carries similar definitions. The DPCO of 2013, Section 2(f), defines a formulation as 'a medicine processed out of, or containing one or more drugs with or without use of any pharmaceutical aids, for internal or external use for or in the diagnosis, treatment, mitigation or prevention of disease' (GoI 2013b).[14] A bulk drug is defined as

> any pharmaceutical, chemical, biological or plant product including its salts, esters, isomers, analogues and derivatives conforming to standards specified in the Drugs and Cosmetics Act, 1040 (23 of 1040) and which is used as such or as an ingredient in any formulation.
>
> (*ibid*.: Section 2[b])

The Department of Pharmaceuticals classifies products under HS Chapters 30, 35, 38, 56, and 96 as formulations and products classified under other chapters (15, 17, 28, and 29) as bulk drugs (Table 2.2). The SITC does not explicitly use the terms 'formulations' and 'bulk drugs', but classifies pharmaceutical products into two groups: Code 542, 'medicaments (including veterinary medicaments)', representing formulations; and Code 541, 'medicinal and pharmaceutical products, other than medicaments of group 542', representing bulk drugs. Code 542 consists of products from HS 30.03 and 30.04. Chapter 30 of the HS, relating to pharmaceutical products, has six subchapters (four digits). The term 'medicaments' applies only to subchapters 30.03[15] and 30.04,[16] indicating that these two subchapters are distinct from the other four subchapters. For the purposes of the present analysis, products classified under SITC Code 542 (which, in the HS classification, include the products under Chapters 30.03 and 30.04) are considered as formulations or dosage forms. Products classified under SITC Code 541 (which, in the HS classification, include select products from Chapter 29 and products in Chapters 30.01, 30.02, 30.05, and 30.06) are considered as bulk drugs or APIs. Our interaction with officials of the BDMA confirmed that HS 30.03 and 30.04 are considered as formulations by the pharmaceuticals industry. Table 2.3 offers a detailed HS classification of bulk drugs and formulations (at the six-digit level).

Our analysis also requires firm-wise data. This was accessed through the Prowess database of the CMIE, described in Chapter 1. Though the Prowess database does not cover small firms, it offers an overall view of the pharmaceuticals trade, since it includes all the major players in the industry. For the present analysis, data on variables such as sales, exports of goods, imports of finished goods, and imports of raw materials were used. Exports of goods and imports of finished goods in pharmaceuticals include both formulations and bulk drugs. Imports of raw materials include intermediates and other raw materials such as speciality chemicals

*Table 2.3* HS codes for bulk drugs and formulations (six-digit level)

| Bulk drugs (SITC 541) | | | | | Formulations (SITC 542) |
|---|---|---|---|---|---|
| 263623 | 293721 | 293941 | 294130 | 300620 | 300310 |
| 293121 | 293722 | 293942 | 294140 | 300630 | 300320 |
| 293610 | 293723 | 293943 | 294150 | 300640 | 300331 |
| 293621 | 293729 | 293949 | 294190 | 300650 | 300339 |
| 293622 | 293731 | 293951 | 300110 | 300660 | 300340 |
| 293624 | 293739 | 293959 | 300120 | | 300390 |
| 293625 | 293740 | 293961 | 300190 | | 300410 |
| 293626 | 293790 | 293962 | 300210 | | 300420 |
| 293627 | 293810 | 293963 | 300220 | | 300431 |
| 293628 | 293890 | 293969 | 300230 | | 300432 |
| 293629 | 293911 | 293991 | 300290 | | 300439 |
| 293690 | 293919 | 293999 | 300510 | | 300440 |
| 293711 | 293929 | 294110 | 300590 | | 300450 |
| 293712 | 293930 | 294120 | 300610 | | 300490 |

*Source:* Compiled by the author using Conversion Table HS 2007 to SITC, Rev. 3, available at UN Statistics Division, http://unstats.un.org/unsd/trade/conversions/HS%20Correlation%20and%20Conversion%20tables.htm (accessed on 23 June 2010). The UN Statistics Division provides conversion and correspondence data between different HS classifications, SITC revisions and between HS and SITC.

for technical applications and solvents. This was confirmed using the annual reports of companies. For example, the classification of finished goods in the annual report of Glenmark (2008–09) includes both bulk drugs and formulations. Similarly, the exports data in the annual report of Matrix (2008–09) include bulk drugs as well as tablets and capsules (formulations). In the annual report of Ranbaxy (2009), the list of products mentioned among 'raw materials used' includes certain intermediates and chemicals.[17] Data from the three sources on pharmaceutical exports and imports discussed in the preceding paragraphs are provided in Table 2.4.

Of the three sources, data provided by Prowess for exports seem to be closest to the reality. We would expect firms engaging in exports to have a minimum amount of investment in R&D. The firms listed in the Prowess database account for 93 per cent of the R&D undertaken in the pharmaceuticals industry.[18] Similarly, the firms listed by Prowess hold 96 per

Table 2.4 Export–import data: similarities and divergences

| | Exports ($ million) | | | | Imports ($ million) | | | |
|---|---|---|---|---|---|---|---|---|
| | COMTRADE* | Prowess | DoP† | DoP‡ | COMTRADE* | Prowess | DoP† | DoP‡ |
| 2004–05 | 2,271.6 | 3,118.5 | 3,972.6 (178,570)§ | 3,832.8 (172,280) | 680.3 | 1,275.9 | 698.3 (31,390) | 1,345.2 (60,470) |
| 2005–06 | 2,761.8 | 3,672.9 | 5,017.2 (222,160) | 4,794.5 (212,300) | 937.8 | 1,689.7 | 1,019.6 (45,150) | 1,824.6 (80,790) |
| 2006–07 | 3,416.1 | 5,124.2 | 5,939.7 (268,950) | 5,668.2 (256,660) | 1,181.5 | 2,118.0 | 1,295.7 (58,670) | 2,256.8 (102,190) |
| 2007–08 | 4,476.7 | 6,653.2 | 7,643.9 (307,590) | 7,294.1 (293,540) | 1,616.3 | 2,601.0 | 1,673.5 (67,340) | 2,940.1 (118,310) |
| 2008–09 | 5,822.7 | 6,543.4 | 8,369.6 (384,330) | 8,671.8 (398,210) | 1,869.6 | 2,537.6 | 1,862.4 (85,520) | 3,362.4 (154,400) |

Notes: *Refers to calendar-year data.

†Before revision.

‡After revision.

§Figures in brackets indicate estimates reported by the Department of Pharmaceuticals (DoP, in Rs million).

Source: Computed by the author based on DESA/UNSD, UN COMTRADE Database (Rev. 3); Prowess, version 4.13, CMIE.

cent of the domestic market.[19] As Prowess covers all the major firms that account for the bulk of activities in the pharmaceuticals industry, exports and imports data provided by Prowess appear to be the most reliable.

With respect to imports data, Prowess figures are higher compared to COMTRADE and Department of Pharmaceuticals figures (before revision). A possible explanation for this could be that Prowess's imports data include figures for raw materials, such as speciality chemicals and solvents, which do not have medicinal properties. It is likely that the imports data provided by COMTRADE and the Department of Pharmaceuticals (before revision) do not take these raw materials into account, since they do not possess medicinal properties. The revised imports estimates of the Department of Pharmaceuticals, however, are higher than the Prowess estimates. Since Prowess does not cover small firms, its imports figures might be lower than actual imports; small firms do not generally engage in exports, but do engage in imports of raw materials.[20] It seems, therefore, that the revised estimates of the Department of Pharmaceuticals are more reliable in the case of imports. However, we refrain from employing the HS codes used by the Department of Pharmaceuticals in arriving at its revised estimates, since the new estimates have not been made public even four years after revision.

## Trends in the pharmaceuticals trade

India has experienced a remarkable growth in the exports of pharmaceutical products in the post-1994 period. The country's share in world exports of pharmaceutical products increased from 1 per cent in 1994 to 2.9 per cent in 2012. India's ranking as a global exporter of pharmaceutical products improved from 17 to 11 during this period.[21] Within the domestic exports basket as well, the share of the pharmaceuticals sector has been increasing: from 2.2 per cent in 1994 to 3.8 per cent in 2012.[22] India does not have any significant imports in pharmaceuticals, and the country does not figure in the list of leading importers of pharmaceuticals in the WTO's *International Trade Statistics*.[23] Table 2.5 shows the trends in exports and imports of pharmaceutical products since 1994.

The Indian pharmaceutical sector has a steadily growing positive trade balance. The surplus has been contributed by the formulations category, which accounted for 83 per cent of pharmaceutical exports in 2012. However, in bulk drugs, the country has had negative trade balances in most years. Whereas formulations account for a major share of exports, bulk drugs make up the larger share of imports.

Most leading exporters of pharmaceuticals are domestic firms, which derive a substantial share of their sales turnover from exports. Table 2.6

*Table 2.5* Export, import and BoT of different categories of pharmaceutical products (in $ million)

| | Bulk drugs | | | Formulations | | | Total | | |
|---|---|---|---|---|---|---|---|---|---|
| | Export | Import | BoT | Export | Import | BoT | Export | Import | BoT |
| 1994 | 101.6 | 251.0 | −149.4 | 484.2 | 47.5 | 436.7 | 585.8 | 298.5 | 287.3 |
| 1995 | 141.2 | 348.1 | −206.9 | 582.9 | 56.9 | 526.0 | 724.2 | 405.1 | 319.1 |
| 1996 | 174.3 | 269.3 | −95.0 | 639.7 | 37.4 | 602.3 | 814.0 | 306.7 | 507.3 |
| 1997 | 222.6 | 324.2 | −101.6 | 724.6 | 64.6 | 660.0 | 947.2 | 388.9 | 558.3 |
| 1998 | 250.5 | 303.5 | −53.0 | 683.2 | 80.7 | 602.5 | 933.7 | 384.3 | 549.4 |
| 1999 | 265.3 | 290.2 | −24.9 | 802.9 | 82.6 | 720.3 | 1,068.2 | 372.8 | 695.4 |
| 2000 | 341.8 | 281.1 | 60.7 | 805.1 | 92.8 | 712.3 | 1,147.0 | 373.9 | 773.1 |
| 2001 | 363.3 | 303.0 | 60.3 | 959.1 | 97.6 | 861.5 | 1,322.4 | 400.5 | 921.9 |
| 2002 | 451.7 | 404.0 | 47.7 | 1,157.1 | 141.9 | 1,015.2 | 1,608.7 | 545.9 | 1,062.8 |
| 2003 | 516.5 | 468.8 | 47.7 | 1,455.4 | 141.2 | 1,314.2 | 1,971.9 | 609.9 | 1,362.0 |
| 2004 | 482.5 | 493.9 | −11.4 | 1,789.1 | 186.4 | 1,602.7 | 2,271.6 | 680.3 | 1,591.3 |
| 2005 | 543.0 | 662.4 | −119.4 | 2,218.8 | 275.3 | 1,943.5 | 2,761.8 | 937.8 | 1,824.0 |
| 2006 | 644.5 | 789.3 | −144.8 | 2,771.6 | 392.2 | 2,379.4 | 3,416.1 | 1,181.5 | 2,234.6 |
| 2007 | 900.8 | 1,101.2 | −200.4 | 3,576.0 | 515.1 | 3,060.9 | 4,476.7 | 1,616.3 | 2,860.4 |
| 2008 | 1,015.0 | 1,203.5 | −188.5 | 4,807.7 | 666.0 | 4,141.7 | 5,822.7 | 1,869.6 | 3,953.1 |
| 2009 | 1,322.1 | 1,312.4 | 9.7 | 4,599.4 | 735.5 | 3,863.9 | 5,921.5 | 2,047.9 | 3,873.6 |
| 2010 | 1,356.9 | 1,598.5 | −241.6 | 5,767.2 | 835.9 | 4,931.3 | 7,124.1 | 2,434.4 | 4,689.7 |
| 2011 | 1,828.6 | 1,799.4 | 29.2 | 7,674.1 | 935.7 | 6,738.4 | 9,502.6 | 2,735.0 | 6,767.6 |
| 2012 | 1,871.0 | 1,908.2 | −37.2 | 8,988.7 | 1,161.0 | 7,827.7 | 10,859.7 | 3,069.2 | 7,790.5 |

*Source:* Computed by the author based on DESA/UNSD, UN COMTRADE database (Rev. 3).

shows that some firms derive more than 80 per cent of their sales from exports of formulations and bulk drugs.

Eight of the ten exporters listed in Table 2.6 are Indian-owned. Ranbaxy and Mylan (earlier Matrix), though they now fall under the ambit of 'foreign-owned' companies, were formerly flagship Indian pharmaceutical firms that were subsequently taken over by MNCs (Ranbaxy was taken over in 2008 and Matrix in 2006).[24] Figure 2.1 shows the export intensity (defined as exports–sales ratio) of MNCs, domestic firms and taken-over firms.[25] The figure reveals that the taken-over firms (previously domestic enterprises) have been the most export-oriented and

*Table 2.6* Leading exporters and importers of pharmaceuticals*

| Exporters in 2011–12 | | | Importers in 2008–09 | | |
|---|---|---|---|---|---|
| Company | Exports ($ Million) | Sales (%) | Company | Imports ($ million) | Sales (%) |
| Ranbaxy Laboratories (F) | 1,027.4 | 70.5 | Sanofi India (F) | 36.1 | 14.4 |
| Dr. Reddy's Laboratories (I) | 961.9 | 71.4 | Jubilant Life Sciences (I) | 34.4 | 6.3 |
| Cipla (I) | 733.7 | 52.2 | Novartis India (F) | 26.1 | 15.5 |
| Mylan Laboratories (F)† | 679.1 | 86.0 | Wyeth (F) | 24.8 | 20.6 |
| Lupin (I) | 602.7 | 56.1 | GSK (F) | 20.7 | 4.4 |
| Aurobindo Pharma (I) | 581.1 | 66.8 | Merck (F) | 14.4 | 12.7 |
| Divi's Laboratories (I) | 319.8 | 86.4 | Cadila Healthcare (I) | 13.7 | 2.6 |
| Sun Pharmaceutical Industries (I) | 290.7 | 59.0 | Abbott India (F) | 11.0 | 3.8 |
| Jubilant Life Sciences (I) | 269.8 | 49.7 | Pfizer (F) | 9.0 | 4.5 |
| Cadila Healthcare (I) | 269.7 | 51.6 | Lupin (I) | 5.6 | 0.5 |

*Notes:* (I), Indian; (F), Foreign.
*Importers of finished goods.
†Matrix Laboratories officially became Mylan Laboratories in October 2011.
*Source:* Prowess, version 4.13, CMIE.

MNCs the least export-oriented. While taken-over firms had an exports–sales ratio of 76 per cent in 2011–12, the ratio for MNCs stood at only 9 per cent.

The fact that MNCs in India do not have significant exports is contrary to the general perception that foreign firms tend to be more export-oriented. Firms investing abroad are expected to show greater export competitiveness, as their presence in foreign markets ensures flexibility, reliability and timeliness in dealing with global buyers, features that are crucial for export success (Kumar and Jayaprakash 2007). This expectation was explicitly articulated in the Statement on Industrial Policy, 1991, which initiated the liberalisation of FDI rules in the pharmaceutical sector. The statement reads: 'Foreign investment would bring attendant advantages of technology transfer, marketing expertise, introduction of modern managerial techniques and new possibilities for promotion of exports' (GoI 1991). From 2001, the year in which 100 per cent FDI was permitted in the pharmaceutical sector, the exports–sales ratio of MNCs has grown only marginally: from 7 per cent to 9 per cent between 2000–01 and 2011–12.

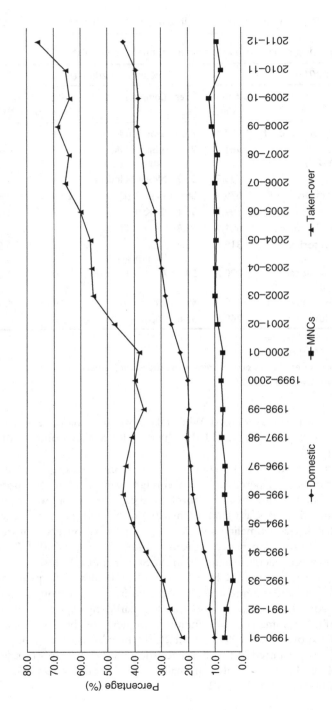

*Figure 2.1* Exports–sales ratio

*Source:* Prowess, version 4.13, CMIE.

With the pipeline of new drugs drying up, and a number of countries emphasising the production of generic drugs, MNCs have been forced to get into the generics business as well. Many have opted to take over leading players in the generics segment, instead of doing it the organic way. This is precisely the reason why taken-over firms in India have been the most export-oriented. Daiichi took over Ranbaxy when the Government of Japan decided to take measures that would help increase the share of generic drugs in the total use of medicines in the public health system from 17 per cent to 30 per cent by 2012. Daiichi Sankyo has its nose in front in the expanding generics market because of Ranbaxy's cheap, high-quality manufacturing facilities (R. Joseph 2008). The phenomenon of MNCs taking over generics firms has not been limited to India alone. Domestic drug companies have been subject to takeover by multinational firms in other countries also. For example, Sanofi Aventis took over Medley in Brazil and Zantiva in the Czech Republic; GSK took over Biotechnology Medical Services (BMS) in Egypt and Pakistan (DIPP 2010). According to a survey of 50 top industry executives reported in the *Financial Times* (2010), 65 per cent of the executives considered that their sector was facing a 'strategic crisis', and 67 per cent saw 'diversification' as a potential solution. Sanofi Aventis has led the field in diversification over the period 2004–09; its non-patented drug sales grew from 5 per cent to 12 per cent between 2004 and 2009 (*ibid.*).

In imports of pharmaceutical goods (excluding raw materials), on the other hand, the leading players are foreign firms. Table 2.6 shows that 7 of the top 10 importers in 2008–09 were MNCs. Taken-over firms had no imports at all. For MNCs as whole, imports of finished products constituted 8 per cent of sales in 2011–12, as compared to 2 per cent in 1994–95,[26] whereas, for domestic firms as whole, imports of finished products has been insignificant.[27]

Major changes have taken place in the destinations of exports from India and the sources of imports into the country. In 1994, the Soviet Union was the single largest exports destination (15 per cent). The US, which was only the third largest export destination accounting for just 7 per cent of total exports of pharmaceutical products, became the single largest export destination by 2012, accounting for more than a fourth of total exports (Table 2.7). With respect to imports, India used to source the bulk of its requirements from Germany, China and the US in 1994; the three countries together met 36 per cent of India's requirements. Over the years, China has replaced other countries as the major supplier. China's emergence as the single largest supplier is

*Table 2.7* Top five destinations for exports and sources of imports in 2012 (bulk drugs and formulations combined)

| Exports | | | Imports | | |
|---|---|---|---|---|---|
| Destinations | $ million | Total exports (%) | Sources | $ million | Total imports (%) |
| US | 3,137.3 | 28.9 | China | 966.2 | 31.5 |
| Russian Federation | 490.9 | 4.5 | Switzerland | 480.5 | 15.7 |
| UK | 395.1 | 3.6 | US | 320.7 | 10.4 |
| South Africa | 315.6 | 2.9 | Germany | 228.9 | 7.5 |
| Nigeria | 287.8 | 2.6 | Italy | 127.9 | 4.2 |
| Others | 6,233.0 | 57.4 | Others | 945.0 | 30.8 |

*Source:* Computed by the author based on DESA/UNSD, UN COMTRADE database (Rev. 3).

remarkable. In 1991, imports from China were insignificant at 0.2 per cent ($0.5 million), and it ranked a low 30 in terms of exports of pharmaceutical products to India.

### Exports of bulk drugs and formulations

The pharmaceutical industry of India has increasingly become export-oriented. The share of exports in sales has grown steadily from 15 per cent in 1993–94 to 45 per cent in 2011–12.[28] The rates of growth of exports of bulk drugs and formulations, respectively, also suggest that the industry has been doing better in the TRIPS period (i.e. after 2005). Figure 2.2 shows the annual rates of growth in exports of bulk drugs and formulations in different periods between 1991 and 2012.

Two major changes in the trends may be seen in Figure 2.2. First, the rate of growth of exports was higher for bulk drugs compared to formulations in the period before 2001, whereas the opposite has been true in the post-2001 period.[29] Second, exports of bulk drugs witnessed a decline until 2005, but this trend was reversed in the post-2005 period, although the growth rate seems to have remained stagnant in the period since 2006. Formulations, on the other hand, exhibited a steady growth in exports throughout.

An important factor contributing to the growth in exports of bulk drugs in recent years has been the outsourcing of API production by MNCs. Much of the publicly known outsourcing undertaken by MNCs has involved APIs. Table 2.8 lists selected cases of pharmaceutical outsourcing.

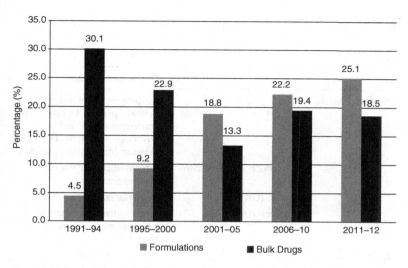

*Figure 2.2* Average annual rate of growth in exports during different periods
*Source:* Prepared by the author based on DESA/UNSD, UN COMTRADE database (Rev. 3).

*Table 2.8* Outsourcing by MNCs

| Indian partner | MNC | Outsourced products |
| --- | --- | --- |
| Cadila Healthcare | Altana (Germany) | Two intermediates for Altana's under-patent molecule Protonix (pantoprazole) |
| | Boehringer Ingelheim (Germany) | Gastrointestinal and cardiovascular products |
| | Mayne (Australia) | Intermediates for oncology products |
| Hikal Ltd | Degussa | Pharmaceutical intermediates and APIs |
| Nicholas Piramal | Advanced Medical Optics (USA) | Neutralising tablets and sterile form-fill-seal (FFS) packs (product name not disclosed) |
| | Allergan (USA) | APIs for levobunolol (Betagan) and brimonidine (Alphagan and Alphagan-D) |
| | AstraZeneca (Sweden) | APIs |
| | Pfizer (USA) | APIs |

*(Continued)*

*Table 2.8* (Continued)

| Indian partner | MNC | Outsourced products |
|---|---|---|
| Dishman Pharma | Solvay (Belgium) | Six projects, of which the primary project involves starting material and advanced intermediate for Teveten (eprosartan mesylate) |
| | AstraZeneca (Sweden) | Intermediate for Nexium (esomeprazole) |
| | GSK (UK) | Intermediates and APIs |
| | Merck (USA) | Intermediate for losartan (to be supplied to its contract manufacturer in Japan) |
| Shasun Chemicals | GSK (UK) | API for ranitidine |
| | Eli Lilly (USA) | APIs for nizatidine, methohexital and cycloserine |
| | Reliant Pharma (USA) | APIs |
| | Alpharma (USA) | APIs and generics |
| | Boots (South Africa) | APIs |
| Lupin Labs | Fujisawa (Japan) | Cefixime |
| | Apotex (Canada) | Cefuroxime axetil, lisinopril |
| | DMS (USA) | APIs for cephalosporins |
| IPCA Labs | Merck (USA) | APIs |
| | Tillomed (UK) | Atenelol |
| Biocon | Bristol Myers Squibb (USA) | APIs |

*Source:* KPMG (2006); Linton and Nicholas (2007).

Foreign companies are keen to outsource their production so as to contain their costs. India has become a favourable destination for outsourcing, since it has the largest number of USFDA-approved plants outside the US. India has more than 160 FDA-approved plants, whereas its competitor China has only about 30 (ICRA 2011). We do not have information on how many of the outsourced APIs are under patent protection, so we cannot derive any firm conclusions regarding the impact of the new patents law on the outsourcing of pharmaceutical production to India.

However, the composition of exports (Table 2.9) shows that formulations account for more than four-fifths of pharmaceuticals exports. While the rate of growth of exports of bulk drugs has recorded an increase in the post-2005 period, the share of bulk drugs in exports has declined

*Table 2.9* Composition of exports (%)

| Year | Bulk drugs | Formulations |
|------|-----------|--------------|
| 1994 | 17.3 | 82.7 |
| 1995 | 19.5 | 80.5 |
| 2000 | 29.8 | 70.2 |
| 2005 | 19.7 | 80.3 |
| 2008 | 17.4 | 82.6 |
| 2009 | 22.3 | 77.7 |
| 2010 | 19.0 | 81.0 |
| 2011 | 19.2 | 80.8 |
| 2012 | 17.2 | 82.8 |

Source: Computed by the author based on DESA/UNSD, UN COMTRADE database (Rev. 3).

consistently since 2000. This raises the question of whether the acceleration in the growth rate of bulk drugs exports in recent years has any significance in terms of the dynamics of the pharma industry in the new environment.

The analysis of revealed comparative advantage (RCA) suggests that the country's advantage lies in formulations, among the two categories of pharmaceutical products (Figure 2.3). The RCA is an index of the export performance of a country with respect to a particular commodity; it captures the comparative advantage of trade in that commodity. The RCA of a particular commodity is measured by the share of that industry in the country's total exports relative to the share of the industry in total world exports. The RCA index may assume values from zero to infinity, with values greater than unity indicating a comparative advantage for that country in a particular commodity. One needs to be cautious in interpreting the RCA results, because an improvement in a country's total exports would bring down the RCA for a particular sector. For our purposes, RCA analysis helps us understand the changing dynamics of exports within the pharmaceutical sector.

The RCA index of the $i$th product for country $j$ in year $t$ is defined as:

$$RCA_{ij}^{(t)} = [(X_{ij}W^{(t)}/X_{io}W^{(t)})/(X_{oj}W^{(t)}/X_{oo}W^{(t)})]$$

where
$X_{ij}W^{(t)}$ = total export of product $i$ by country $j$ to the world in year $t$
$X_{io}W^{(t)}$ = total export of product $i$ by all countries in year $t$
$X_{oj}W^{(t)}$ = total export by country $j$ to the world in year $t$
$X_{oo}W^{(t)}$ = total export of all products by all countries in year $t$

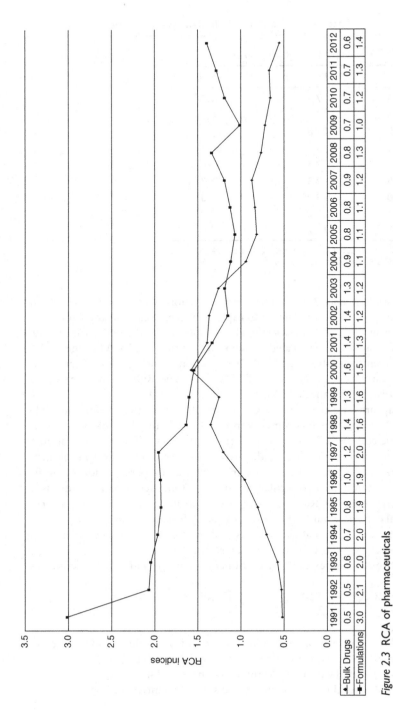

| | 1991 | 1992 | 1993 | 1994 | 1995 | 1996 | 1997 | 1998 | 1999 | 2000 | 2001 | 2002 | 2003 | 2004 | 2005 | 2006 | 2007 | 2008 | 2009 | 2010 | 2011 | 2012 |
|---|---|---|---|---|---|---|---|---|---|---|---|---|---|---|---|---|---|---|---|---|---|---|
| Bulk Drugs | 0.5 | 0.5 | 0.6 | 0.7 | 0.8 | 1.0 | 1.2 | 1.4 | 1.3 | 1.6 | 1.4 | 1.4 | 1.3 | 0.9 | 0.8 | 0.8 | 0.9 | 0.8 | 0.7 | 0.7 | 0.7 | 0.6 |
| Formulations | 3.0 | 2.1 | 2.0 | 2.0 | 1.9 | 1.9 | 2.0 | 1.6 | 1.6 | 1.5 | 1.3 | 1.2 | 1.2 | 1.1 | 1.1 | 1.1 | 1.2 | 1.3 | 1.0 | 1.2 | 1.3 | 1.4 |

*Figure 2.3* RCA of pharmaceuticals

Source: Computed by author using data from DESA/UNSD, UN COMTRADE database (Rev. 3).

Figure 2.3 provides two indications that tell the story of the changing dynamics of the Indian pharmaceutical industry. First, the RCA index for bulk drugs shows upward movement till 2000 and the reverse trend after 2001. Since 2004, the value of the RCA index for bulk drugs is below unity. We also saw that the share of bulk drugs in pharmaceutical exports began to decline after 2000. Second, the RCA index for formulations shows a decline till 2005 and a gradual acceleration from 2006. Further, the index never falls below unity.[30] It is startling that, in the post-2005 period, the comparative advantage indicator for formulations has shown upward movement. This is contrary to what was anticipated by many observers.

The changing trends in pharmaceutical exports, when combined with the removal of restrictions on imports of pharmaceutical products and removal of the requirement of local production of bulk drugs, is likely to have affected the production dynamics of the pharmaceutical industry. But it is hard to establish this relationship due to limitations in the production data. The Department of Pharmaceuticals data on production are based on selected drugs; moreover, the data are presented in terms of quantity. The *Annual Report 2012–13* of the Department of Pharmaceuticals states that one of the functions of the NPPA is 'to collect/maintain data on production', and that 'NPPA compiles the annual data on production of selected monitored bulk drugs' (GoI 2013c: 23). Annexure I of the *Annual Report* provides the data on production compiled by NPPA (*ibid.*: 99–102). It contains data on 96 bulk drugs. The data are provided in terms of million tons of value (*ibid.*). We cannot relate production data based on quantity to trade data that are available mostly in terms of value. The only option, then, is to rely on the production data made available by industry sources. The *Annual Publications* of IDMA provide data on the production of formulations and bulk drugs. However, IDMA stopped releasing this data a few years ago.[31] The data on production available from IDMA until 2009 shows that the growth dynamics of pharmaceuticals production has changed in the post-1994 period (Figure 2.4).

It may be seen from Figure 2.4 that growth in the production of bulk drugs has been considerably lower since 2005–06 as compared to earlier periods.[32] Expansion in exports of bulk drugs (Figure 2.2), along with a decline in production, indicates more imports. Firms are increasingly importing bulk drugs, intermediates and fine chemicals, as against relying on indigenous production as they did earlier. Prowess data on imports of raw materials show that the share of imported raw materials in the total sales turnover has grown from 9 per cent in 1990–91 to

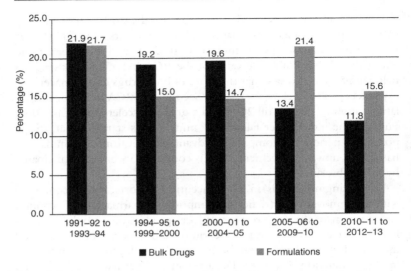

*Figure 2.4* Average annual growth rate in production (at current prices)
Source: Computed by author based on data available in IDMA (2004) for data up to 2002–03, and IDMA (2014) for data from 2003–04 to 2012–13.

11 per cent in 2000–01, and further to 13 per cent in 2011–12. There are different levels of value addition in bulk drugs manufacturing. The Indian bulk drugs industry seems to be focusing on the higher end of the value chain. The abolition of the ratio parameter linking the production of formulations to indigenous production of bulk drugs from basic stages, alongside reductions in import duty, has eased the constraints on imports of bulk drugs and other raw materials. Import duty on organic chemicals including bulk drugs has been reduced from 120 per cent in 1990–91 to 7.5 per cent in 2007–08 (Jha 2007).

Another important factor contributing to the decline in domestic bulk drugs production has been the implementation, in July 2005, of Schedule M of the Drugs and Cosmetics Act, 1940, which lays down GMPs for the pharmaceuticals industry in India. As a consequence, a number of bulk drug manufacturers in the SME category had to shut down their operations. By January 2006, 70 firms were reported to have shut down in the state of Andhra Pradesh alone, on account of lack of implementation of the GMP (*Times of India* 2006). Thousands of firms were reported to have shut down by the end of 2009 due to their inability to comply with the GMP standards (Pharmabiz 2009). Complying with the GMP would cost at least Rs 2 million for an SME firm – a cost that most SMEs find beyond their reach. During my interactions with SME pharma representatives, it was revealed that not more than 1 per cent of SME pharma firms would be able to implement Schedule M.[33] Reportedly, no new SME pharmaceutical units came up during the three-year period ending 2009, except in excise-free zones (*ibid.*). The SME sector has been a major producer of bulk drugs in India.

The bulk drugs segment is highly competitive, with a large number of players; hence, the returns are very low. The Hathi Committee (GoI 1975) had worked out the capital invested–turnover ratio for bulk drugs and formulations manufacturing, respectively. It estimated a ratio of 1 : 1 for bulk drugs at best, and 1 : 2.6 for formulations on average; the ration for formulations in some cases could be as high as 1 : 7.2. Given these facts, and with the ratio parameter no longer in force, firms in India tend to concentrate on the production and export of formulations. They rely on imports for sourcing cheap raw materials. A detailed discussion of the imports segment is provided later in this chapter, in the section on imports of bulk drugs and formulations.

Exports of bulk drugs have been characterised by more diversified destinations. The share of the top five export destinations declined from 44 per cent in 1994,[34] to 22 per cent in 2012. The top five destinations in 2012 were USA (8 per cent), Turkey (5 per cent), Bangladesh (3 per cent), Brazil (3 per cent), and China (3 per cent).

Unlike bulk drugs, the growth in formulations exports has been driven mostly by expansion in exports to selected countries. In 2012, the US alone accounted for one-third (33 per cent) of total formulations exports, worth US$2,986 million.[35] In 1995, on the other hand, the export strategy was focused on a more diverse range of countries. Russia, the top export destination in 1995, accounted for only 14 per cent of total exports of formulations from India in that year. The share of the top three export destinations including Russia in 1995 was only 30 per cent, lower than even the share that the US holds now.[36]

The US has become the most desired exports destination for both bulk drugs and formulations. However, formulations account for the lion's share of exports to the US – 95 per cent in 2012. In order to market a generic drug in the US, a company needs to file an Abbreviated New Drug Application (ANDA). When filing an ANDA, a company is required to certify that its product does not infringe any patent rights, or that the patent is invalid (para. IV certification). If the company successfully proves that the patent is invalid, or if it is the first to get approval for the generic version, it gets market exclusivity for 180 days. During this period, no other generics company is permitted to enter the market. This exclusivity is available under the Hatch-Waxman Act.

A successful first-to-file para. IV ANDA can bring immense profit to a company. For example, Dr. Reddy's, the first Indian company to market a generic (fluoxetine 40 mg) in August 2001 under the 180-day exclusivity provision, saw its sales of generics increasing from Rs 304 million in 2000–01 to Rs 4,066 million in 2001–02. The sale of fluoxetine 40 mg contributed 81 per cent of its total generics sales, and about half of Dr. Reddy's operating profit in 2001–02 (Chaudhuri 2007). In fact, Ranbaxy was the first to obtain the 180-day exclusivity, but could not launch the product in time because the patent holder obtained an injunction against Ranbaxy.[37] Patent litigation under para. IV is highly risky, since failure means the loss of several years of hard work and huge legal expenses. However, encouraged by the success of Dr. Reddy's, a number of firms have taken steps towards registering themselves as the first movers in the generics market, often gaining a huge market share. In November 2009, Ranbaxy introduced the generic version of GSK's skin medicine Valtrex under the 180-day market exclusivity condition. This enabled the company to secure 74 per cent of the US$1,400 million market before the expiry of exclusivity (*LiveMint* 2010a). The launch of a generic of Aricept (an Alzheimer's drug, whose patent is held by Eisai Co.) after its patent expired on 25 November 2010 was expected to earn Ranbaxy about US$200 million (*Economic Times* 2010a). Table 2.10 gives an overview of some recent cases in which Indian companies obtained 180-day marketing exclusivity in the US.

Until recently, only a few companies like Ranbaxy and Dr. Reddy's had filed ANDAs in their own names. Companies like Cipla had filed ANDAs in the names of their marketing partners in the USA. This situation has changed dramatically in recent times, and more companies are engaged in securing ANDAs on their own. From 161 ANDAs filed by four companies – Ranbaxy, Dr. Reddy's, Wockhardt, and Lupin – in the last quarter of 2003, the number went up to 701 ANDAs filed by 17 companies by the second quarter of 2007 (Chaudhuri 2007). Moreover, ANDA approvals obtained by Indian firms as a percentage of total approvals have also risen sharply, from 7 per cent in 2001 to 21 per cent in 2006, and further to 30 per cent in 2008 (*ibid.*; *Business Standard* 2009). The success of Indian firms in obtaining 180 days' exclusivity gives a definite boost to Indian exports of formulations. Exports of olanzapine (the generic of Zyprexa by Dr. Reddy's) and atorvastatin (the generic of Lipitor by Ranbaxy) are reported to have increased the growth in total pharmaceutical exports to 20 per cent in the third quarter of the

*Table 2.10* Selected drugs for which Indian companies have obtained 180-day market exclusivity in the US

| Company | Year of launch | Brand | Innovator | Innovator's sales/ year ($ million) |
| --- | --- | --- | --- | --- |
| Sun and Glenmark | 2007 | Trileptal | Novartis | 700 |
| Dr. Reddy's | 2008 | Imitrex | GSK | 1,000 |
| Dr. Reddy's* | 2011 | Zyprexa | Eli Lilly | 3,200 |
| Sun | 2008 | Protonix | Altana | 2,300 |
| Lupin | 2008 | Altace | Bayer | 800 |
| Sun | 2009 | Effexor XR | Wyeth | 2,300 |
| Ranbaxy | 2009 | Flomax | Boehringer Ingelheim | 1,300 |
| Ranbaxy | 2010 | Lipitor | Pfizer | 8,000 |
| Ranbaxy | 2010–11 | Aricept | Eisai | 1,600 |
| Glenmark | 2010–11 | Zetia | Schering-Plough/ Merck | 1,200 |
| Glenmark | 2010–11 | Tarka | Abbott/ Sanofi-Aventis | 72 |
| Glenmark | 2010–11 | Cutivate | Nycomed | 37 |

*Note:* *Dr. Reddy's obtained 180-day exclusivity for its drug olanzapine (generic version of Zyprexa) (20 mg tablets). Teva got authorisation for its olanzapine tablets of 2.5 mg, 5 mg, 7.5 mg, 10 mg and 15 mg.

*Source:* R. Joseph (2012: 67); Dr. Reddy's (2011) for information on Zyprexa, which was launched in 2011.

financial year 2011–12, as compared to the average quarterly growth rate of 15–16 per cent in the first two quarters (Nandakumar 2012). Dr. Reddy's reported an increase in profit of 88 per cent (on a quarter-on-quarter basis) on account of the sale of the Zyprexa generic in the US (Pilla 2012).

Companies also engage in developing non-infringing process for ANDA filing. Matrix Laboratories was the first Indian company to develop a non-infringing process for manufacturing citalopram. The company was able to reap huge benefits from its sales of the product, amounting to Rs 5,600 million till 2005–06. Another commercially successful example is the cefotaxime process developed by Lupin (Chaudhuri 2007).

Data from ANDAs and drug master files (DMFs) submitted to the USFDA provide indications of the extent to which Indian firms are seeking opportunities in the US market. The leading 10 pharmaceutical firms in India received 537 ANDA approvals between 2001 and 2012, one-fourth of which came with 180-day market exclusivity. A detailed analysis of ANDAs and DMFs filed by the top 10 Indian pharmaceutical companies is provided in Chapter 3.

India has the largest number of USFDA-registered pharmaceutical plants outside the US (GoI 2012c). As of December 2012, India had 546 company sites registered at USFDA (Pharmexcil 2012). Recent market estimates indicate that there may be further acceleration of Indian exports to the US. About 250 Indian generics products were launched in the US market in 2008, as opposed to 93 in 2003 (KPMG 2006). Up until the end of the 1980s, Indian firms focused extensively on the rest of the world markets, especially the USSR, where there was little patent protection and registration requirements were lax. The accumulation of enhanced technologies and production capabilities, coupled with the change in the global patent regime, has led to a gradual shift of focus to the highly lucrative US generics market, while retaining the old markets.

Indian firms have also begun to establish their presence in Europe, especially the UK. This is confirmed by data obtained from the Medicines and Healthcare Products Regulatory Agency (MHRA) for 2001–12. The two leading firms, Ranbaxy and Dr. Reddy's, have led the way here too, and they have been joined by three other firms, viz., Aurobindo Pharma, Nicholas Piramal and Orchid Healthcare (Dhar and Gopakumar 2008). Ranbaxy obtained the largest number of approvals (400), followed by Dr. Reddy's Laboratories (251). Table 2.11 lists the year-wise approvals obtained by the top three Indian firms from MHRA.

The preceding discussion points to the increasing presence of leading Indian firms in the generics industry in some of the larger markets for drugs in the world. Though Indian engagement is expanding in the European Union (EU), this market has generally been viewed as problematic compared to the US due to various kinds of barriers, for example, different regulatory approval requirements within the community, linguistic difficulties and complex pricing dynamics (Sampath 2008). No wonder, then, that Europe has been losing its prominence as an export destination.

The share of Europe in India's exports of formulations has seen a drastic decline: from nearly about two-thirds in 1991 to less than one quarter in 2012 (Table 2.12). On the other hand, Africa and America

Table 2.11 Year-wise approvals obtained from MHRA by the top three Indian firms

| Company | 2001 | 2002 | 2003 | 2004 | 2005 | 2006 | 2007 | 2008 | 2009 | 2010 | 2011 | 2012 | Total |
|---|---|---|---|---|---|---|---|---|---|---|---|---|---|
| Ranbaxy | 62 | 24 | 32 | 65 | 21 | 12 | 52 | 39 | 21 | 36 | 27 | 9 | 400 |
| Dr. Reddy's | – | 7 | 13 | 20 | 17 | 28 | 21 | 31 | 36 | 37 | 22 | 19 | 251 |
| Aurobindo | – | – | – | 2 | 17 | 5 | 0 | 25 | 12 | 57 | 33 | 0 | 151 |

*Source:* Compiled by the author based on the marketing authorisations granted by MHRA, Department of Health, Government of UK. Month-wise marketing authorisations issued by the MHRA are available at http://www.mhra.gov.uk/Howweregulate/Medicines/Licensingofmedicines/Informationforlicenceapplicants/Otherusefulservicesandinformation/Listsofapprovedproducts/Marketingauthorisations/index.htm (accessed on 21 February 2011).

*Table 2.12* Region-wise share in exports of formulations

| Year | Europe | Africa | America | Asia | Oceania |
|------|--------|--------|---------|------|---------|
| 1991 | 63.8 | 8.0 | 7.1 | 20.6 | 0.6 |
| 1992 | 51.3 | 16.7 | 7.3 | 23.7 | 1.0 |
| 1993 | 48.6 | 15.8 | 8.4 | 26.2 | 1.1 |
| 1994 | 45.8 | 15.1 | 8.9 | 29.6 | 0.7 |
| 1995 | 41.1 | 16.2 | 10.8 | 31.2 | 0.6 |
| 1996 | 41.5 | 15.5 | 10.8 | 31.5 | 0.8 |
| 1997 | 39.8 | 17.4 | 10.2 | 31.9 | 0.8 |
| 1998 | 28.2 | 21.3 | 12.4 | 37.0 | 1.1 |
| 1999 | 31.8 | 19.3 | 11.3 | 36.1 | 1.5 |
| 2000 | 31.2 | 22.6 | 12.3 | 32.4 | 1.5 |
| 2001 | 28.2 | 21.1 | 20.3 | 29.1 | 1.3 |
| 2002 | 28.5 | 22.3 | 22.2 | 25.6 | 1.1 |
| 2003 | 27.7 | 19.1 | 27.1 | 24.8 | 1.0 |
| 2004 | 30.8 | 20.1 | 25.1 | 22.8 | 1.0 |
| 2005 | 33.2 | 20.8 | 20.3 | 24.1 | 1.5 |
| 2006 | 29.6 | 23.1 | 25.5 | 20.6 | 1.2 |
| 2007 | 27.7 | 21.5 | 31.4 | 18.2 | 1.2 |
| 2008 | 31.5 | 23.3 | 27.7 | 16.3 | 1.3 |
| 2009 | 24.6 | 23.5 | 31.8 | 18.0 | 2.0 |
| 2010 | 24.0 | 24.4 | 34.4 | 15.0 | 1.9 |
| 2011 | 24.7 | 22.3 | 35.9 | 14.8 | 2.0 |
| 2012 | 22.5 | 21.3 | 39.6 | 14.3 | 2.1 |

*Source:* Computed by the author based on DESA/UNSD, UN COMTRADE database (Rev. 3).

are becoming major export destinations; the share of exports to these regions combined has grown from 15 per cent in 1991 to 24 per cent in 1994, and to 61 per cent in 2012. More than 80 per cent of exports to America are destined for North America, especially the US. We may also see from Tables 2.12 and 2.13 that exports to Asia and its subregions have experienced a decline between 2000 and 2012. Exports to BRICS partners (Brazil, Russia and China) have also shown a decline over this period. Overall, we may conclude that North America and Africa have been driving the growth of Indian pharmaceutical exports. South America and Asia, including subregions and regional blocs within Asia, seem to be relatively less significant for pharmaceutical exports.

Table 2.13 Share in exports (formulations): selected regions and groupings

| | North America | South America | West Asia | SAARC | BIMSTEC | ASEAN | BRICS |
|---|---|---|---|---|---|---|---|
| 1991 | 6.6 | 2.5 | 7.4 | 7.3 | 7.4 | 4.5 | 0.2 |
| 1992 | 6.7 | 3.7 | 8.5 | 7.7 | 8.5 | 5.5 | 13.8 |
| 1993 | 6.9 | 5.3 | 8.6 | 8.0 | 8.6 | 5.3 | 21.7 |
| 1994 | 7.6 | 6.2 | 8.1 | 7.8 | 8.1 | 8.2 | 18.9 |
| 1995 | 8.4 | 6.0 | 8.0 | 7.4 | 8.0 | 8.7 | 16.1 |
| 1996 | 8.7 | 5.2 | 8.2 | 7.5 | 8.2 | 8.9 | 18.5 |
| 1997 | 6.8 | 6.1 | 8.3 | 8.0 | 8.3 | 8.0 | 16.4 |
| 1998 | 8.4 | 6.4 | 9.7 | 9.2 | 9.7 | 10.0 | 10.2 |
| 1999 | 6.9 | 6.8 | 9.3 | 7.9 | 9.3 | 10.6 | 17.0 |
| 2000 | 7.3 | 5.7 | 10.3 | 8.6 | 10.3 | 9.7 | 15.6 |
| 2001 | 14.2 | 5.1 | 8.6 | 7.4 | 8.6 | 8.6 | 16.5 |
| 2002 | 15.4 | 4.7 | 7.6 | 6.9 | 7.6 | 7.9 | 14.9 |
| 2003 | 22.2 | 4.6 | 7.5 | 7.6 | 7.5 | 6.8 | 13.4 |
| 2004 | 19.1 | 5.6 | 6.5 | 6.2 | 6.5 | 6.8 | 14.0 |
| 2005 | 13.2 | 6.4 | 6.7 | 6.7 | 6.7 | 6.6 | 15.1 |
| 2006 | 18.0 | 4.3 | 6.4 | 6.4 | 6.4 | 6.3 | 15.6 |
| 2007 | 25.1 | 3.9 | 5.6 | 5.2 | 5.6 | 5.8 | 13.2 |
| 2008 | 21.4 | 3.7 | 5.1 | 4.8 | 5.1 | 5.3 | 13.7 |
| 2009 | 26.2 | 4.0 | 5.2 | 4.5 | 5.2 | 6.4 | 11.9 |
| 2010 | 30.2 | 3.5 | 2.4 | 3.8 | 4.8 | 5.5 | 11.4 |
| 2011 | 32.1 | 3.1 | 1.9 | 3.8 | 4.8 | 5.7 | 12.8 |
| 2012 | 35.5 | 3.4 | 1.8 | 3.2 | 2.9 | 5.6 | 11.2 |

Source: Computed by the author based on DESA/UNSD, UN COMTRADE database (Rev. 3).

## Global initiatives for the enforcement of IPRs

The renewed vigour that is visible globally with respect to IP enforcement, supposedly to aid the anti-counterfeiting drive, will have implications for the Indian pharmaceuticals industry, given that Africa is a major export focus. The recent anti-counterfeiting initiatives at various levels – WHO, the Anti-Counterfeiting Trade Agreement (ACTA), some free trade agreements (FTA) with EU, etc. – attempt to eliminate the distinctions between substandard drugs (a quality issue), counterfeit drugs (a trademark issue) and generic drugs (a patents issue). In the process, legitimate generics (for which no patents exist in the exporting country or the importing country) have been targeted under the counterfeits label. Such initiatives, which are supported by the pharma lobbies, have found takers even in developing countries, especially in East Africa. Members of the Eastern African Community (EAC) attempted to bring in an anti-counterfeit law at the regional level by proposing the EAC Anti-Counterfeit Bill of 2010.[38] Some members of the EAC also attempted to enact their own national anti-counterfeit legislations, such as the Kenya Anti-Counterfeit Act of 2008, the Tanzania Merchandise Marks Regulations Act of 2008, and the Uganda Anti-Counterfeit Bill of 2011 (UNDP 2012). Kenya adopted the Anti-Counterfeit Act, 2008, according to which copies or generic versions of all products having patent protection in Kenya or elsewhere may be considered 'counterfeit' in case of an IP dispute with the patent holder. The act defined counterfeiting as

> taking the following actions without the authority of the owner of intellectual property right subsisting in Kenya or elsewhere in respect of protected goods: (a) the manufacture, production, packaging, re-packaging, labelling or making, whether in Kenya or elsewhere, of any goods whereby those protected goods are imitated in such manner and to such a degree that those other goods are identical or substantially similar copies of the protected goods; . . . (d) in relation to medicine, the deliberate and fraudulent mislabelling of medicine with respect to identity or source, whether or not such products have correct ingredients, wrong ingredients, have sufficient active ingredients or have fake packaging.
>
> (Government of Kenya 2008: Section 2)

This definition is problematic for generic drugs, as they carry the same active ingredients as the originator drug, as well as carrying the same chemical names. So, the chances are very high that even legitimate generic drugs may be construed as infringing IPRs due to their relation to the identity and source of active ingredients.[39] This means that a genuine drug exported from India to Kenya would be classified as a counterfeit drug if a company that does not hold a patent for that particular drug either in India or in Kenya, but does hold the patent in a third country, raises a dispute over it. Indian pharmaceuticals exporters have expressed concern that the Kenyan anti-counterfeiting act may sound the death knell for India's pharmaceutical exports to Africa, as other nations may follow suit. In fact, following the passage of the act in Kenya, a few African countries – Nigeria, Uganda and Libya – moved towards banning imports of drugs from India (Lakshmi 2009).

However, the High Court of Kenya at Nairobi ruled in 2012 that the Anti-Counterfeit Act was unconstitutional.[40] The Kenyan act was challenged in the High Court by three HIV-infected patients, on the grounds that the act would infringe upon the fundamental rights to life and human dignity guaranteed by the Constitution of Kenya. They argued that 90 per cent of the AIDS patients in the country depended on imported generic drugs for treatment. The act would adversely affect the import of such drugs, since it did not distinguish between counterfeit drugs and generic drugs. Substantiating their argument, the petitioners pointed out that similar provisions in the law of other countries had resulted in customs authorities in European ports seizing HIV generic drugs destined for countries like Brazil and Vanuatu. The court ruled that the provisions of the act 'threaten to violate the right to life of the petitioners as protected by Article 26(1), the right to human dignity guaranteed under Article 28 and the right to the highest attainable standard of health guaranteed under Article 43(1)'.[41] The judgement pointed out that that the act did not distinguish between counterfeit and generic drugs. Further,

> the right to life, dignity and health of people like the petitioners who are infected with the HIV virus cannot be secured by a vague provision in a situation where those charged with the responsibility of enforcement of the law may not have a clear understanding of the difference between generic and counterfeit medicine.[42]

The export of formulations was not affected adversely by the implementation of TRIPS provisions. Indeed, formulations exports grew at higher rates in the post-2005 period. North America and Africa have been the two regions driving the accelerated pace of exports of formulations, together accounting for more than half of all such exports. Exports to India's IBSA[43] partners – Brazil and South Africa – have also seen remarkable growth. The expiry of blockbuster patents in the US and the success of Indian firms in obtaining 180-day market exclusivity by garnering first-to-file status have been major factors boosting exports from India. Exports to Europe have shown a trend of revival in recent years. However, the overzealous drive to enforce IPRs outside WTO under the banner of anti-counterfeiting initiatives has cast a shadow on the exports prospects of Indian generics, especially to Africa. As discussed earlier, the anti-counterfeit law that some countries in East Africa are in the process of adopting does not maintain the distinction between substandard and trademark counterfeits and patents infringement.

## Imports of bulk drugs and formulations

The analysis of imports data presented in Table 2.5 revealed that a major change has occurred in the composition of imports. The share of bulk drugs in imports has declined steadily from 84 per cent in 1994 to 62 per cent in 2012. The share of formulations, on the other hand, showed a corresponding increase. Analysis of the data also revealed that the rate of growth of total imports was higher during the period after 2001: 20.8 per cent average annual growth rate between 2002 and 2012, as compared to 7.2 per cent between 1994 and 2001. Table 2.14 gives a breakdown of the rates of growth of imports in the different periods.

Table 2.14 allows us to make the important observation that imports of formulations have been growing at a higher rate than bulk drugs. The surge in the import of formulations was a major cause of concern in India soon after the country became a party to the TRIPS Agreement. However, although formulations imports have been growing at higher rates, this has not adversely affected the BoT, since exports have also been growing. The import of formulations would have grown even faster had Indian legislators not incorporated provisions in the Patents Act to prevent the filing of frivolous patents (evergreening)[44] and had they not allowed the continued production of generics of mailbox drugs.[45] We will discuss these safeguards in more detail in the following paragraphs.

Evergreening has been a fundamental factor underlying the apprehensions in India about the adverse impacts of the new patents law. It was feared that the product patent system would become an instrument in the hands of foreign firms to exercise their monopoly power through filing frivolous patents. Normal tactics used in evergreening include the invention of salts, esters, polymorphs, etc., of existing molecules. The

*Table 2.14* Average annual growth rate of imports (%)

|             | Total | Bulk drugs | Formulations |
| ----------- | ----- | ---------- | ------------ |
| 1994–2001   | 7.2   | 6.1        | 13.4         |
| 2002–12     | 20.8  | 18.8       | 26.2         |

*Source:* Computed by the author based on the import data presented in Table 2.5.

intense deliberations in the Parliament of India attending the process of amending the Patents Act, 1970, resulted in the incorporation of Section 3($d$) into the act. This section excludes the following from patentable inventions:

> The mere discovery of a new form of a known substance which does not result in the enhancement of the known efficacy of that substance or the mere discovery of any new property or new use for a known substance or of the mere use of a known process, machine, or apparatus unless such known process results in a new product or employs at least one new reactant.
>
> *Explanation.* – For the purposes of this clause, salts, esters, ethers, polymorphs, metabolites, pure form, particle size, isomers, mixtures of isomers, complexes, combinations and other derivatives of known substance shall be considered to be the same substance, unless they differ significantly in properties with regard to efficacy.[46]

This clause has resulted in the denial of patents in a number of cases in India. The denial of a patent to Novartis for the beta crystalline form of imatinib mesylate (Glivec) was the most prominent of these cases, testing the sanctity of Section 3($d$). The highest court of India in its final judgement upheld the validity of this section, commenting that the provision was crucial for preventing bad patents. A detailed discussion of the Glivec case is provided in Chapter 4.

The amended Patents Act also provides that generic drugs, for which patent rights are in force, manufactured in India before 1 January 2005 would continue to be produced and marketed despite the existence of the patent on the drug. Section 11A.7 of the amended Patents Act provides that:

> the patent holder shall only be entitled to receive reasonable royalty from such enterprises which have made significant investment and were producing and marketing the concerned product prior to the 1st day of January, 2005 and which continue to manufacture the product covered by the patent on the date of grant of the patent and no infringement proceedings shall be instituted against such enterprises.[47]

These two sections of the amended Patents Act have played an important role in checking the import of formulations. Section 3($d$) ensures that the number of patents granted are kept to a minimum by incorporating provisions for checking bad patents. Section 11A.7 ensures that generics will be available for patented drugs, if the concerned generics were produced in India prior to 2005. The import of expensive, patented formulations are not a viable option for MNCs if less expensive generics are available in the market.

An analysis of the patents granted by USFDA makes the picture clearer. The USFDA approved 305 new medical entities (NMEs) between 1995 and 2004. Of these 305 entities, the patents for 298 had expired before 1995. Therefore, these 298 molecules or their minor modifications could not be patented in India, which meant that Indian firms could produce and market these drugs in India. Of the seven post-1995 NMEs, Indian firms obtained marketing approval for three entities in India prior to 2005 (see Gopakumar 2010). Although MNCs could obtain patents on these three molecules, Indian firms were able to produce them in India due to the provisions of Section 11.A.7 of the Patents Act. Thus, effectively, MNCs would be able to exercise patent monopoly only on 4 out of the 298 NMEs. Since the Supreme Court of India has upheld the sanctity of Section 3(d) of the Patents Act, India can continue to apply the high threshold level of patentability criteria. This ensures that not too many drugs can be patented for which domestic production cannot provide generic substitutes. Therefore, the probability that formulations imports will rise to a level that threatens the BoT is a distant one. A detailed discussion of patentable pharmaceutical inventions is provided in Chapter 4.

In the import of bulk drugs, interesting transitions took place after the patents reforms of the mid-1990s. China became the single largest supplier of bulk drugs from 1994. In 1994, China's share was 14.7 per cent (Figure 2.5). Over a period of time, India's import dependence for bulk drugs became centred on one country – China. By 2007, China's share in Indian imports of bulk drugs reached 59 per cent. This is in contrast to the situation prevailing in the beginning of the 1990s, when India's import dependence with regard to bulk drugs was more diversified. Imports of bulk drugs from the US, the largest supplier of bulk drugs to India in 1991, accounted for only 11 per cent. The top five countries exporting bulk drugs to India in 1991 had a combined share of only 48 per cent. India's dependence on China for bulk drugs is represented in Figure 2.5.

There are many factors contributing to the increased dependence on China for sourcing bulk drugs. The cost advantage is the factor driving Indian manufacturers to shun indigenous production and engage in imports. For example, theophylline from China is 10 per cent cheaper

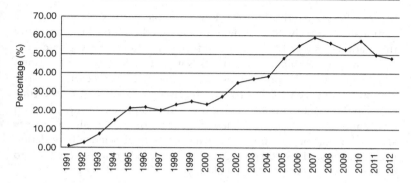

*Figure 2.5* Share of China in India's import of bulk drugs

*Source:* Computed by the author using data from DESA/UNSD, UN COMTRADE database (Rev. 3).

compared to the price of indigenous production. Chinese firms are able to sell bulk drugs at lower prices not only due to the state subsidies – for example, power subsidies – that they enjoy, but also due to the availability of better technologies. For example, Indian firms still use sugar for fermentation (an essential process in the production of bulk drugs), whereas technology available in China enables its firms to use cauliflower, which is much cheaper.[48] Besides, a number of incentives are given to exporters of bulk drugs by the Chinese government. Apart from electricity subsidies, Chinese bulk drug exporters receive a 13 per cent cash incentive.[49]

The report of the Task Force on Strategy for Enhancing Exports of Pharmaceutical Products (GoI 2008a) pointed out that the fermentation sector, one of the segments of biotechnology that was instrumental in shaping the Indian antibiotics segment in the early decades of growth of the Indian pharmaceutical industry, had moved to China due to lower energy costs there. In general, China has been stronger in the area of biology, rapidly improving its skills in this area. Companies producing APIs in China are similar to those in India, except that they have an advantage owing to China's status as a dominant force in fermentation technology. Government support for biotechnology has played an important role in the emergence of the Chinese bulk drugs industry.

China began to explore the potential of biotechnology from the mid-1990s onward. Government expenditure on R&D in the biotechnology sector came mainly from its national programmes for science and technology, including the National Basic Research Program (also called the 973 Program), the National Key Technologies R&D Program, the National High-tech R&D Program (also called the 863 Program), and the National Natural Science Foundation. In 2009, the Chinese government spent 29 billion yuan on its National Basic Research Program, which supported 10 projects on drugs and vaccines in that year. The National High-tech R&D Program received state funding to the tune of 5.1 billion yuan in 2009. This programme supported 40 projects on drugs and 2 on vaccines. Fermentation technology was also a priority area within this programme. The National Natural Science Foundation in 2010 approved 13,000 projects, of which 3,163 projects were focused on drugs, with funding of one billion yuan (Zhe and Lifeng 2011).

While the strategy of importing from cheaper locations makes economic sense, it could spell trouble for the industry if an adequate supply of raw materials is not guaranteed in the long term. The threat becomes more credible when imports are being sourced from a single country; an interruption in supply from that country could put the whole industry in jeopardy. The report of the task force on pharmaceuticals exports (GoI 2008a) pointed out that in certain categories of products, up to 70 per cent of the requirement was met through imports from China. In 2008, a crackdown on the chemicals industry in China to enforce environmental legislation resulted in supply shortages. The subsequent hike in prices affected not only the bottom lines of Indian companies, but even the very existence of many firms. Due to the supply shortage and rising prices of raw materials, about 50 bulk drug manufacturing units were shut down, while others cut down on the manufacturing of loss-making drug categories (*Economic Times* 2008). The dependence on imports of intermediates and bulk drugs from China has been such that India does not have the domestic manufacturing capacity to meet the demand for these products, if supplies from China cease for unforeseen reasons.

The task force on pharmaceuticals exports recommended that India must reduce its dependence on China for these intermediates. It is necessary to identify alternative markets that are equally competitive. Alternatively, there is a strong need to review domestic capacities for the supply of drug intermediates, so that the Indian drug industry is not overdependent on imports from a single country. The report of the task force suggested that India should create a policy environment where SMEs could position themselves appropriately to address the back-end needs of the pharmaceuticals industry.

The increasing dependence on imports of bulk drugs, which seems undesirable *prima facie*, needs to be analysed in the context of the changing dynamics of the industry. The import dependence of the pharmaceuticals industry before the mid-1970s was on account of lack of domestic manufacturing capabilities. The situation has changed in the meantime, and the current import dependence is due not so much to a lack of capabilities, but to the availability of cheaper intermediates and bulk drugs in foreign countries. The increasing export orientation of the Indian industry has forced firms to look for cheaper inputs to maintain their competitive advantage in the international market. The rising dependence on bulk drugs, intermediates and other raw materials is an outcome of the shift in the export orientation of the industry towards formulations. The export potential of Indian-made formulations relies on the 'Brand India' image, i.e. good-quality medicine at low prices.[50]

When production is oriented to the domestic market, firms have had few incentives for reducing their cost of production. This is because about 50 per cent of the drugs in the retail market in India are governed by a cost-based price control system. (In 1970, all drugs were placed under price control; the number came down to 90 per cent 1979, 70 per cent in 1987 and 50 per cent in 1995.) Such a system of price control assures firms a pre-defined rate of return. It also means that firms have greater incentive to spend on promoting their products rather than innovating to reduce the cost of production. As Indian firms increasingly enter foreign markets, cost becomes a highly sensitive factor; the high domestic production costs of raw materials and intermediates leads them to import cheaper raw materials so as to reduce the cost of production for export. As the industry gradually sheds its focus on the bulk drugs segment, it has little to gain from the 'Brand India' image in this segment. Therefore, there is little compulsion to produce these drugs within India.

The view that increasing export orientation with a focus on formulations results in the increased import of bulk drugs, intermediates and other raw materials, is strengthened by the observation of a positive association between export orientation and imports of raw materials. The ratio of exports to the import of raw materials (Figure 2.6) shows that taken-over firms i.e. the most export-oriented firms, have the highest ratio. On the other hand, MNCs, which are the least export-oriented firms, have the lowest ratio.[51]

In recent times, leading producers of bulk drugs have entered into the formulations business in partnership with foreign firms. Aurobindo Pharma, a major producer of bulk drugs, entered into an agreement with AstraZeneca in 2010 and with Pfizer in 2009 for the supply of a number of formulations. This business is expected to fetch Aurobindo US$350–500 million in coming years (*Economic Times* 2010b). To meet the additional demand, Aurobindo is increasingly engaged in the import

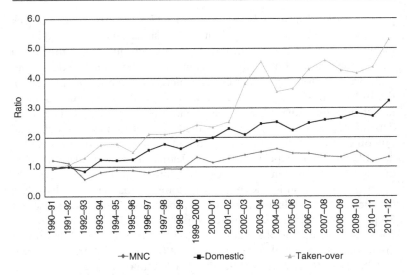

*Figure 2.6* Ratio of exports to imports of raw materials
Source: Computed by the author using data from Prowess, version 4.13, CMIE.

of raw materials. The share of imports of raw materials in the sales turnover of the company increased from 31 per cent in 2000–01 to 42 per cent in 2008–09. Table 2.15 lists the leading importers of raw materials in the pharmaceuticals sector in India. Most of the top exporters of pharmaceuticals (finished goods; see Table 2.6) have figured in the list of top 10 importers of raw materials.

Though we do not have precise data to support this view, the available indicators suggest that the industry is focusing on the higher end of the value chain in the production of bulk drugs. Separate estimates of the production of final bulk drugs and their intermediates are not available. Yet, the increase in imports of pharmaceutical raw materials and the simultaneous acceleration in the growth of exports of APIs in recent years, especially to the US, suggests that imported raw materials and intermediates are processed into final APIs in FDA-approved plants, and then exported to clients in the US and other countries.

Although imports of formulations have registered a higher rate of growth in recent years, this is limited to 5 per cent of the total production of formulations. The MNCs have been the largest importers of formulations into India. Switzerland is the major source of supply, accounting for 36 per cent (US$421 million) in 2012.

*Table 2.15* Largest importers of raw materials in 2011–12

| Company | Imports ($ million) | Percentage of sales |
| --- | --- | --- |
| Aurobindo Pharma | 275.1 | 31.6 |
| Cipla | 189.7 | 13.5 |
| Mylan Laboratories | 179.2 | 22.7 |
| Ranbaxy Laboratories | 144.2 | 9.9 |
| Dr. Reddy's Laboratories | 137.4 | 10.2 |
| Lupin | 123.9 | 11.5 |
| Jubilant Life Sciences | 94.6 | 17.4 |
| Orchid Chemicals & Pharmaceuticals | 91.3 | 26.2 |
| Ind-Swift Laboratories | 88.6 | 33.3 |
| Arch Pharmalabs | 83.0 | 27.3 |

*Source:* Prowess, version 4.13, CMIE.

To summarise, it had not been expected that the change in IP statutes would lead to a surge in imports of bulk drugs and other raw materials, and a corresponding decline in the domestic production of these items. With the change in IP laws, firms facing a 'do or die' scenario began to look for markets outside India. Gradually, the focus shifted to the production of formulations, a very lucrative and at the same time very competitive market. Companies sought cheaper sources of bulk drugs and other raw materials, especially China. As a result, the bulk drugs segment in India continues to have a negative trade balance. While the decline in import duties and elimination of ratio parameters linking the production of formulations to the indigenous production of bulk drugs facilitated imports, the implementation of GMP standards led to the closure of a number of small-scale units manufacturing bulk drugs, leading to reduced domestic production.

In the formulations category, on the other hand, the anticipated surge in imports did not occur. This was due to the adoption of a high threshold of patentability criteria in the patents law. Further, the provision for continued manufacturing of generics of patented drugs (through the mailbox system) in cases where companies had invested in production and marketing prior to 2005, left a smaller number of patented drugs for which no substitutes were available in India. Wherever substitutes are available, foreign firms are less likely to engage in imports of these drugs, so as to maintain their price competitiveness.

## Conclusion

The Indian pharmaceutical industry has witnessed a structural change in its export orientation since the reforms of the mid-1990s. While the industry has become more export-oriented, the focus has shifted from bulk drugs to formulations. Further, the export strategy is now primarily focused on one country – the US. The evidence shows that RCA indices for formulations have been increasing in the post-2005 period. This runs counter to the apprehensions engendered by the introduction of product patents in the pharmaceuticals sector in India. The changes in export orientation have caused changes in the production structure; the emphasis is now on the formulations segment. The production of bulk drugs and other raw materials is on the decline, and the pharmaceuticals sector has become more import-dependent in these areas. Imports of these items are drawn primarily from a single country – China. The production capabilities achieved by the bulk drugs segment, with the support of deliberate policy interventions over a period of three decades, appear to have been lost in the wake of economic reforms in the country.

The new export strategy, focused on a single country, is likely to have strategic implications for the Indian pharmaceutical industry in the long run. Any difficulty in exporting to the US would jeopardise the industry. There are indications that exports of drugs to the US may not continue in the same vein as before. Reports show that the current GMP (cGMP) standards of the US are shifting focus to 'quality by design', whereby conventional, manually managed processes in drug manufacturing are to be replaced by computer-managed automatic production processes (Mathew 2014). Such requirements would make exports from India very difficult. It is time for the Indian pharmaceuticals industry to take cognisance of the growing number of incidents of Indian drug manufacturing units falling under the USFDA scanner. The export focus needs to shift away from a single country to a number of countries, especially those in neighbouring regions.

Similarly, dependence on one country for imports of bulk drugs and raw materials will also have strategic implications. A situation has now arisen in which the production of formulations is entirely dependent on the supply of bulk drugs and raw materials from China. This makes the Indian pharmaceuticals industry extremely vulnerable. As Y. K. Hamied, chairman of Cipla, the legendary Indian generics firm, put it, 'if China decided one bright day to stop export to India, we would be finished. The pharma industry is zero both domestic and export and we are looking at that danger objectively.'[52] As the pharmaceutical industry plays a vital role in public health programmes, the universal health care programme of India depends to a great extent on the vibrancy of the Indian pharmaceutical industry for the supply of affordable, quality medicines.

## Notes

1 The market power effect reduces the elasticity of demand facing a foreign firm and ordinarily induces the firm to export less of its patentable product. The market expansion effect increases the elasticity of demand, encouraging firms to export more.

2 Data on imitative abilities include scientists, engineers and technicians engaged in R&D (total number and per capita), and R&D expenditure as percentage of GNP.

3 The cost of building a new manufacturing facility in India that complies with international regulatory norms is about one-fourth the cost of setting up a similar facility in the US or Europe. The cost of an Indian-based laboratory analyst/chemist is one-fifth to one-eighth the US cost. Higher-level Indian scientists are well trained, yet earn about a third of their western counterparts' salaries.

4 Chaudhuri uses data provided by the Directorate General of Commercial Intelligence and Statistics (DGCI&S), employing the HS of commodity classification. Chapter 30 of the HS code includes formulations; a list of 359 products (at the eight-digit level) consisting of items from HS Chapters 15, 17, 28, and 29 are used to classify bulk drugs.

5 BDMA data available at http://www.bdmai.org/statistics.php (accessed on 11 April 2008).

6 Import data at the eight-digit level are given on pages 38–96 of the report. Export data at the eight-digit level are provided on pages 98–148. The aggregate exports and imports figures are given on page 97.

7 The import data were 'estimated'.

8 Department of Chemicals and Petrochemicals, http://chemicals.nic.in/pharma1.htm (accessed on 10 October 2014).

9 The Department of Pharmaceuticals made available (personal communication, 8 February 2010) the revised estimates for a period of five years from 2004–05 to 2008–09.

10 A marginal decline was seen in the export estimates, except for 2008–09.

11 Even the latest annual report (2012–13) of the Department of Pharmaceuticals (GoI 2013c) does not carry the revised import estimates.

12 This was confirmed by officials at the International Trade Statistics Section of the WTO.

13 314.3(b) of Title 21 of the Code of Federal Regulations. Title 21 of the Code of Federal Regulations relates to food and drugs. It defines formulations in the process of defining drug products. A drug product is defined as 'a finished dosage form, for example, tablet, capsule or solution that contains a drug substance, generally, but not necessarily, in association with one or more other ingredients'.

14 As the DPCO's objective is price control of essential medicines, medicines for the treatment of animals and those included in the Ayurveda, Siddha, Unani and homeopathic systems are excluded from its purview.

15  'Medicaments (excluding goods of heading 3002, 3005 or 3006) consisting of two or more constituents which have been mixed together for therapeutic or prophylactic uses, not put up in measured doses or in forms or packings for retail sale' (DGCI&S 2012).
16  'Medicaments (excluding goods of heading 3002, 3005 or 3006) consisting of mixed or unmixed products for therapeutic or prophylactic uses, put up in measured doses (including those in the form of transdermal administration systems) or in forms or packings for retail sale' (*ibid.*).
17  The compound '6 APA' is one of the intermediates mentioned in the Ranbaxy annual report. It is a key intermediate used in the production of semi-synthetic penicillin antibiotics. See Glenmark (2008–09), Matrix, *Annual Report 2008–09*, and Ranbaxy (2009).
18  In 2005–06, private sector R&D expenditure in pharmaceuticals was Rs 28,269 million (DST 2007–08). The firms listed in Prowess, on the other hand, had R&D investments of Rs 26,354 million.
19  The domestic Indian pharmaceuticals market was worth Rs 504,100 million in 2007–08 (GoI 2008–09). The firms listed in the Prowess database, on the other hand, had domestic sales (total sales – exports) of Rs 487,263 million.
20  This was revealed during my interactions with SME Pharma Industries Confederation (SPIC).
21  Computed by the author based on DESA/UNSD, UN COMTRADE database (Rev. 3).
22  Computed by the author based on DESA/UNSD, UN COMTRADE database (Rev. 3).
23  *International Trade Statistics*, an annual publication of the WTO, lists the major exporters and importers commodity-wise. India does not figure in the list of leading importers of pharmaceuticals in *International Trade Statistics*. See, for example, WTO (2010: 76, 2012: 94, 2013: 92, 2014: 87).
24  See Table 1.6 in Chapter 1.
25  Multinational corporations are firms established in India with greater than 50 per cent foreign-owned shares. Prowess shows the shareholding pattern of most firms. Where information on shareholding was absent in the Prowess database, a web search was conducted to ascertain the MNC/domestic status of firms. There are 39 pharmaceutical firms in the list of MNCs. The FDI Policy of 2013 (GoI 2013a) identifies a firm as 'owned by resident Indians' only if more than 50 per cent of the capital is owned by resident Indian citizens, or by Indian companies ultimately owned and controlled by resident Indian citizens. Accordingly, we used the 50 per cent shareholding criterion to identify MNCs and domestic firms. Five erstwhile Indian firms have been grouped in the category of taken-over firms – Matrix (Mylan), Ranbaxy, Dabur (Fresenius Kabi Oncology), Shantha Biotechnics, and Paras. Two other taken-over firms are not included in this category because they sold off only selected product lines and not the entire firm. The five firms categorised as taken-over firms are not included in the category of either MNCs or domestic firms. Of these five firms, only Matrix, Ranbaxy and

Dabur have a separate existence from their parent firms; therefore, post-takeover data is available for only these firms. However, we have also included the other two taken-over firms in our analysis, to demonstrate that taken-over firms were well established in the exports market and were targeted for takeover for this reason.

26  Computed by the author based on data from Prowess, version 4.13, CMIE.

27  For domestic firms, imports constituted 0.6 per cent of sales in 1994–95 and 0.4 per cent of sales in 2011–12. Computed by the author based on data from Prowess, version 4.13, CMIE.

28  Based on Prowess data, version 4.13.

29  The disintegration of the Soviet Union, a major importer of formulations from India, in 1991 contributed to the low rate of growth of exports of formulations during 1991–94.

30  The year 2009 was exceptional, on account of seizures of pharmaceutical exports from India. For details see Rediff.com (2009).

31  This was communicated to me by the IDMA head office in Mumbai.

32  Data on production are provided in Figure 1.1 in Chapter 1.

33  I have had regular interactions with SPIC members over several years, beginning from the end of 2008. This particular point was made in an email from the Secretary General of SPIC in the context of a discussion on the implementation of Schedule M.

34  The countries in question were Germany (14 per cent), Hong Kong (11 per cent), USA (8 per cent), the Netherlands (7 per cent), and Canada (4 per cent).

35  The other four countries were the Russian Federation (6 per cent), the UK (4 per cent), South Africa (3 per cent), and Nigeria (3 per cent). The top five export destinations together constituted half (49 per cent) of the entire exports of formulations from India in 2012.

36  Germany accounted for 9 per cent of exports and USA 7 per cent, in 1995.

37  Ranbaxy was successful in challenging the patent held by GSK on Ceftin (an antibiotic). A suit was filed by GSK in the US District Court of New Jersey in October 2000. The court issued a preliminary injunction, which prevented Ranbaxy from marketing its generic version. In 2001, however, Ranbaxy launched its product commercially after the US Court of Appeals for the Federal Circuit vacated the preliminary injunction. After a full trial, the district court ruled that Ranbaxy's product did not infringe GSK's patent, and that Ranbaxy was not required to pay any damages.

38  A regional intergovernmental organisation of five countries – Burundi, Kenya, Rwanda, Tanzania, and Uganda – the EAC has its headquarters in Arusha, Tanzania.

39  Generic medicines contain the same chemical ingredients as the patented drug, and therefore carry the same chemical names. This makes genuine generic drugs prone to being treated as counterfeits, because they have identical chemical ingredients and the same chemical names as the patented medicines.

40  *Patricia Asero Ochieng, Maurine Atieno and Joseph Munyi vs the Attorney General*, High Court of Kenya at Nairobi, Petition no. 409 of 2009,

http://kelinkenya.org/wp-content/uploads/2012/04/Judgment-Petition-No-409-of-20092.pdf (accessed on 18 October 2014).

41  *Ibid.*, para. 87 of the judgement.

42  *Ibid.*, para. 84 of the judgement.

43  The forum for international cooperation between India, Brazil and South Africa.

44  The term 'evergreening' in the literature on patents refers to the strategy often used by patent holders to extend the life of a patent by making minor modifications to the product. As a result, a number of patents are obtained at different periods to protect what is essentially the same product. This gives rise to a situation where the product continues to remain under patent protection long after the expiry of the initial patent. Evergreening is a strategy widely adopted by pharmaceutical MNCs to prevent generics firms from manufacturing and supplying generic drugs when the patent expires.

45  The 'mailbox provision' refers to the requirement, under the TRIPS Agreement, that countries that did not have product patents in pharmaceuticals and chemicals had to have in place a mechanism for accepting product patent applications with effect from 1 January 1995. Applications in the mailbox would be examined for grant of patents after the patents law of the concerned country was made TRIPS-compatible. The mailbox system offers scope for exclusive marketing rights – a five-year, patent-like monopoly for products covered by product patent applications made under the mailbox system. A company securing exclusive marketing rights has the exclusive right to sell or distribute the article or substance covered in the patent application in the country in question.

46  The Patents Act, 1970, Chapter II, Section 3, http://ipindia.nic.in/ipr/patent/eVersion_ActRules/sections/ps3.html (accessed on 18 October 2014).

47  The Patents Act, 1970, Chapter IV, Section 11A.7, http://ipindia.nic.in/ipr/patent/eVersion_ActRules/sections/ps11.html (accessed on 18 October 2014).

48  This was revealed during my interactions with an IDMA representative.

49  Data quoted by Y. K. Hamied, chairman of Cipla, during the stakeholders' meeting (including civil society and representatives of the domestic Indian pharmaceutical industry) held on 24 November 2013 in Mumbai, organised by the Lawyers Collective.

50  India launched a massive 'Brand India' campaign in African countries to regain their confidence in the wake of the initiatives by MNCs to equate Indian generics with counterfeits. This information was obtained from officials in the Department of Commerce, Ministry of Commerce and Industry, Government of India.

51  The correlation coefficient of exports and imports of raw materials was 0.99 between 1994–95 and 2008–09 (for all firms combined).

52  Dr Hamied made this remark this during a stakeholders' meeting (attended by members of civil society and the Indian domestic pharmaceuticals industry) on 24 November 2013 in Mumbai. The meeting was organised by the Lawyers' Collective.

# Chapter 3

# Pharmaceutical R&D in India

An important aspect of the policy reforms in the Indian economy since 1991 has been the change in perceptions about the respective roles of the public and private sectors. In the pre-liberalisation phase, the public sector was assigned a leadership role in pharmaceuticals, while the private sector was required to support the efforts of the state. In the liberalisation phase, the public sector has been assigned an inferior position, while private sector firms take a leadership role and are expected to make commercially sensible decisions.

The Industrial Policy Resolution of 1956 classified industries into three categories based on the priority assigned to them. Schedule A industries were reserved exclusively for the public sector; Schedule B consisted of industries in which the public sector would play a leading role and the private sector was expected to supplement the state's efforts and Schedule C consisted of all other industries, whose future development was left to private initiative. The pharmaceutical industry was categorised as a Schedule B industry. Private industry was also encouraged, though it was strictly regulated through industrial licensing. The leadership role of the public sector was further emphasised in the Industrial Policy Statement, 1977:

> the public sector will be charged with the responsibility of encouraging the development of a wide range of ancillary industries, and contribute to the growth of decentralised production by making available its expertise in technology and management to small scale and cottage industry sectors.
>
> (GoI n.d.)

The Industrial Policy Statement, 1977, also provided a perspective on technology capability building. In those priority areas where Indian skills and technology were not adequately developed, 'preference would be for outright purchase of the best available technology and then adapting such technology to the country's needs' (*ibid.*). The import of foreign technology was subject to the setting up of indigenous R&D facilities to enable appropriate adaptation and assimilation of such technologies. Moreover, the government also proposed to monitor all foreign collaborations through a national registry set up in the Secretariat of the Foreign Investment Board.

In pursuit of these policies, the Government of India established five public sector companies, of which two played very important roles – Hindustan Antibiotics Ltd (HAL) and Indian Drugs and Pharmaceuticals Ltd (IDPL).[1] Technical assistance from USSR helped to set up IDPL, while HAL was established with technical assistance from WHO and the UN International Children's Emergency Fund (UNICEF). These two PSUs played a major role in building up technical competence in the industry, as well in establishing a strong bulk drugs industry in the country. According to Anand (1988), IDPL and HAL created a new environment for the pharmaceuticals sector, fostering confidence that India could manufacture bulk drugs in a major way. The prevailing university system in India did not provide the specialised training required by the pharmaceuticals industry. In this context, IDPL and HAL encouraged universities to impart specialised training in pharmaceuticals by creating a demand for skilled labour; further, they sparked industrial development in upstream and downstream businesses by generating the demand for specialised capital and other services (S. Smith 2000). It was this dynamism that led to the creation of a bulk drugs manufacturing industry in Hyderabad, where IDPL's synthetic drug plant is located (Chaudhuri 2005a).

Considerable efforts were also made by HAL and IDPL to adapt and assimilate the technologies supplied by their sponsors to Indian requirements. Modifications were required on account of technological imperfections and the physical and economic climate into which the imported technology was implanted (Joshi 1977). The government also insisted on the mutual exchange of technologies developed in the laboratories of IDPL and HAL from time to time (Parthasarathi 2007). When it was found that the technology agreements with their respective sponsors were prohibiting the transfer of technologies between the two firms, the government found a way around this bottleneck by transferring scientists from one company to the other. Thus, when Merck & Co. of the US, which had provided the technology to the streptomycin unit of HAL, objected to the sharing of the technology with IDPL, and on the other hand the USSR objected strongly to the application of Merck's technology in the IDPL plant, the government appointed a senior HAL technologist to work in IDPL's antibiotics plant (*ibid.*). The technologies available in these firms also spilled over into the private sector through the movement of scientists and technicians from public sector companies to private firms. Some of the founders of private sector bulk drugs manufacturing companies had earlier worked in public sector companies. For example, Dr Anji Reddy, founder of Dr. Reddy's Laboratories, had previously worked in IDPL.

The public sector research laboratories set up under the auspices of CSIR – especially the Central Drug Research Institute (CDRI), the Indian Institute of Chemical Technology (IICT) and the National Chemical Laboratory (NCL) – also contributed considerably to the growth of the Indian pharmaceuticals industry. These organisations developed laboratory-level processes that were later transferred to private industry, scaling up the technologies at the industry level. The public laboratories also conducted research on the problems referred to them by Indian companies. The process technologies developed by the CSIR laboratories include technologies for ciprofloxacin, omeprazole, salbutamol, vitamin B6, lamivudine, diclofenac sodium, and azithromycin. Almost all the top pharmaceutical companies in India have used the services of the CSIR laboratories (Chaudhuri 2005a). J.M. Khanna and Bansi Lal, who headed the R&D divisions of Ranbaxy and Nicholas Piramal, respectively, had both worked at CDRI before joining these firms (*ibid.*).

The reforms initiated in the pharmaceuticals sector from 1994 onwards did away with the leadership role of the public sector. The Statement on Industrial Policy, 1991, called for a limited role for the public sector, and stated that the priority areas of growth for public enterprises in the future would be 'technology development and building of manufacturing capabilities in areas which are crucial in the long term development of the economy and where private sector investment is inadequate' (GoI 1991: para. 32). In line with the vision of a greater role for the private sector in the economy, the policy also called for limiting the role of the state from that of a regulator to a facilitator:

> Government policy and procedures must be geared to assisting entrepreneurs in their efforts. This can be done only if the role played by the government were to be changed from that of only exercising control to one of providing help and guidance by making essential procedures fully transparent and by eliminating delays.
>
> (*ibid.*: para. 21)

As opposed to earlier industrial policies, the policy of 1991 viewed foreign investment and technology collaborations involving MNCs as important channels for building technology competence. A detailed discussion of these policy changes is provided in Chapter 1.

The new IPR regime, although introduced due to external compulsions, seems to have complemented the strategy of giving a prominent role to private enterprises, with the state withdrawing from its role of regulator. With a strong patents regime in place, pharmaceutical firms are expected to invest more substantially in R&D. It has been argued by proponents of the product patent regime that stronger patent protection would stimulate innovation in pharmaceutical products (Levin *et al.* 1987; Prasad 1999; Prasad and Bhat 1993).

What are the likely implications of these reforms for the future development of the Indian pharmaceuticals industry? The industry has already mastered skills in reverse engineering and now needs to step into new drug development. Analysing pharmaceuticals industries in 27 countries, Ballance, Pogany and Forstner (1992) classify the Indian pharmaceutical industry in the group that is not active in discovering new chemical entities, but has the technological capabilities necessary to reverse engineer existing drugs. If Indian firms do not possess the skills and other resources required for developing new drugs, it is very likely that they will collaborate with MNCs. Foreign investment and foreign technology collaborations are viewed as important means of competence building in the Indian industry. What will the position of Indian firms be in such alliances? Will they be collaborators on equal terms, enabling an independent path to growth, or will they be subordinate collaborators, entailing a dependent path to development?

Another issue of concern is whether Indian firms will find commercial opportunities in all therapeutic segments. By building alliances with MNCs, the R&D emphasis of Indian firms is likely to be on global diseases, resulting in the neglect of diseases that are more prevalent in developing and least developed countries. There are two views on this issue. According to Aggrawal and Saibaba (2001), and Prasad and Bhat (1993), Indian firms will find opportunities in all therapeutic areas, including those catering predominantly to developing countries. These authors argue that the lack of product patent rights in pharmaceuticals in India has been responsible for discouraging Indian firms, which are otherwise capable of developing new drugs, from venturing into new drug development.

However, other scholars make a careful distinction between therapeutic areas where the new patent regime is likely to incentivise firms, and those areas where it may not. According to this view, R&D decisions are guided by commercial considerations. Neglected diseases, or diseases prevalent mainly in developing countries, do not constitute an attractive market for the pharma majors. For instance, Keayla (1994) and Dhar and Rao (1993) argue that developing countries have very low purchasing power, hence diseases that are predominant in these countries do not offer adequate market incentives for R&D. The UK's CIPR (2002) reports that large companies are unwilling to pursue a line of research unless the potential outcome is a product with annual sales of the order of US$1 billion. Studies have shown that MNCs are not interested even in filing patents in countries where the market is not attractive. A study of 15 antiretroviral drugs, conducted across 53 African countries, found that patenting prevalence was only 21.6 per cent (Attaran and Gillespie 2001). In this context, it is pertinent to explore how the R&D scenario is unfolding in the Indian pharmaceutical sector.

## Changing trends in R&D

The global pharmaceuticals industry is highly research-intensive. Innovative firms spend on average about 15 per cent of their sales turnover on R&D.[2] However, R&D expenditure as a percentage of sales turnover (R&D intensity) among Indian pharmaceutical firms remained at less than 2 per cent until the beginning of the 2010s. The report of the Hathi Committee (GoI 1975) observed that R&D intensity was only 1.1 per cent in 1973. Perhaps this low R&D intensity is explained by the fact that Indian companies were then engaged primarily in the manufacture of generics and the development of non-infringing processes, and not in new drug development, which involves huge investments. The R&D intensity of the Indian industry began to increase from 2000–01, and reached its peak in 2005–06 (Figure 3.1). This increase is entirely accounted for by the private sector; the R&D intensity of public sector pharmaceutical firms still remains below 2 per cent. Since the R&D intensity of Indian public sector firms is very low, and the share of the public sector in total industrial investment in R&D (public and private combined) is negligible,[3] the focus of analysis in the following sections will be on private industry.

The stagnation of R&D intensity after 2005–06 needs detailed analysis, as this was the period when R&D intensity was expected to increase due to the incentives created by the introduction of product patent rights. Additionally, there were other incentives like tax benefits, grants and soft loans awaiting firms engaged in R&D. A firm-wise analysis

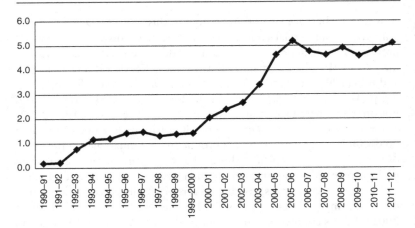

*Figure 3.1* R&D–sales ratio in the pharmaceutical industry in India (percentage)
*Source:* Prowess, Version 4.13, CMIE

using Prowess data shows that the decline is attributable to two firms – Dr. Reddy's and Ranbaxy (Figure 3.2). In 2005–06, these two firms accounted for one-third (33 per cent) of the total R&D investment by the pharmaceutical industry.

It is possible that firms were investing in new facilities, technologies and equipment (capital expenditure), accounting for the growth of R&D intensity until 2005–06. Once this investment had been undertaken, the need for capital expenditure may have declined in subsequent years. This could explain the decline in R&D intensity after 2005.[4] Figure 3.3 shows the trends in R&D capital expenditure as a percentage of total R&D expenditure at Dr. Reddy's, Ranbaxy and all other firms taken together.

It is clear from Figure 3.3 that the change in R&D capital expenditure does not explain the decline in R&D intensity after 2005–06. There has been no systematic decline in the share of capital expenditure after 2005–06 to justify the stagnation in R&D intensity. Actual R&D capital and current expenditure has been increasing since 2005–06 for all firms except Ranbaxy and Dr. Reddy's.[5] At Ranbaxy, however, both capital and current expenditure declined after 2005–06.[6] The R&D intensity of the company declined from 19 per cent in 2005–06 to 6 per cent in 2011–12. Since Ranbaxy accounted for one-fourth (24 per cent) of the total R&D spending in the pharmaceutical industry in 2005–06, the decline in its R&D spending considerably impacted the overall trend in the R&D intensity of the industry.

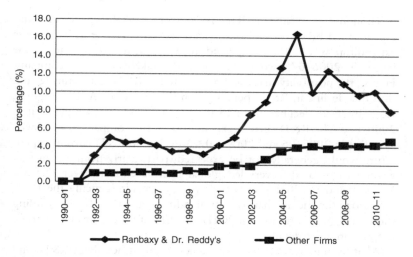

*Figure 3.2* R&D intensity of Dr. Reddy's, Ranbaxy and other firms
*Source:* Prowess, Version 4.13, CMIE.

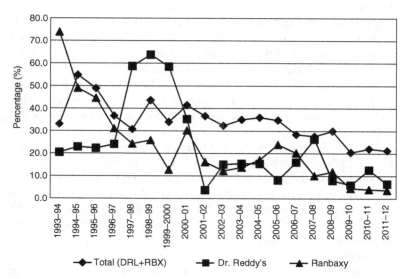

*Figure 3.3* R&D capital expenditure (% of total R&D expenditure)
*Source:* Prowess, Version 4.13, CMIE

Though the decline in Ranbaxy's R&D capital expenditure may be explained by the rationale provided earlier, a decline in its revenue expenditure would not be expected. It should be noted that the decline began in 2006–07, two years before the takeover of the company. Hence, the possibility that takeover resulted in R&D restructuring, and thus in a decline in R&D spending, can be ruled out.[7] At Dr. Reddy's, R&D intensity declined from 18 per cent in 2004–05 to 6 per cent in 2006–07.[8] The R&D current expenditure of the company also showed a decline in 2005–06 and 2009–10.[9] A decline in R&D current expenditure would generally not be expected, particularly from a firm that wanted to be a 'discovery-led global pharmaceutical player'.[10] Since Ranbaxy and Dr. Reddy's are the two key firms influencing the R&D scenario in the Indian pharmaceutical industry, and their R&D spending shows unexpected trends, the R&D scenario of these firms needs to be analysed in more detail.

What prompted these two companies to invest heavily in R&D, and what later forced them to reduce this allocation of resources? Dr. Reddy's and Ranbaxy were pioneers in new drug development in the Indian pharmaceuticals industry. Dr. Reddy's developed an anti-diabetic molecule (DRF 2593), which the company out-licensed to Novo Nordisk in 1997 for pre-clinical and clinical development (Dr. Reddy's 2004). Dr. Reddy's also out-licensed two other anti-diabetic molecules – DRF 2725 to Novo Nordisk in 1998 (Dr. Reddy's 2002a) and DRF 4158 to Novartis in 2001 (Dr. Reddy's 2002b). Similarly, Ranbaxy out-licensed its first compound (RBx 2258, for the treatment of benign prostatic hyperplasia) in 2002 to Schwarz Pharma (Ranbaxy 2002). When a molecule is out-licensed, the subsequent expenditure on R&D is incurred by the licensee. The license holder gets upfront and milestone payments and, in some cases, royalty payments upon the commercialisation of the product.

These deals brought substantial financial returns to both companies. Dr. Reddy's deal with Novartis (DRF 4158) contained a package of US$55 million in upfront and milestone payments (Dr. Reddy's 2002b). Ranbaxy's deal with Schwarz Pharma provided US$48.3 million worth of returns to the company, of which US$6.3 million was upfront and the remaining was in the form of milestone payments over a period of five to six years (Ranbaxy 2002). Ranbaxy was also to receive royalty payments on the commercialisation of the drug (*ibid.*). Out-licensing seemed to be a highly lucrative business model, since the cost of development of molecules up till the pre-clinical stage was relatively cheaper, and the prospects of returns from out-licensing were huge. It is reported that the cost incurred by Dr. Reddy's in developing the first eight molecules until the pre-clinical stage was only US$57 million (Chaudhuri 2005a). On average, the cost per molecule was only US$7 million. Excited by the initial out-licensing deals, both companies boosted their allocations to R&D, resulting in their R&D intensity growing many times as compared to the late 1990s.

The trouble began when licensees encountered problems at the pre-clinical and clinical development stages. In 2003, Novo Nordisk suspended the trials on DRF 2725 after finding tumours in the pre-clinical studies. In the same year, Novartis also decided to discontinue the development of DRF 4148. In 2004, Novo Nordisk decided to terminate further clinical development of DRF 2593, as the phase II results did not suggest a sufficient competitive advantage for the molecule (balaglitazone) compared to existing products. Schwarz Pharma in 2004 discontinued trials on Ranbaxy's molecule (RBx 2258) due to disappointing results in phase II. These setbacks forced the two companies to review their R&D strategy, and the direct outcome of this review was pruning R&D expenditure.

The failure of the so-called 'out-licensing business model' also manifested in other forms. Dr. Reddy's removed the line 'discovery-led global pharmaceutical company' from its grandiose vision statement (Dr. Reddy's 2005a: 6), instead emphasising a strategic initiative called 'The Viable Vision', with the aim of transforming the organisation into an 'ever-flourishing company' (Dr. Reddy's 2009: 22). In 2009, Dr. Reddy's shut down its R&D office in Atlanta, USA. In the same year, the company transferred its research division based in Hyderabad to a Bangalore-based subsidiary, Aurigene, which offers research services to pharma firms. Dr. Reddy's now has only 30 scientists working on new drug development, compared to 280 in the early years of the 2000s (Bisserbe 2010).

Why did these companies out-license the molecules, instead of developing them in-house until the last stages? Do they have the science and technology (S&T) skills and other resources required to develop new chemical entities (NCEs)? Analysis of the stages involved in the development of new drugs, and the skills required at each stage, offers some clues as to where the Indian pharma industry stands in terms of its ability to develop new drugs. Figure 3.4 illustrates the stages involved in the R&D process of new drugs.

In stages 1 and 2, biology studies are conducted to understand how a disease works. This leads to the identification of the specific targets, the inhibition of which plays a crucial role in treating that particular

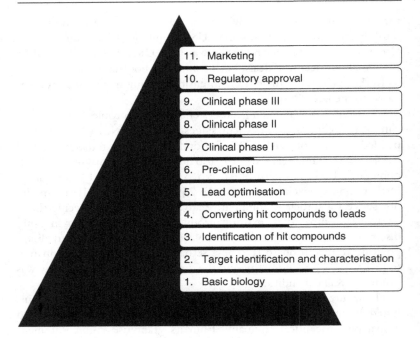

*Figure 3.4* R&D process for developing new drugs
*Source:* Adapted from Kettler, White and Jordan (2003).

disease. In stages 3–5, teams of chemists, pharmacologists and biologists engage in screening thousands of compounds, or chemically or genetically engineer new ones, to generate potential compounds. Molecules with desirable properties are further modified to enhance the activity or minimise side effects (this process is known as lead optimisation) (PhRMA 2007).

Pre-clinical testing (on animals, stage 6) and clinical trials (on humans, stages 7, 8 and 9) are conducted to determine the efficacy and safety of the molecule. During the pre-clinical phase, studies of how the drug moves through a living organism are conducted by examining four key processes – absorption, distribution, metabolism, and excretion. Pre-clinical studies also involve chemistry tests to establish the purity of the compound; manufacturing tests to determine what would be involved in the production of the drug on a large scale; and pharmaceutical tests to explore dosing, packing and formulation (e.g. as a pill, inhaler, injection, etc.). Pre-clinical studies take from three to six years.[11]

Phase I clinical trials are conducted on a small group of 20–100 healthy volunteers to determine the safety profile of the drug. Phase II trials involve 100–500 volunteer patients. Studies in this phase aim to establish the efficacy of the drug. Phase III involves a larger group of patients, from 1,000 to 5,000. The volunteers are closely monitored at regular intervals to confirm that the drug is effective and to identify side effects. During phase III, toxicity tests and long-term safety evaluations are also carried out. Clinical trials take from about two to six years.

Once all three phases of clinical trials are completed, the company applies for regulatory approval. Only one in every 10,000 potential compounds investigated gets regulatory approval. It takes about 15 years of effort and R&D expenditures of US$1 billion to develop a successful drug (PhRMA 2007). A recent study pegs the figure at US$2.6 billion (Tufts CSDD 2014). The clinical phase is the most expensive stage of new drug development. Forty per cent of R&D expenses are incurred during this phase. On average, basic research accounts for 27 per cent of total R&D expenditure, development of production processes 19 per cent, implementation of regulatory requirements 7 per cent, and other expenses 7 per cent.[12] Adequate skills in biology and medicinal chemistry are fundamental prerequisites for venturing into new drug development.

In a study conducted for the Commission for Intellectual Property Rights, Innovation and Public Health of the WHO, Chaudhuri (2005a) analyses in detail the preparedness of the Indian pharmaceutical industry for new drug R&D. Chaudhuri finds that the Indian industry lacks the biology skills required in stages 1 and 2, as well as the medicinal chemistry skills to carry out research in stages 2 to 9. The capabilities possessed by Indian companies in new drug research from stage 6 onwards relate to the manufacturing aspects of compounds, including process chemistry, scaling up, manufacturing process development, and formulation development of proper dosage forms.

How did leading Indian firms like Dr. Reddy's and Ranbaxy manage to develop new molecules up to the pre-clinical stage before out-licensing, if they did not have the skills to conduct R&D from stages 1 through 5? The molecules developed by these firms did not constitute completely new families of drugs. Rather, they were new molecules within existing families of drugs that had already been well researched. By working on already established targets and developing new drugs within families that have been extensively researched, a company reduces some of the uncertainty involved in new drug research (Abrol, Prajapathi and Singh 2011; Chaudhuri 2005a). This model of R&D is known as 'analogue research'. Japanese pharma firms had resorted to this strategy very successfully when they ventured into new drug development (*Business World* 2006). Dr. Reddy's anti-diabetic compound DRF 2593 (balaglitazone) falls in the family of glitazone. Glitazones are the only approved anti-diabetic agents that are known to act as insulin sensitisers. Glenmark's GRC 3886 (oglemilast) belongs to the family of PDE4 inhibitors.[13] Similarly, Wockhardt's WCK 771 and WCK 2349 belong to the family of antibiotics known as fluoroquinolones.[14] Fluoroquinolones are broad spectrum antibiotics used in the treatment of a number of bacterial infections.

It follows that the argument that Indian firms are capable of innovating NCEs, and are in a position to take advantage of product patent rights, is misplaced. Estimates by PhRMA suggest that out of 10,000 molecules synthesised, only 20 reach the pre-clinical stage, only 10 go through to the clinical trials stage, and only one ultimately gets approval for marketing.[15] Going by this estimate, a company should have a minimum of 20 molecules at the pre-clinical stage if a successful molecule is to be expected. Since Indian firms use the analogue research strategy, they also carry the additional burden of proving enhancement of efficacy over existing drugs. In their effort to develop molecules within existing families of drugs, it is possible that some molecules may be developed with therapeutic activities that are already offered by other drugs on the market. So, the failure of many out-licensed molecules is only to be expected in the process of new drug development.

Indian companies also lag behind in their ability to invest in R&D. There have been reservations about the US$1 billion benchmark;[16] R&D costs in India can be much lower. McKinsey & Company estimates that the cost of R&D in India would be only 40–60 per cent of similar costs in the US, while the CDRI estimates that R&D in India would cost only 30 per cent of the cost in the US (Chaudhuri 2005a). But the fact is that R&D investments by India's largest R&D spenders are way below the yardstick of 30–60 per cent of R&D costs in the US. The combined R&D investment of India's top 10 pharma R&D investors during the last 10 years amounts to only 40 per cent of Pfizer's investment in R&D in one year.[17] And this investment by Indian firms includes R&D expenses towards the production of generics and novel drug delivery systems (NDDS).

The myth about the capacity of Indian firms to innovate new drugs also resulted in the failure to form dedicated R&D companies. By hiving off R&D units and creating new R&D companies, parent firms are expected to raise more funds. This insulates parent firms from the risks associated with the failure of research projects. Dr. Reddy's established Perlecan, India's first integrated drug development firm, in 2005 in collaboration with Citigroup Venture and ICICI Venture, putting together US$52.2 million. Dr. Reddy's shifted four of its experimental drugs to Perlecan. Of the four molecules, the development of three drugs had to be stopped due to their potential side effects. The remaining molecule did not prove to be more effective than drugs already on the market. In 2008, Citigroup and ICICI pulled out of Perlecan, and Dr. Reddy's had to buy back their shares. The Perlecan debacle need not come as a surprise, because the success of such a venture requires a large number of experimental drugs. Further, the financial outlay of the company was also very small. The failure of the out-licensed molecules further inhibited private venture capital from coming forward to support pharma R&D initiatives. A few companies like Nicholas Piramal also established separate R&D companies, but are now in the process of re-merging the R&D units with the parent firm. Ranbaxy, Torrent and Wockhardt had floated plans for spinning off R&D units. However, in the wake of the Perlecan debacle, these companies have not gone ahead with the implementation of these plans (*LiveMint* 2010b). Though a number of Indian pharma firms have invested in R&D for the development of new drugs, only Zydus Cadila has been successful in bringing out a new drug based on 100 per cent indigenous R&D from lab to market. The company obtained marketing approval from the Drug Controller General of India (DCGI) in 2013 for the drug Lipaglyn (saroglitazar) for the treatment of patients suffering from diabetic dyslipidemia (Zydus Cadila 2013). Zydus Cadila has obtained a patent on this drug, which is available in the Indian market at Rs 25.90 per tablet. The company is reported to have spent US$250 million in the development of Lipaglyn over a period of 12 years (BioSpectrum 2013).

The preceding discussion raises a number of questions. Does the paucity of skills and resources indicate a bleak prospect for the Indian pharmaceutical industry? Has the strategy of Indian drug firms really contributed to strengthening the innovative capability of the Indian pharmaceuticals sector? What can Indian firms do to overcome these constraints? The following section analyses emerging R&D strategies in the pharmaceutical sector in India.

## Emerging R&D strategies

Whereas in the pre-reform era, the government had provided the direction and necessary support to the pharmaceuticals industry, now firms are expected to stand on their own feet and take decisions based on commercial considerations. Indian pharmaceutical firms have been engaging in various kinds of business collaborations in R&D with MNCs. Such collaborations may be expected in the new environment, where foreign technology and capital are viewed favourably as accelerating the process of competence building. But the important issue is whether such alliances result in actual competence building. Broadly, there are three kinds of alliances involving MNCs – contract research and manufacturing services (CRAMS), collaborative research projects (CRPs), and out-licensing and in-licensing.

## Contract research and manufacturing services

Contract research and manufacturing services are essentially outsourcing arrangements. They include activities such as manufacturing APIs and formulations, chemistry and biology research for new drug compounds, pre-clinical trials and clinical trials. The CRAMS market in India was estimated at US$2.5 billion in 2009[18] and is expected to reach US$6.6 billion by 2013 (Frost & Sullivan 2007).

Many factors have been forcing MNCs to outsource their production to India. The cost of manufacturing is substantially lower in India – as low as 35 per cent of US costs and 28 per cent of the cost in Europe (ICRA 2011). India also has the largest number of USFDA-approved manufacturing plants outside the US.[19] Multinational companies like AstraZeneca and Eli Lilly have already announced plans to outsource a substantial part of their manufacturing activities to countries like India. In 2010, the contract manufacturing market in India was estimated at US$2.3 billion (*ibid.*). Top global pharma firms like Pfizer, Merck, GSK, Sanofi Aventis, Novartis, and Teva largely depend on Indian firms for the supply of many of their APIs and intermediates (FICCI 2005). A list of leading firms engaged in contract manufacturing in pharmaceuticals and the type of products covered has been provided in Table 2.8 (see Chapter 2).

Earlier, it was mainly the smaller Indian firms which engaged in contract manufacturing. Lately, however, larger firms like Dr. Reddy's have also entered this business as part of much wider marketing and R&D collaborations. The alliance between Dr. Reddy's and GSK provides the latter exclusive access to Dr. Reddy's diverse portfolio and its future pipeline of more than 100 formulations in therapeutic segments such as cardiovascular diseases, diabetes, oncology, gastroenterology, and pain management. The drugs will be manufactured by Dr. Reddy's and licensed and supplied by GSK in various developing countries in Africa, the Middle East, Asia Pacific, and Latin America. In some markets, the drugs will be co-marketed by both companies (GSK 2009). Revenues will be shared with Dr. Reddy's as per the agreement. Similar contract manufacturing alliances involving marketing tie-ups exist between Astra-Zeneca and Torrent, Pfizer and Aurobindo, Pfizer and Biocon, and Boehringer Ingelheim and Cipla. The financial terms of these deals are often not disclosed; hence, it is not possible to gauge the actual size of the contract manufacturing business vis-à-vis the wider alliances. As part of its alliance with Napo Pharmaceuticals of USA, Glenmark agreed to develop the crofelemer compound used to treat diarrhoea, obtaining the licence for exclusive supply of Napo's global requirement of the API for the crofelemer drug.[20]

The contract research business in India was estimated at US$1.5 billion in 2010 (ICRA 2011). The market for contract research in India has been growing at a more rapid pace compared with the global contract research market. Between 2007 and 2010, when the global contract research market grew at a compound annual growth rate (CAGR) of 19 per cent, reaching US$25 billion in 2010, the corresponding CAGR of the market in India was 65 per cent, reaching US$1.5 billion by 2010. The low cost of conducting research in India is an important factor encouraging the outsourcing of research to India. As suggested earlier, R&D activities in India are estimated to be 60–65 per cent cheaper compared to the corresponding costs in the US. Labour costs in India are about 10–15 per cent of similar costs in the US. Upfront capital requirements in setting up R&D projects in India are 25–50 per cent lower, due to the use of locally fabricated equipment and the availability of high-quality local technology/engineering skills (IBEF 2011: 10). The cost advantage of conducting clinical trials in India is higher than 50 per cent during phase I studies and higher than 60 per cent during phase II and phase III studies (ICRA 2011). More than half (52 per cent) of all contract research in India takes place in clinical trials.[21]

Other factors also make India an attractive destination for clinical trials. India's large population is ethnically and genetically diverse, and suffers from various ailments (Grace 2004). India has six of the seven genetic varieties of the human race, and a large, treatment-naïve (untreated) population looking for cure or better treatment (Srinivasan and Sachin 2009). The country also has a large English-speaking population along with a well-developed communication network with information technology capabilities, which are an advantage in conducting clinical trials. The number of contract research organisations (CROs) in India has grown from 20 in 2005 to 100 in 2008, and the number was expected to rise to 150–200 by 2012. Table 3.1 lists the leading CROs in India.

*Table 3.1* Leading CROs in India

| Companies in contract research (excluding clinical trials) | Companies in contract research (clinical trials) |
| --- | --- |
| Aurigene (Dr. Reddy's) | Clinigene (Biocon) |
| Syngene (Biocon) | Jubilant Clinsys (Jubilant Organosys) |
| GVK Biosciences | WellQuest (Nicholas Piramal) |
| Jubilant Organosys | Synchron |
| Divi's Laboratories | Vimta Labs |
| Vimta Labs | Lambda (Intas) |
| Suven Life Sciences | SRL Ranbaxy |
| Dr. Reddy's Laboratories | Reliance Life Sciences |
| Nicholas Piramal | Asian Clinical Trials (Suven Life Sciences) |
| Shasun Chemicals | Metropolis |
| Avra Labs | Quintiles |
| Procitius Research | Manipal Acunova |

*Source:* Abrol, Prajapathi and Singh (2011); GoI (2006); O. R. S. Rao (2007).

Contract research arrangements are entered into for fixed periods and for identified therapeutic areas. The service provider receives research funding and milestone payments. Indian companies with proven strengths in selected areas of drug discovery, but unprepared to step into new drug development on their own, tend to enter into this type of collaboration. The outsourcing company bears the entire risk of failure of the project; likewise, it owns the compound developed through the partnership.

A number of mid-level Indian firms are actively engaged in the contract research business. Jubilant Organosys, a Bangalore-based company, has research collaborations with two leading MNCs and a foreign university. It entered into a five-year contract, starting in 2009, with Astra-Zeneca to help add to its pre-clinical pipeline in neuroscience. Jubilant is expected to earn US$220 million in upfront and milestone payments. Of this, US$20 million is up front, with an annual payment of US$3 million coming in during the first two years. The company could potentially earn up to US$200 million as and when it meets certain targets in developing drugs under the deal. This deal also provides for royalties from AstraZeneca on the successful sale of any drug (*Business Line* 2009).

Jubilant has a similar arrangement with Eli Lilly for a period of nine years, starting 2005. However, Jubilant will receive only upfront and milestone payments and not royalties in this case (Jubilant LifeSciences 2009a). The company also entered into a multifaceted partnership with Duke University in 2009. Under this partnership, Jubilant and Duke agreed to jointly select a set of research projects that synergise the research capabilities of Duke University and the development capabilities of Jubilant (Jubilant LifeSciences 2009b). Jubilant is expected to translate the discoveries of Duke scientists into clinical therapies (*ibid.*).

GVK Biosciences, a Hyderabad-based contract research firm offering drug discovery services, started with bioinformatics and then moved into providing medicinal chemistry services. According to a Planning Commission report (GoI 2006), GVK Biosciences proposes in future to begin a collaborative research programme where it can partner with virtual companies not having any fixed assets. Virtual companies work with specialist service providers and sell off the molecule whenever they get an optimum price.

Contract research arrangements thus provide a source of revenue for Indian partners, but their contribution in terms of competence building is uncertain. In these arrangements, Indian firms are expected to perform discrete tasks in drug research and are not exposed to the whole process of new drug development. Further, the products developed out of these partnerships are owned exclusively by the outsourcing firm, denying Indian firms the opportunity to benefit from future gains accruing from the product.

Firms offering clinical trial services, unlike those offering drug discovery services, essentially perform the administrative work of conducting clinical trials (Srinivasan and Sachin 2009). They recruit researchers and train them, provide them with supplies, coordinate study administration and data collection, organise meetings, ensure that the trial is conducted in compliance with clinical protocols, and ensure that the sponsor receives clean data from all trial sites. It is the responsibility of the sponsor to monitor the study results emerging from different study sites.

Clinical trials in India are regulated under Schedule Y of the Drugs and Cosmetics Rules, 1945, and are monitored by the DCGI. For new drugs developed in India, clinical trials have to be conducted in India from phase I. For obtaining marketing approval for a drug that has already been approved in other countries, phase III trials have to be conducted in India on a sample of 100 people to assess the impact on the Indian ethnic population. Till 2005, the year in which Schedule Y of the Drugs and Cosmetics Rules was amended, clinical trials of drugs developed outside India were permitted only with a 'phase lag', i.e. phase III trials would be permitted in India only when phase III trials had been completed elsewhere (Srinivasan and Sachin 2009). This restriction served the twin purposes of safeguarding against the initiation of unnecessary clinical trials in India and also forcing companies to conduct R&D in India if they wished to perform clinical trials in the country from the early stages. The amended rules enable parallel global clinical trials, allowing firms to conduct clinical trials in India without the phase lag. In just one year, from 1 April 2009 to 31 March 2010, the DCGI granted 237 permissions for global clinical trials in the country (Rajya Sabha 2010). With effect from 15 June 2009, the registration of applicants in the clinical trial registry maintained by the Indian Council of Medical Research (ICMR), New Delhi, has become mandatory for conducting clinical trials in India. As per the clinical trial registry maintained by ICMR, a total of 1,542 clinical trials had been registered in India as of February 2013 (Rajya Sabha 2013).

Do Indian pharmaceutical firms benefit from the liberalised clinical trial regulation mechanism in the country? The pharmaceutical industry could benefit if clinical trials offered an opportunity for the industry to build competence. Abrol, Prajapathi and Singh (2011) find that clinical trials by MNCs are concentrated in phase III, where the scope for competence building is extremely limited. (Domestic firms are only just beginning to enter into phase I trials.) Phase III trials are designed primarily to confirm the preliminary evidence accumulated in phase II, namely, that a drug is safe and effective for use for the intended indication, by conducting trials on a larger population. New safety and effectiveness assessments are not conducted in phase III trials.

Abrol, Prajapathi and Singh (2011) further argue that India's health infrastructure and health care personnel, developed over more than 60 years, are increasingly being utilised for the benefit of MNCs. In the process, patients in India have been exploited in clinical trials. In June 2011, the DCGI suspended the clinical trial of an anti-cancer drug being conducted by the Hyderabad-based firm Axis Clinicals. The trial was reported to be in violation of the Schedule Y requirement of obtaining the informed consent of the people on whom trials are conducted. The illegal trial came to light when at least nine women from Guntur district of Andhra Pradesh reported health problems to a local doctor (*India Today* 2011). Companies secure huge cost savings by neglecting to inform the people involved about the trials and documenting their informed consent. Schedule Y and the Guidelines for Good Clinical Practices for clinical research in India both require the sponsor to meet compensation requirements in case any harm is caused to subjects during the trials.

Another area of business relating to clinical trials is clinical data management. Managing clinical trial data requires multidisciplinary skills – information technology, clinical terminology and physician skills (O. R. S. Rao 2007). A number of leading information technology firms like Tata Consultancy Services, Cognizant, Satyam, HCL, Infosys, and IBM, and clinical trial companies like Quintiles and Manipal Acunova, have entered this area. Pharmaceutical MNCs like GSK have established clinical data management units in India. GlaxoSmithKline operates the Clinical Data Management Centre, India, established in 1996 and Biomedical Data Sciences India established in 1999 (GSK 2005). The services offered by this category of firms range from protocol development to data management, analysis and reporting, through to manuscript writing. In 2007, this business was estimated at US$100 million, growing at 80 per cent per year (O. R. S. Rao 2007). Clinical data management services have not been included in our discussion of CRAMS in this chapter; however, this segment may be the fastest growing business category in CRAMS.

The contract research taking place in India in itself does not result in any technology transfer, and in that sense it does not amount to competence building. However, the business provides an opportunity to firms to improve their skills in specialised areas of new drug discovery and development, as well as helping to strengthen their finances. In the long run, companies which offer integrated drug development, research, clinical trials, and manufacturing outsourcing services, like Dr. Reddy's, Nicholas Piramal, Suven Life Sciences, and Biocon (see Table 3.1), may be able to synergise the strengths they have accumulated in the various stages of drug discovery and development. Firms providing services in the initial stages of drug development have the opportunity to synergise the skills developed and the profits accumulated so as to move into higher levels of new drug R&D. An example of this is Suven Life Sciences (discussed further later in this chapter).

## Collaborative research projects

There is only a thin line differentiating contract drug discovery and development services and CRPs. In contract research, a firm provides discovery services in a number of therapeutic areas. In CRPs, on the other hand, the Indian firm focuses on selected therapeutic areas. A firm may have collaborative tie-ups with more than one MNC. In CRPs, the MNC and its Indian partner jointly discover drug molecules and develop them. Moreover, in CRPs, unlike in CRAMS, risk is shared proportionally. The MNC works closely with the Indian partner in the discovery process, while clinical development is the MNC's responsibility. The Indian company gets upfront payments and milestone and royalty payments depending on the progress made and the commercialisation of the drug. However, the compound is owned by the MNC.

A few mid-level Indian firms are involved in CRPs. Suven Life Sciences, which started out as a generics company, then moved into CRAMS, and finally entered into CRPs, offers the best example. Suven Life Sciences focuses its research on central nervous system (CNS) disorders. Research on CNS disorders like Alzheimer's disease or depression is very difficult, as quantitative measurement is not possible, unlike diseases such as hypertension. Thus, research into CNS diseases requires expertise. Suven has brought in Eli Lilly as its collaborator in CNS research. In 2011, the company now has 16 molecules in the discovery pipeline, with one molecule in phase II clinical trials (Suven Life Sciences 2014: 5).[22]

In CRPs, royalty is an essential component of the arrangement, unlike in CRAMS. Royalties ensure a steady stream of income to Indian firms. As in CRAMS arrangements, Indian firms tend to be subordinate allies in CRPs, entitled only to a fraction of the total benefits accruing from the product. Since Indian firms work jointly with MNC partners, however, the chances of building up specialised skills are better compared to CRAMS. The royalty payments involved are often in double-digit percentages, and this constitutes a major incentive for Indian firms to enter into CRPs (Sukumar 2009).

### Out-licensing and in-licensing

#### Out-licensing

The discovery and development of new drugs requires huge financial resources and availability of expertise. As a result, in most cases, Indian companies have collaborated with MNC partners at the more advanced stages of drug development, i.e. clinical development. Out-licensing is the strategy most widely adopted by major Indian firms. They develop the molecule independently up to a certain stage, and then license it out to an MNC partner for further development. Indian firms receive upfront and milestone payments and, depending on the terms of the contract, royalties upon the successful marketing of the drug. In some cases of out-licensing, Indian firms have been entitled to marketing rights and contract manufacturing opportunities. The Ranbaxy–Schwarz Pharma deal on the RBx 2258 compound gave Schwarz exclusive marketing rights in Europe, Japan and the United States, while Ranbaxy retained the rights for the rest of the world. The deal also allowed Ranbaxy to manufacture and supply finished formulations of the drug to Schwarz Pharma (*Economic Times* 2002).

Out-licensing was considered a win-win strategy because, on the one hand, it augmented the scarce financial and research resources available to Indian firms, while on the other hand it gave MNCs access to promising compounds at considerably lower prices. With the NCE pipeline of MNCs drying up, and profit margins hitting record lows due to competition from generics firms, MNCs have been forced to look for new compounds. In fact, many of these companies started up compound acquisition departments. The out-licensing business was initiated in India by Dr. Reddy's and Ranbaxy. They were later joined by others, like Glenmark. Glenmark's GRC 15300 molecule was out-licensed to Sanofi Aventis in 2010, and the molecule had entered phase II proof of concept trials after successfully completing phase I trials. Glenmark received US$20 million as upfront payment for the deal and was expecting another US$325 million as milestone payments depending upon the progress of the molecule. But Sanofi Aventis terminated the deal with Glenmark in the January–March quarter of 2014 following the failure of the molecule in the phase II proof of concept trial (Unnikrishnan and Ananthanarayanan 2014).

With the experience of consecutive setbacks in out-licensing deals, Indian firms became more careful in their outsourcing deals and in selecting partners. One of the emerging strategies is to collaborate with smaller and specialised research companies rather than collaborating with MNCs (Chaudhuri 2007). Dr. Reddy's entered into an agreement with Rheoscience, a subsidiary of Denmark-based Nordic Bioscience, for the development of balaglitazone (DRF 2593), which had been abandoned by Novo Nordisk (Dr. Reddy's 2004, 2005b). The molecule is currently at an advanced stage of phase III trials. In many cases, companies pursue the development of drugs independently. When Merck decided to shift focus away from anti-diabetic research, it returned to Glenmark a molecule (GRC 8200, melogliptin) that it had licensed in 2006. Glenmark had been paid US$31 million up front for this deal in 2006. When Merck pulled out from the deal in 2008, Glenmark decided to develop the drug on its own (Glenmark 2008), managing to take the GRC 8200 molecule up to phase III clinical trials.[23] Even while Glenmark was developing the molecule on its own, the company was looking for a suitable partner to take the molecule forward. A press release stated that 'Glenmark continues to be in discussions with various licensing partners to take the molecule forward' (Glenmark 2009: 2).

Piramal Life Sciences has followed a similar strategy in the case of cancer drugs. The company is striving to develop cancer drugs which would cost about US$100 million, as compared to the global standard of about US$1 billion (*Economic Times* 2009). At present, the company has four molecules in different phases of clinical trials.[24] Piramal Life Sciences' strategy is to opt for out-licensing only in the case of non-cancer drugs, and that too after a compound passes phase II. The company has learned that MNCs are not willing to pay much for compounds out-licensed in the initial stages of development (*ibid.*). Whenever out-licensing is required, most Indian firms now seek to develop the molecule until phase II of trials. The valuation rises considerably when a molecule passes phase II.[25] Suven Life Sciences is pursuing the same strategy in its CNS candidates developed in-house (*LiveMint* 2009). At the same time, this strategy carries risks, since failures at higher levels of R&D mean greater losses. The growing confidence among Indian pharmaceutical firms may be an indication of their growing innovative as well as financial capabilities.

Zydus Cadila is the first Indian company to have brought out a drug from an indigenously discovered and developed NCE. The company received the approval of Indian authorities in June 2013 for the marketing of saroglitazar (brand name Lipaglyn), the first drug in the world to treat diabetic dyslipidemia.[26] Cadila completed the entire process of discovery and development over a period of 10 years, involving an investment of US$250 million (Unnikrishnan 2013).

How will Indian firms be able to develop further in-house molecules, if they do not have the required S&T skills? Non-resident Indians (NRIs) who have experience in the new drug development projects of MNCs are increasingly becoming resource persons for Indian pharmaceutical firms. Several of the new drug development projects of Indian companies are headed by NRIs with experience in pharma MNCs. For instance, Rajinder Kumar and Rashmi H. Barbhaiya, prior to heading the R&D division of Ranbaxy, had worked at GSK and Bristol Myers Squibb, respectively (Chaudhuri 2005a). Uday Saxena, president and chief executive officer of Reddy US Therapeutics Inc., a subsidiary of the Dr. Reddy's group since 2002, earlier worked with AtheroGenics Inc., a bio-pharmaceutical company located in Georgia, USA. There, Saxena directed several drug discovery and early development programmes. He was also associated with the Parke-Davis Research Division in Michigan, where he was responsible for establishing a discovery programme in inflammation and atherogenesis.[27] Similarly, Somesh Sharma, managing director of Piramal Life Sciences, previously worked with the monoclonal antibody and vaccine unit at Anosys Inc.[28] It is estimated that 15 per cent of those working in the laboratories of pharmaceutical companies in the US and Europe are of Indian origin (Chaudhuri 2005a).

*In-licensing*

In a few rare cases, molecules have been in-licensed for clinical development. Glenmark has an in-licensing deal with San Francisco–based Napo Pharmaceuticals for Napo's proprietary anti-diarrhoeal molecule crofelemer. Diarrhoea is the most commonly reported gastrointestinal symptom in HIV-infected patients. About 15–30 per cent of the HIV/AIDS-infected population is affected by diarrhoea. Napo has granted Glenmark development and commercialisation rights for crofelemer in 140 countries, including India (outside USA, Europe, China, and Japan) (Glenmark 2005). Glenmark successfully completed phase III clinical trials in the US and obtained FDA approval for its drug to treat HIV-associated diarrhoea in 2013 (Glenmark 2012–13). The company is in the process of obtaining regulatory approval for the drug in a number of emerging markets. The same molecule is currently undergoing phase III clinical trials for adult acute infectious diarrhoea including cholera.[29]

It is important to note that the IP rights for the composition of matter and formulation of the compound lie with Napo. Glenmark has the licence to develop and commercialise the drug in certain geographical areas. The deal also contains a contract manufacturing provision, wherein Glenmark is to be the exclusive supplier of Napo's global API requirements for the manufacture and sale of crofelemer (Glenmark 2005). Glenmark also received US$15 million for upgrading its crofelemer API manufacturing unit. As with the other collaboration models, in-licensing is also principally a business opportunity for Indian firms, rather than a means of building competence through joint ownership of the technologies generated out of the partnerships.

In all kinds of partnerships involving MNCs, Indian pharmaceutical firms have always had a subordinate status. In the long run, this may result in Indian firms developing a dependency relationship with the MNCs. This can have many deleterious consequences for the country. Being the trusted allies of MNCs in the latter's global strategy, Indian companies may lose interest in the therapeutic areas that do not have global presence (for example, tropical country diseases). Local allies may also refrain from exercising compulsory licensing provisions, the TRIPS instrument to counter any abuse of the monopoly rights granted by patents.

The R&D efforts of Indian companies are not confined only to new drug development. Substantial efforts are directed to the development of generics and NDDS.

## Other areas of R&D

### Development of generics

The most important factor leading to the expansion of the Indian generics industry has been the acceptance of its low-priced drugs by consumers the world over. The share of exports in sales turnover grew from 15 per cent to 45 per cent between 1993–94 and 2011–12. The approvals obtained by Indian firms in regulated markets, especially in the US, offer the best illustration of R&D efforts in the generics business.

Firms are keen to enter regulated markets, despite the stringent standards involved, because they offer better economic prospects. The doors of the generic drugs market in the US were thrown open in 1984 when the Drug Price Competition and Patent Restoration Act (better known as the Hatch-Waxman Act) came into force. This legislation facilitated the entry into the market of generic versions of previously approved innovator drugs.

Two sets of data indicate the extent to which Indian firms are seeking opportunities in the US market – ANDA approvals and DMFs. Generic drug applications are termed 'abbreviated' because they are generally not required to include pre-clinical and clinical data to establish safety and efficacy. They are required only to demonstrate the bioequivalence of the product. When filing an ANDA, a company is required to certify that its product does not infringe any patent rights, or that the patent is invalid (para. IV certification). If the company successfully proves that the patent is invalid, or if it is the first to get approval for the generic version, it gets market exclusivity for 180 days. During this period, no other generic company is permitted to enter the market.

On the other hand, a DMF is a package of proprietary information that is voluntarily filed by a firm with the USFDA. A DMF indicates the future intention of a company to market a product in the US. There are five types of DMFs: type I, which includes information relating to manufacturing site, facilities and operating procedures; type II, relating to drug substance, drug substance intermediate, and material used in the preparation or drug product; type III, relating to packaging material; type IV, relating to excipient (the material carrying the active ingredient), colourant, flavour, essence, or material used in the preparation; and type V, including FDA-accepted reference information. Type II DMF applications indicate the number of drugs that a firm is interested in supplying to the US market. Table 3.2 lists ANDA approvals, including first-time generic approvals with 180-day exclusivity, and DMF filings by leading Indian firms.

Table 3.2 ANDA approvals, first-time generic approvals (180-day exclusivity) and DMF filings by leading Indian firms

| Company | 2001 | | 2002 | | 2003 | | 2004 | | 2005 | | 2006 | | 2007 | | 2008 | | 2009 | | 2010 | | 2011 | | 2012 | | Total | | DMF* |
|---|---|---|---|---|---|---|---|---|---|---|---|---|---|---|---|---|---|---|---|---|---|---|---|---|---|---|---|
| Aurobindo | 0 | 0 | 0 | 0 | 0 | 0 | 2 | 1 | 7 | 2 | 9 | 1 | 27 | 1 | 19 | 3 | 18 | 3 | 17 | 0 | 16 | 3 | 29 | 8 | 99 | 11 | 163 |
| Dr. Reddy's | 5 | 1 | 4 | 2 | 3 | 0 | 3 | 3 | 6 | 2 | 14 | 4 | 13 | 2 | 13 | 1 | 17 | 4 | 11 | 6 | 14 | 7 | 20 | 6 | 83 | 31 | 188 |
| Ranbaxy | 3 | 1 | 11 | 3 | 15 | 9 | 14 | 5 | 15 | 5 | 6 | 2 | 14 | 6 | 3 | 1 | 7 | 3 | 3 | 1 | 2 | 1 | 2 | 0 | 81 | 46 | 105 |
| Sun | 0 | 0 | 0 | 0 | 0 | 0 | 0 | 0 | 0 | 0 | 7 | 0 | 10 | 3 | 21 | 2 | 17 | 5 | 12 | 0 | 15 | 5 | 11 | 4 | 67 | 10 | 86 |
| Wockhardt | 0 | 0 | 0 | 0 | 4 | 0 | 0 | 0 | 4 | 1 | 6 | 0 | 13 | 1 | 18 | 0 | 14 | 1 | 5 | 0 | 6 | 0 | 11 | 3 | 64 | 3 | 46 |
| Glenmark | 0 | 0 | 0 | 0 | 0 | 0 | 0 | 0 | 0 | 0 | 4 | 0 | 9 | 2 | 5 | 0 | 9 | 1 | 19 | 3 | 12 | 3 | 10 | 2 | 46 | 6 | 55 |
| Lupin | 0 | 0 | 0 | 0 | 3 | 0 | 2 | 2 | 5 | 0 | 6 | 3 | 7 | 2 | 4 | 1 | 1 | 0 | 12 | 3 | 15 | 0 | 11 | 3 | 40 | 11 | 122 |
| Orchid | 0 | 0 | 0 | 0 | 0 | 0 | 0 | 0 | 9 | 0 | 9 | 0 | 4 | 1 | 3 | 0 | 3 | 2 | 2 | 0 | 0 | 0 | 4 | 1 | 30 | 3 | 87 |
| Matrix† | 0 | 0 | 0 | 0 | 0 | 0 | 1 | 0 | 0 | 0 | 0 | 0 | 1 | 0 | 2 | 1 | 3 | 1 | 10 | 1 | 0 | 0 | 1 | 0 | 17 | 3 | 159 |
| Cipla | 0 | 0 | 0 | 0 | 0 | 0 | 0 | 0 | 0 | 0 | 0 | 0 | 2 | 0 | 4 | 0 | 3 | 1 | 1 | 0 | 2 | 0 | 4 | 1 | 10 | 1 | 93 |
| Total | 8 | 2 | 15 | 5 | 25 | 9 | 22 | 11 | 46 | 10 | 61 | 10 | 100 | 18 | 92 | 9 | 92 | 21 | 92 | 14 | 30 | | 45 | | 537 | 125 | 1,104 |

Notes: Figures in shaded columns indicate first-time generic approvals.

*Type II DMF.

†For 2011 and 2012, data provided under the name of Mylan Laboratories.

Source: USFDA, ANDA (Generic) Drug Approvals, Previous Years, http://www.fda.gov/Drugs/DevelopmentApprovalProcess/HowDrugsareDevelopedand Approved/DrugandBiologicApprovalReports/ANDAGenericDrugApprovals/ucm050527.htm (last accessed on 3 November 2014). Data for ANDA approvals (not first-time generics) since 2007 accessed from USFDA, Drug Approval Reports, http://www.accessdata.fda.gov/scripts/cder/drugsatfda/index. cfm?fuseaction=Reports.ReportsMenu (last accessed on 3 November 2014); DMF data accessed from USFDA, Drug Master Files (DMFs), http://www.fda. gov/Drugs/DevelopmentApprovalProcess/FormsSubmissionRequirements/DrugMasterFilesDMFs/default.htm#download (accessed on 3 November 2014).

The leading 10 firms in India received 573 ANDA approvals between 2001 and 2012, of which a quarter obtained the 180-day market exclusivity provision. Ranbaxy and Dr. Reddy's led the way in filing ANDAs and DMFs, and were later followed by other firms. Ranbaxy and Dr. Reddy's stand out for their aggressive approach to challenging patents and obtaining market exclusivity. Fifty-seven per cent of Ranbaxy's and 33 per cent of Dr. Reddy's ANDA approvals carry market exclusivity, as against an average of 12 per cent for other firms. An illustrative list of innovators' exclusive markets thrown open to Indian generics with 180-day exclusivity is provided in Table 2.10 (Chapter 2). The leading firms also have a large number of DMF filings, an indication of their interest in the US market. These 10 firms account for nearly half of the DMF filings by all pharmaceutical firms in India.[30]

However, Ranbaxy performed badly in terms of ANDA approvals and first-time generic approvals in the later years of the 2000s. After the FDA found irregularities in the data submitted by Ranbaxy, the company signed a consent decree in December 2011 agreeing to incorporate corrective measures. Ranbaxy was imposed a fine of US$500 million in May 2013 by the US Department of Justice for the supply of adulterated drugs in the country and for making false statements to the FDA.[31] Three of Ranbaxy's plants in India have been placed under import alert by the FDA – the plants at Paonta Sahib, Batamandi and Dewas. Para. IV filings involving patent litigations are a high-risk, high-return strategy. A failure leads to the loss of years of hard work and the incurring of huge legal expenses.

### Novel drug delivery systems

Developing NDDS for existing drugs has been a priority area of research for most leading firms in India. Developing an NDDS is relatively easy and involves a smaller investment than new drug development. An NDDS can be developed in three to four years with an investment of US$20–50 million (Dhar and Gopakumar 2008). Regulatory requirements in the case of NDDS involve only the establishment of the product's bioequivalence with the 'normal' brand. This means essentially that the drug, in its new mode of delivery, should yield a similar concentration in the blood as the original drug, hence producing the same effect on the body. Several Indian firms are working in this area – JB Chemicals, Cadila Healthcare, Zydus Cadila, Morepen Laboratories, Neuland Laboratories, and Aurobindo.

Ranbaxy has exhibited the most remarkable success in the development of NDDS. The company developed an improved version of ciprofloxacin, a drug developed by Bayer AG. The drug was under patent protection until 2003. Ranbaxy developed a once-a-day formulation instead of the multiple-dose-a-day formulation offered by Bayer. Ranbaxy's formulation promised better patient compliance and was therefore considered to be a major step forward. Recognising this improvement, Bayer entered into a licensing agreement with Ranbaxy in 1999 for the latter's version of ciprofloxacin. Ranbaxy received US$65 million from Bayer over a four-year period, with an initial payment of US$10 million (Dhar and Gopakumar 2008). The agreement gave Bayer AG worldwide marketing rights for ciprofloxacin except India and the Commonwealth of Independent States, where Ranbaxy Laboratories secured marketing rights.

Alembic's once-a-day NDDS for Belgium-based UCB's anti-epileptic drug Keppra is another success story. In 2007, Alembic entered into a licensing agreement with UCB for US$11 million. Alembic would also receive royalty payments on sales of its product (*Economic Times* 2007). Dabur Pharma developed a nanotechnology-based anti-cancer NDDS, Nanoxel, for the widely used anti-cancer treatment drug paclitaxel. Dabur's NDDS entered clinical trials in Europe and US in 2007 (*Business Standard* 2007). Nanoxel is currently in the portfolio of Fresenius Kabi (Singapore), a unit of the European health care company Fresenius SE, which took over Dabur Pharma in 2008.

We have seen that the Indian pharmaceutical industry has been growing more R&D-intensive from the beginning of the 2000s. Has the new patent regime been the driver of this increased focus on R&D? Data on R&D investment in new drug development are not available separately; as a result, we cannot draw any conclusions based on R&D expenditure. However, a few studies have attempted to address this question by analysing information accessed from pharmaceutical companies and data on their patenting behaviour. On the basis of interactions with senior officials of leading Indian pharmaceutical companies, Chaudhuri (2005a) concludes that the increase in R&D intensity has been an outcome of the fear of shrinking market opportunities, rather than a result of the incentives offered by the new patents regime. Companies fear they will no longer be able to reverse engineer existing products and therefore undertake to produce new drugs.

Abrol, Prajapathi and Singh (2011) analyse the patenting behaviour of Indian pharmaceutical firms in the US Patents and Trademark Office. They find that chemistry-driven process research resulting in non-infringing processes for APIs, the introduction of cost-effective routes, the reduction of impurity levels, new dosage forms and formulations, and NDDS are the main research priorities of Indian firms. Of the 1,159 patents granted to 35 firms from India between 2000 and 2007, product patents constituted only 5 per cent; dosage forms constituted 44 per cent, new forms of substances 24 per cent, and processes 18 per cent. The study also concludes that the Hatch-Waxman Act of 1984 still continues to be 'the most important stimulus for domestic pharmaceutical firms to invest in the process of learning, competence building and innovation making activity' (*ibid*.: 334).

Another way to address this question is to analyse the therapeutic areas of new drug R&D undertaken by Indian firms. If the patents regime in India has been the driving force of R&D, firms would find market opportunities in developing drugs for diseases that are relevant in the Indian context. On the other hand, if the patent regime in developed countries (i.e. the regime that prevailed before TRIPS) has been the driver, we would expect Indian firms to invest more heavily in drugs for global diseases. The following section analyses the new drug R&D of Indian firms in terms of therapeutic areas.

## Therapeutic areas of new drug R&D

Table 3.3 lists the new molecules being developed by leading pharma firms in India.

Table 3.3 shows that the R&D efforts of Indian pharmaceutical firms are concentrated in global chronic disease conditions such as cancer and diabetes. Though there are two molecules for malaria and tuberculosis (TB), these compounds have not been the outcome of purely corporate considerations. Ranbaxy's anti-malarial compound (arterolane) came out of its partnership with the Medicines for Malaria Venture (MMV), a global public health funding agency. Ranbaxy obtained approval from the DCGI to initiate phase III human clinical trials in India. The firm also plans to seek regulatory approval in other countries outside India for the phase III trial.[32] However, when MMV pulled out of the project in 2007 after a review of the preliminary data, Ranbaxy pursued the development of the drug its own. The bulk of the anti-malarial project cost was financed by MMV, which is estimated to have spent about US$13–15 million on this project (Unnikrishnan 2007). When MMV withdrew, the Department of Science and Technology (DST) of the Government of India came forward to collaborate in the project, with an offer of Rs 110 million (Mathew 2007).

Lupin, the only company engaged in the development of TB drugs, has been the world leader in their production. It is also a preferred supplier to the Global Drug Facility, which supplies drugs to more than

Table 3.3 Compounds of Indian companies at different stages of development

| Compound | Therapeutic area | Status |
|---|---|---|
| **Dr. Reddy's[a]** | | |
| DRF 2593 | Metabolic disorders | Ongoing: phase III |
| Several compounds | Respiratory disorders | Ongoing: phase I |
| DRL 17822 | Metabolic disorders / cardiovascular disorders | Ongoing: phase I |
| **Ranbaxy[b]** | | |
| RBx 11160 (arterolane) | Anti-malaria combination drug (arterolane maleate and piperaquine phosphate) | Obtained marketing approval in India |
| MMP-9 MMP-12 | COPD inhibitor | Phase II (proof of concept) in India Recruitment of patients under way in EU |
| **Glenmark[c]** | | |
| GRC 15300 | TRPV3 inhibitor | Phase I (out-licensed to Sanofi Aventis) |
| mPGES-1 inhibitors | Chronic inflammatory conditions | Pre-clinical trials |
| GRC 17536 | TRPA1 inhibitor | Pre-clinical trials |
| GBR 401 | Lymphomas and leukaemias | Completed pre-clinical trials |
| GBR 500* | Multiple sclerosis and inflammatory disorders | Ongoing: in phase II |
| GRC 15300 | Osteoarthritic pain, neuropathic pain, skin disorders | Ongoing: in phase II |
| GBR 600* | Antiplatelet, adjunct to PCI/acute coronary syndrome | Ongoing: completed pre-clinical trials |
| GBR 900* | Chronic pain | Pre-clinical trials |
| GBR 830* | Autoimmune diseases | Pre-clinical trials |
| Vatelizumab | Ulcerative colitis | In phase II |
| Crofelemer | Anti-diarrhoeal | Successfully completed phase III Obtained FDA approval |

(Continued)

Table 3.3 (Continued)

| Compound | Therapeutic area | Status |
|---|---|---|
| **Biocon**[d] | | |
| Nimotuzumab | Oncology | In market |
| Itolizumab | Autoimmune diseases | In market |
| IN 105 (oral insulin)* | Diabetes | Ongoing: phase II |
| BVX-20 | Oncology | Phase I |
| Fusion proteins | Oncology | Pre-clinical trials |
| **Wockhardt**[e] | | |
| WCK 771 | Anti-infective | Ongoing: in phase II |
| WCK 2349 | Anti-infective | Ongoing: in phase II |
| WCK 4873 | Anti-infective | Completed pre-clinical trials |
| **Piramal Enterprises**[f] | | |
| P1446A | Malignant melanoma | Phase I |
| P7170 | Oncology | Investigational drug |
| PL225B | Oncology | Investigational drug |
| P1736-05 | Diabetes | Phase II completed in India |
| P7435 | Diabetes | Phase II completed in India |
| P1187 | Type II diabetes | Investigational new drug |
| **Lupin**[g] | | |
| LL 2011# | Anti-migraine (Amigra) | Ongoing: in phase III |
| LL 4218 | Anti-psoriasis (Desoside-P) | Ongoing: in phase II |
| LL 3858/4858# | TB (Sudoterb) | Ongoing: in phase I |
| LL 3348 | Anti-psoriasis (herbal desoris) | Ongoing: in phase II |
| Unnamed | Diabetes type 2 | Ongoing: in pre-clinical trials |
| Unnamed | Rheumatoid arthritis | Ongoing: in pre-clinical trials |
| **Zydus Cadila**[h] | | |
| Lipaglyn Saroglitazar | Diabetes and cardiac | Successfully completed phase III trials. Now available in the Indian market |

(Continued)

*Table 3.3* (Continued)

| Compound | Therapeutic area | Status |
|---|---|---|
| Lipaglyn Saroglitazar | Lipodystrophy (fat redistribution) | Entered phase III |
| ZYH7 | Cholesterol | Completed phase II |
| ZYG19 | Diabetes | Ongoing: in phase I |
| ZYDPLA1 | Diabetes | Ongoing: in phase I |
| Collaborative programme with Prolong Pharma* | Anaemia | Ongoing: in phase I |
| Collaborative programme with WHO* | Rabies | Ongoing: in phase I |
| Collaborative programme with Pieries AG* | Oncology | In pre-clinical development stage |

*Notes:* *Biologics

#These molecules are phytopharmaceuticals (originating from plants)

*Source:*

aBased on the company's annual reports over nine years beginning 2001–02. See http://www.drreddys.com/media/annual-reports.html (accessed on 3 November 2014). In its *Annual Report 2012–13*, Dr. Reddy's does not offer molecule-wise, detailed information.

bBased on Ranbaxy's annual reports for eight years beginning 2002. See http://www.ranbaxy.com/investor-relations/financial-information/annual-report/ (accessed on 3 November 2014).

cBased on Glenmark's *Annual Report 2012–13*, http://www.glenmarkpharma.com/Common/pdf/Glenmark_AR_FY13.pdf (accessed on 3 November 2014).

dBased on Biocon's *Annual Report 2013*, http://www.biocon.com/docs/Biocon_Annual_Report_2013.pdf (accessed on 3 November 2014).

eBased on Wockhardt's *Annual Report 2011–12*, http://www.wockhardt.com/pdf/Annual-Report-2011-2012-f932f.pdf (accessed on 3 November 2014).

fBased on Piramal's *Annual Report 2012–13*, http://piramal.com/sites/default/files/PEL-Annual-Report-FY2013.pdf (accessed on 3 November 2014).

gBased on Lupin's annual reports for five years from 2004–05. See http://www.lupinworld.com/archives-annual-report.htm (accessed on 3 November 2014).

hBased on Zydus Cadila, 'New molecular entities in development', http://www.zyduscadila.com/discovery.html (accessed on 30 December 2014).

50 countries. For the development of the TB drug, Lupin has entered into partnerships with public-funded research institutions (Chaudhuri 2005a). Under the New Millennium Indian Technology Leadership Initiative (NMITLI) programme of CSIR, the expertise of Lupin and 12 institutional partners was synergised in TB research for the development

of new targets, drug delivery systems, enhancers, and therapeutics. Lupin's TB candidate is the first success in developing a new TB therapy to be achieved over the last 40 years globally.[33]

Unfortunately, Lupin is now in the process of shedding its TB research programme. 'We were not satisfied with the way the programme was running,' Nilesh Gupta, executive director of Lupin, said in an interview to *Business World*. 'Our focus will now be on diabetes and anti-inflammatory research. Globally these are hot areas' (Bisserbe 2010). Until recently, Lupin had focused on TB and sporiasis drug research. However, the development of molecules that do not qualify for western markets has progressed very slowly over the past five years, since Lupin began reviewing its R&D strategy. Globally, pharmaceutical companies have registered decreasing interest in R&D on tropical diseases. The withdrawal of Indian firms from such research should also be seen in this context. Of the four TB molecules that are in different stages of clinical development around the world, with the exception of Lupin's molecule (LL3858), the other three emerged out of sponsorship by public institutions and global health initiatives.[34]

Policies initiated in India's pharmaceuticals sector from the mid-1990s have opened the doors to the globalisation of the country's pharma industry. Indian pharma firms have become an integral part of the global R&D and production network of MNCs. In other words, they have become partners in 'non-equity modes of international production and development'.[35] Indian firms have been able to participate in the process because of the strengths they had accumulated during the earlier policy regime. With globalisation, Indian pharmaceutical firms have shifted their focus away from the domestic market, and are increasingly aligning themselves with the R&D strategies of MNCs. The orientation of Indian firms has also changed, from being the competitors of foreign firms during the earlier policy regime, to being subordinate collaborators of MNCs in the new regime.

This reorientation of the R&D focus of the Indian pharma industry poses a number of challenges to public health management in the country. With the withdrawal of the private sector from neglected diseases, public health faces a serious crisis. The introduction of product patent rights in pharmaceuticals has not attracted investment into research on diseases more common to India, as had been argued by proponents of the new patent regime when TRIPS was negotiated in the Uruguay Round. The following section discusses the role of the public sector in addressing the market failure of the new patent regime in the country.

## The role of the public sector

There are essentially two ways in which the public sector can address the market failure issue. First, public sector pharma companies are encouraged to undertake R&D for drugs for neglected diseases. Second, additional incentives in the form of public–private partnerships (PPPs) can be provided to the private sector to encourage it to conduct R&D for neglected diseases.

The first option is not feasible, since most of the earlier champions of the pharmaceuticals industry have become sick enterprises. The Board for Industrial and Financial Reconstruction declared HAL, IDPL and BCPW as sick units. A few other units, such as Bengal Immunity, Smith Stanistreet Pharmaceuticals Ltd and Maharashtra Antibiotics and Pharmaceuticals Ltd, have also been shut down (Rajya Sabha 2005). In spite of recommendations from various agencies for the revival of pharma PSUs, the latest being from the High-Level Expert Group (HLEG) on Universal Health Coverage of the Planning Commission, no steps have been taken in this direction. One of the recommendations of the HLEG was to 'ensure drug and vaccine security by strengthening the public sector and protecting the capacity of Indian private sector companies to produce low cost drugs and vaccines needed for the country' (GoI 2011b: 132). The HLEG report observes that the increasing number of acquisitions of Indian pharmaceutical firms by MNCs, and the growth of strategic alliances between Indian firms and MNCs, is leading to a restructuring of the Indian pharmaceutical industry. In order to reduce the vulnerability arising out of this restructuring, the report recommends the revival of PSUs like IDPL and Hindustan Antibiotics Ltd by infusing more capital into the sick units and granting them autonomous status.

The strategy of the government in addressing market failure has been to resort to the second option – PPPs. It is believed that public–private partnerships will synergise the strengths of public-funded R&D institutes, such as the CSIR laboratories, universities and academic institutions, on the one hand, and the pharma industry on the other. An example of a PPP initiative in the pharmaceuticals sector is the Drugs and Pharmaceuticals Research Programme (DPRP) of the DST, instituted in 1994–95. Under this programme, research is conducted jointly by a publicly funded R&D institution and a pharma company, with the DST monitoring the collaborative research project. The public-funded institution provides its existing R&D facilities and the services of its R&D personnel to the collaborating private firm. However, the recurring expenses associated with the collaborative project incurred by the public-funded institution are shared between the public-funded institution and the private firm. The private firm incurs 30 per cent of the recurring costs. The remaining 70 per cent of recurring expenses incurred by the public-funded institution are funded by the DST. The entire capital expenditure associated with the collaborative research project incurred by the public-funded institution is funded by the DST. But the private firm has to fund the entire capital and recurring expenditure, if any part of the project is pursued solely by the private firm.

Since 2009–10, 15 collaborative research projects have been approved by the DPRP.[36] Since the launch of the DPRP in 1994–95, 101 collaborative projects had been sanctioned until 2010 for drugs for TB, malaria, diarrhoea, diabetes, psychosomatic disorders, kala-azar, cataract, dementia, HIV/AIDS, arthritis, Japanese encephalitis, hepatitis-B, anti-fungal drugs, antivirals, anti-cancer drugs, antibacterials, anti-rabies drugs, anti-obesity drugs, anti-asthma drugs, and a vaccine for dengue (DST 2011). However, despite a large number of projects being sanctioned, no NCE has been developed out of this collaborative programme (Chaudhuri 2010). The projects undertaken as part of the DPRP initiative are isolated research projects dealing only with particular aspects of drug development. Nevertheless, the studies have generated insights that may be of use in future research (Chaudhuri 2005a). Perhaps this is precisely what is expected of the programme, whose two-pronged approach involves 'exploratory drug design and drug development on candidate molecules already identified on the one hand and providing cutting edge to Indian Industry through innovative process for known/generic drug as well as crucial intermediates on the other'.[37]

Other factors may also be involved in the absence of new products emerging from the DPRP PPP initiative. Laboratories belonging to CSIR, like the CDRI, have not experienced a great deal of interaction with the pharmaceutical industry in the area of new drug development. Since 1947, 17 new drugs have been developed in India, of which 15 emerged from public sector institutions like CDRI and HAL.[38] These institutes developed the drugs, conducted clinical trials in India, obtained marketing approval in India, and licensed the drugs to Indian firms for marketing. But none of the drugs has been commercially successful (Chaudhuri 2010). A major constraint has been the lack of commercial orientation on the part of these institutes. Domestic firms find it difficult to promote the product primarily because of the 'Indian' tag (Chaudhuri 2005a). Cipla's experience with deferiprone (brand name Kelfer), a drug used for the removal of iron from blood, is a case in point.

Cipla introduced Kelfer in India in 1995. The company faced huge problems in promoting the product in India. Deferiprone was originally developed by Robert Hilder and George Kontoghiorghes of the UK in 1983. Phase I and phase II trials were conducted in Switzerland and England. Cipla obtained the licence for the development of the drug, and phase II and phase III trials were conducted in India. When it came to obtaining marketing approval and promoting the product, however, Cipla faced problems essentially because of the 'Indian' tag of its product. Reportedly, Cipla faced the question, 'Where else has it been approved?', not only from the DCGI but also from doctors. Finally, Cipla had to bring George Kontoghiorghes to India to impress upon the DCGI the merits of its product.[39] Perhaps the eagerness of Indian firms to engage in out-licensing should be seen not merely as a result of a lack of skills and resources, but also from the point of view of the wider drug innovation environment in the country.

Other PPPs from which pharma firms can benefit are NMITLI (an initiative of the CSIR) and the Small Business Innovation Research Initiative (SBIRI) of the Department of Biotechnology. Under the NMITLI scheme, 42 pharmaceutical R&D projects were sanctioned between 2005 and 2011 involving 287 partners (222 in the public sector and 65 in the private sector) (Abrol, Prajapathi and Singh 2011). Similarly, SBIRI had sanctioned 32 R&D projects in pharmaceuticals until May 2008. Abrol, Prajapathi and Singh (*ibid.*) analyse the R&D projects initiated under the NMITLI and SBIRI programmes. They observe a relative lack of focus on neglected diseases, the priority areas of the research projects being concentrated on global chronic disease conditions.

The PPPs have succeeded in establishing linkages between public sector laboratories and research institutions and the pharmaceuticals industry. These partnerships, however, have been catering to the industry's need to participate effectively in the global R&D networks of pharma MNCs, rather than to the country's need to develop new therapies for neglected diseases. Thus, PPPs have not offered an effective means of addressing the market failure. Ablaquin, the anti-malarial drug developed by CDRI and licensed to Nicholas Piramal, still has not entered the US$800 million anti-malarial market. The government's efforts to develop technologies for neglected diseases will be futile if the manufacturing industry is averse to these technologies. Mechanisms such as advance purchase commitments might incentivise the industry to engage in the commercialisation of such technologies.

The Open Source Drug Discovery (OSDD) project is an innovative PPP initiative launched in 2008 by the CSIR. It focuses on discovering novel therapies for neglected diseases. Initially, the project started with TB as its primary area of focus. The Government of India committed Rs 459.6 million to this project during the 11th Five Year Plan period (2007–12).[40] The Planning Commission of India extended the project to the 12th plan period (2012–17) and earmarked Rs 1,583.8 million for it. The cost of the project, as of 31 March 2015, is expected to be Rs 509.6 million (CSIR 2014). The OSDD also receives funds from non-governmental sources. In October 2013, the Sir Dorabji Tata Trust announced a grant of Rs 28.6 million to support students and young researchers to contribute to OSDD (*ibid.*).[41] The OSDD project involves a portal that provides an open source platform for scientists, doctors, technocrats, software professionals, and students to share knowledge. More than 8000 members from 130 countries are registered at the portal (*ibid.*). Anyone who registers can submit project proposals to the community. If a proposal gets through the review process, it will receive funding from OSDD. The project can be based at any of the partnering institutions.[42]

The OSDD now has 82 molecules in the pipeline, including 2 at the hit to lead stage and 1 in clinical trials (Thomas 2012). One ambitious OSDD project was the decoding of the genetic structure of mycobacterium tuberculosis, which has become resistant to conventional multidrug TB therapy. This pathogen carries about 4,000 genes, of which the functions of only 500 were known (J. Joseph 2011). The project has successfully mapped the entire genetic structure of the pathogen. This will lead to a better understanding of the bacterial multiplication process and thus to much more effective anti-TB drugs.

While developing a drug, OSDD may collaborate with other public-funded institutes in India, or with CROs or industry partners, or other partners with experience in the field. In the case of partnerships with public research institutions, the data generated from the clinical trials are made available to the public. Collaboration with other partners is subject to the condition that any drugs developed in the process will be made available to generics manufactures without any IPR strings attached. Currently, phase II clinical trials of a new combination TB therapy involving PA-824, moxifloxacin and pyrazinamide are under way in collaboration with the National Institute of TB and Respiratory Diseases, New Delhi, and GVK Biosciences, Hyderabad (CSIR 2014).

Researchers associated with the project are allowed to file patents on their innovations, subject to the condition that OSDD will be assigned a worldwide, royalty-free, non-exclusive licence for further development. The advantage of the OSDD approach is that, since the funding comes from the government, the prerogative of setting priorities lies with the government.

Some other initiatives to develop drugs for neglected diseases are funded mainly by philanthropic organisations. The Drugs for Neglected Diseases Initiative (DNDi) is one such programme. A non-profit R&D organisation launched in 2003, DNDi focuses on developing new drugs for neglected diseases.[43] The initiative is funded by public, private and philanthropic institutions, including the Department for International Development, the Sasakawa Peace Foundation, and the Bill and Melinda Gates Foundation. Unlike OSDD, DNDi has also entered into partnership agreements with a number of pharmaceutical companies, biotech firms, and initiatives such as the TB Alliance to secure access to compound libraries and unpublished data. Using this data, it identifies potential molecules for treating neglected diseases in collaboration with public and private sector institutions. For example, the TB Alliance provided DNDi access to a select library of 70 nitroimidazoles. In collaboration with the CDRI in India, DNDi tested these molecules for their antileishmanial activity (DNDi 2011b). Within nine years of its launch and with EUR120 million, DNDi had developed six new treatments for neglected diseases, which constituted improvements upon existing treatments.[44] It had also built a promising pipeline including 11 NCEs (Menghaney 2012b).

The DNDi's business model is based on product development partnerships. The IP generated in the course of these partnerships may be individually or jointly owned by DNDi and/or its partners; however, DNDi secures non-exclusive, sub-licensable, royalty-free licences on the IP generated from these partnerships. The advantage of this model is that a lot of time is saved in the drug development process through ensuring access to compound libraries and other data. On the flip side, the lack of assurance of funding for future research projects and the influence exerted by donors in setting priorities are some of the challenges faced by DNDi (Menghaney 2012b).

In recent years, a proposal was floated at the WHO in the light of the report of the Consultative Expert Working Group (CEWG) on Research and Development: Financing and Coordination .[45] The proposal suggested establishing a binding treaty to finance and coordinate R&D efforts so as to meet the health needs of developing countries.

The proposal suggested that all countries commit at least 0.01 per cent of their GDPs for this purpose. Developed countries were opposed to the idea of a binding agreement. Deliberations on the proposal are still under way.

In this context, a discussion of the proposed Protection and Utilisation of Publicly Funded Intellectual Property Bill, 2008, would be useful. This bill was presented in Parliament by the Ministry of Science and Technology, Government of India, and is currently being reviewed by the Parliamentary Standing Committee on Science, Technology, Environment and Forests. Modelled on the Bayh-Dole Act (the US Patents and Trademark Law Amendments Act), the bill is better known as the Indian Bayh-Dole. The objectives of the bill include, among others: (*a*) commercialisation of IP created out of publicly funded R&D; (*b*) promotion of a culture of innovation in the country; and (*c*) minimising the dependence of universities, academic and research institutions on government funding.

The objectives of the bill are laudable, but imposing strictures on public-funded R&D projects alone will not serve the purpose. First and foremost, the innovation environment has to be ripe enough to promote indigenous innovation. In India, in the pharmaceuticals sector at least, the environment has to be made conducive so as to overcome the stigma of the 'Indian' tag, which we discussed in an earlier section. Further, a move in the direction outlined in the bill would only exacerbate what is popularly known as the 90/10 gap.[46] It has already been shown that the focus of R&D in India is heavily tilted towards global diseases and that private industry is moving away from investing in R&D for tropical diseases. One study (Lanjouw and MacLeod 2005) found that Indian companies were investing only 10 per cent of their total R&D funds to develop drugs for diseases that are more prevalent in developing countries.[47]

In most cases of drug development, the basic research is done in research institutions and laboratories. The molecules thus developed are then licensed to the industry. If the commercialisation of research is overemphasised, the focus of public-funded research may also narrow down to very selective therapeutic areas in which the industry has an interest. Researchers would be inclined to concentrate their efforts on issues of interest to the industry, especially those that promise immediate returns. Further, an exclusive focus on IP and its commercialisation would lead our pillars of learning and research to operate like businesses. Some universities in the US, like Columbia University and Duke University, have been spending more over time on patent litigation than on research (Prakash 2009).

Apart from PPPs, other incentives are also available for R&D in the pharmaceutical sector. The current DP provides incentives for R&D in the form of exemption from price control. Section 32 of the DPCO of 2013 provides for exemption from price control in the following cases:

(i) a manufacturer producing a new drug patented under the Indian Patent Act, 1970 (39 of 1970) (product patent) and not produced elsewhere, if developed through indigenous R&D, for a period of five years from the date of commencement of its commercial production in the country.

(ii) a manufacturer producing a new drug in the country by a new process developed through indigenous R&D and patented under the Indian Patent Act, 1970 (39 of 1970) (process patent) for a period of five years from the date of the commencement of its commercial production in the country.

(iii) a manufacturer producing a new drug involving a new delivery system developed through indigenous R&D for a period of five years from the date of its market approval in India.

The DPRP also provides soft loan schemes for pharma industry R&D projects and grants-in-aid for clinical trials for projects geared to developing drugs for neglected diseases. The loan scheme became a part of the DPRP in 2006, when the Government of India decided to dissolve the Pharmaceutical Research and Development Support Fund (PRDSF).

The Pharmaceutical R&D Committee, under the chairmanship of R. A. Mashelkar, had proposed a mechanism for establishing organic linkages between private and public research institutions and laboratories, with a view to synchronising and synergising national R&D efforts in pharmaceuticals. The committee recommended the creation of an autonomous Drug Development Promotion Foundation, with a one-time contribution of Rs 500 million from the government, and an annual outlay of Rs 1,000 million which was to be generated by imposing a surcharge of 1 per cent on the MRP of formulations. The government did not, however, accept this recommendation. Instead, it established the PRDSF in 2004 with an initial corpus of Rs 1,500 million. The interest accruing on this fund was to be utilised to support collaborative research projects and extending soft loans. However, since the interest accrued was not sufficient to support the R&D initiatives of the pharma industry, the government dissolved the PRDSF corpus in January 2006, and replaced it with an annual budgetary allocation of Rs 1,500 million. Given that the DPRP and the PRDSF were serving the same purpose, the PRDSF was merged with the DPRP.

Under the soft loan programme, loans up to 70 per cent of the requirement are extended to firms engaged in R&D in drugs and pharmaceuticals. The loans are offered at concessional rates (simple rate of interest of 3 per cent, repayment in 10 equal annual instalments, etc.). The ownership of the IP generated out of these projects is based on the terms agreed upon in each case. Some projects funded under this programme are at advanced stages of clinical trials.[48] Ranbaxy's RBx 11160 (an anti-malaria combination drug) is in phase III clinical trials in India and Thailand. Lupin's LL 2011 (an anti-migraine drug) is also in phase III trials, and LL 4218 (an anti-psoriasis drug) is in phase II clinical trials. Dr. Reddy's 7295 (for the treatment of advanced and metastatic cancers of the colon, pancreas, stomach, and lung) has entered clinical trials.[49]

The grant-in-aid programme was constituted specifically to incentivise R&D in neglected diseases, when it was found that the collaborative programme and the DPRP's loan scheme were not attracting investment in research on neglected diseases. As compared to the other schemes of the DPRP, however, there are very few takers for the grant-in-aid scheme. Despite grants having been made available to conduct clinical trials, which is the most expensive phase in the process of new drug development, only two companies – Ranbaxy and Bharat Serum and Vaccines – availed of this facility in the six years starting 2004–05.[50]

Firms engaging in R&D in India also benefit from various provisions for tax and duty exemptions. Firms possessing in-house R&D facilities and recognised by the Department for Scientific and Industrial Research (DSIR) are eligible for 150 per cent weighted exemption on R&D expenditure under Section 35 (2AB) of the Income Tax Act. This provision is extended to depreciation on investment in land and buildings for dedicated research facilities, expenditure incurred in obtaining regulatory approvals and the filing of patents abroad, and expenditure incurred on clinical trials in India. As of now, this facility is available till 2015 (GoI 2005c). The R&D-intensive companies (gold standard companies) are eligible for 200 per cent weighted tax exemption. Gold standard companies are identified on the basis of certain criteria, for instance, investing at least 3 per cent of their sales turnover in R&D, employing at least 200 scientists in India, having filed at least 10 patent applications in India based on research done in India, etc. Similarly, reference standards (i.e. the specimens used in testing by the pharmaceutical industry to help ensure the identity, strength and quality of products) and reference books imported for R&D are exempt from import duty.

The creation of an incentive-based system for pharma R&D has not succeeded in attracting investment by Indian pharma companies in research on tropical neglected diseases. Their involvement in global production and development networks allows these firms to find better opportunities in drugs relating to selected chronic disease conditions. We will turn now to another aspect of the reforms in the pharmaceuticals sector in India, namely, the emphasis placed on foreign investment. Currently, 100 per cent foreign investment is permitted in pharmaceuticals under the automatic route. Have these incentives had any impact on the R&D priorities of pharmaceutical firms? The following section analyses the impact of the liberalisation of foreign investment on R&D in India.

## Foreign investment in R&D

A major limitation to studying the impact of the liberalisation of foreign investment on R&D in India is the availability of data. Most foreign R&D companies in India are not listed companies. As a result, information on the R&D focus of these firms is not available publicly. In a first-of-its-kind study in India, the DSIR and the Indian Institute of Foreign Trade (IIFT) in 2005 jointly framed a questionnaire on foreign R&D centres in India. Of the 119 foreign R&D centres that responded to the questionnaire, 46 firms belonged in the category of biotechnology and pharmaceuticals. Of these 46, those firms working exclusively on pharmaceuticals are listed in Table 3.4, along with their R&D activities.

The foreign R&D centres in India claim to be conducting R&D in various therapeutic segments. But it is not clear in which stage of drug development their R&D is concentrated. A few firms, like Indus BioSciences and PharmaNet Clinical Services India, seem to be engaged in the development of processes, delivery systems and derivatives. However, we do not have clarity on the R&D activities of the affiliates of MNCs such as AstraZeneca and Novartis.

Using data from FDI Market Intelligence, Abrol, Prajapathi and Singh (2011) attempt to figure out the R&D focus of foreign firms in India. They find that R&D activities account for the highest number of projects (36 out of 83) in a range of business activities, such as manufacturing, business services and design. After exploring the FDI transactions in these R&D projects, the study concludes that 'a large number of R&D investment projects are focused on developing facilities for phase III clinical trials and other such modules that only integrate Indian talent and facilities into foreign pharmaceutical firms' global objectives' (*ibid*.: 342). Thus, it emerges that liberalisation of foreign investment has led to the outsourcing of clinical trials to India, rather than to investment in R&D for the development of new drugs from basic stages.

*Table 3.4* Foreign R&D centres in India and the technologies developed by them

| Company | Technologies developed |
|---|---|
| AstraZeneca R&D | 1. Cardiovascular<br>2. Infection<br>3. Neuroscience<br>4. Obstetrics and gynaecology<br>5. Oncology<br>6. Respiratory |
| Merck Development Centre | 1. Antibiotics<br>2. Antimalarials<br>3. Cardiologicals<br>4. Cough and cold formulations<br>5. Dermatologicals<br>6. Haematinics<br>7. Neurologicals<br>8. Oral rehydration solutions<br>9. Non-steroidal anti-inflammatory drugs |
| Novartis India | 1. Arthritis and bone metabolism<br>2. Cardiovascular and metabolic diseases<br>3. Dermatology/immunopathology<br>4. Infectious disease<br>5. Nervous system disorders<br>6. Oncology<br>7. Ophthalmics<br>8. Transplantation |
| Novo Nordisk India | 1. Insulin analogues – Novomix 30 and NovoRapid (in 2003)<br>2. Insulin delivery device – NovoLet<br>3. A third-generation durable insulin delivery device – NovoPen |
| PharmaNet Clinical Services India | 1. Drug-eluting stents<br>2. Implantable drug/device delivery systems<br>3. Catheter-based drug delivery technologies<br>4. Co-packaged combination products |
| Pliva Research India | 1. Anti-infectives<br>2. Cytostatics<br>3. Diuretics<br>4. Various APIs<br>5. Nutraceuticals |
| Roche Scientific Company India | 1. Transplantation<br>2. Oncology<br>3. Hepatitis<br>4. HIV |

(*Continued*)

*Table 3.4* (Continued)

| Company | Technologies developed |
| --- | --- |
| Gangagen Biotechnologies | Library of over 400 bacteriophages which kill a variety of bacteria present in over 1,100 clinical isolates |
| Indus BioSciences | 1. Carbohydrate derivatives<br>2. Heterocyclic building blocks<br>3. Reagents and building blocks<br>4. Chiral agents and building blocks<br>5. Nitriles, acids and amidines<br>6. Pyridines, piperidines, pyrimidines, and indazoles |
| John F. Welch Technology Center (GE ) | Improved diagnostic and treatment protocols |

*Source:* DSIR-IIFT (2005).

Data available for the listed subsidiaries of MNCs[51] shows that their R&D intensity is very low (Figure 3.5). It is even lower than the R&D intensity of public sector pharmaceutical firms in India, which do not engage in any R&D for new drug development. It may be argued that MNC subsidiaries in India need not make R&D investments in new

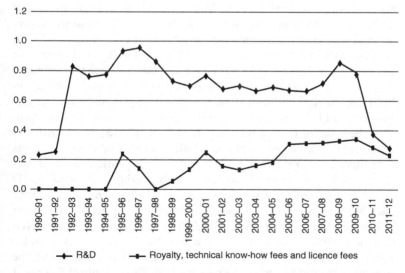

*Figure 3.5* Expenditure on R&D, royalty, technical know-how fees, and licence fees (percentage of sales of MNCs)

*Source:* Prowess, Version 4.13, CMIE.

drug development, since their parent firms are already doing this. In such cases, one would expect the subsidiaries to pay royalty and licensee fees to their parent firms for using the latter's technologies. But here again, the data shows that the expenditure of these firms on royalty, technical know-how fees and licence fees is low and has declined in the 2000s compared to the second half of the 1990s.

As the figure illustrates, MNCs' investment in R&D royalty, technical know-how and licence fees has been very low in India. With the product patent regime in place, we would have expected these firms to invest substantially in R&D in India, so as to benefit from the cost advantage that the country offers. It is possible that some firms prefer to keep their R&D infrastructure in their home countries intact, and not invest in new locations, especially developing countries. In such cases, we would expect their subsidiaries in India to spend substantial amounts as royalty and licence fees. The expenditure on royalty and licence fees would increase also because these subsidiaries would be the exclusive suppliers in India of the patented drugs of their parent firms.

However, both R&D investment and spending on royalty and licence fees has been very low. Though investments in R&D and expenditure on royalty and technical know-how showed an accelerating trend in the 1990s, they declined in the 2000s. Indeed, R&D investment by MNC subsidiaries in India has reached the level that existed in the pre-liberalisation period. It is true that MNCs had threatened that they would reassess their R&D strategy in India in the context of implementation of Section 3(*d*) of the Patents Act, 1970, and the granting of CLs. In any case, MNCs have never been major investors in R&D in India. The low expenditure on royalty and licence fees may indicate that patented drugs do not account for a significant share of the medicine market in India. This is attributable to Section 3(*d*), which prevents evergreening, and Section 11.A.7, which provides more space for generic competition.

In the wake of the Supreme Court of India (2013) judgement that incremental innovations in pharmaceuticals cannot be patented unless such innovations exhibit improvements in therapeutic efficacy, it was alleged that MNCs would step back from making India their R&D hub.[52] In the context of the Supreme Court judgement on the Glivec case, Novartis is reported to have threatened that it would not invest in R&D in India (Krishnan 2013b). The fact is, however, that MNCs have never attempted to make substantial R&D investments in India. The R&D investment of Novartis in India in 2012, a year before the Supreme Court judgement, was only Rs 2.9 million, or just 0.3 per cent of its sales turnover in the country (Selvaraj 2013).

Available evidence indicates that liberalisation of foreign investment *per se* has not resulted in competence building. Global pharma players are opening their centres in India primarily to derive benefit from the advantages that India offers in conducting clinical trials and also to take advantage of the innovative capabilities of Indian firms. In the process, the need to develop new therapies for neglected tropical diseases has been left entirely neglected.

## Conclusion

The increasing R&D intensity in the Indian pharmaceutical sector during the first half of the 2000s generated the impression that India was making significant inroads into new drug development. However, examination of the reasons for the decline in, and subsequent stabilisation of, R&D intensity in the post-2005 period reveals the structural weaknesses of the Indian pharma industry, which prevents it from entering new drug development in a major way. The Indian pharma industry lacks the technological as well as the financial capabilities required for the development of new drugs. The enthusiasm of two leading Indian firms – Ranbaxy and Dr. Reddy's – resulted in the spurt in overall R&D investment by the pharma industry. The challenges that these pioneering firms faced in new drug development led to the decline in R&D investment. A large number of Indian pharma firms are collaborating with MNCs to build their R&D capabilities and overcome their constraints in the development of new drugs. Apart from R&D collaborations, many firms have also entered into manufacturing and marketing collaborations with MNCs. This has led to the globalisation of the Indian pharmaceutical industry, in the sense that it has now become a part of the global production and development network of MNCs.

The globalisation of Indian private sector pharma firms, and the decline of the public sector, raises new challenges for the country. Involvement in the global production and R&D network entails that the focus of the Indian private sector is increasingly aligned with the interests of MNCs. Indian companies therefore tend to focus more on global diseases, which are the principal focus of MNCs, while neglecting the tropical diseases that still constitute a substantial part of the disease burden in developing countries. As trusted allies of MNCs in the latter's global strategy, Indian private sector companies refrain from exercising compulsory licensing provisions, the TRIPS instrument that helps to counter abuse of patent monopoly rights as well as to address national health emergencies. The exercise of compulsory licensing would constitute a critical policy instrument in ensuring affordable access to medicines in India. With the demise of the public sector and the globalisation of the private sector, there are serious challenges to ensuring access to affordable medicines in the country.

Under the new policy regime, R&D for neglected diseases has become a major challenge. Despite the incentives offered by PPPs, soft loans, grants-in-aid, and other schemes catering to pharmaceutical R&D, firms have not come forward to invest in developing new drugs for neglected diseases. The success of the OSDD programme depends on the willingness of the industry to take the product to the market. Since private sector firms are staying away from the neglected diseases market, the role of the public sector is becoming more significant. The outcome so far of the reforms that abridged the role of the public sector and brought the private sector to prominence indicates that the revival of public sector firms may be an important measure for safeguarding public health in the country.

## Notes

1  The other three public sector companies were Bengal Chemical and Pharmaceutical Works Ltd (BCPW), founded in 1901; Rajasthan Drugs and Pharmaceuticals Ltd (RDPL) (a subsidiary of IDPL) and Karnataka Antibiotics and Pharmaceuticals Ltd (KAPL), a joint venture of HAL and the Karnataka State Industrial and Investment Development Corporation. These are all central public sector units (PSUs). There are also a number of state pharmaceutical PSUs.
2  Based on data provided by IRI (n.d.). Of the top 1,000 global companies in different industries investing in R&D, 10 pharmaceuticals firms were selected on the basis of their R&D intensity. Daiichi Sankyo of Japan, the top-ranking firm among these 10, spent 22 per cent of its turnover on R&D, whereas Johnson & Johnson of the US, the lowest-ranking firm, spent 9 per cent on R&D.
3  Investment in R&D by public sector pharmaceutical companies accounts for less than 0.5 per cent of total R&D investment by public as well as private sector pharmaceutical companies. This estimate is based on Prowess data.
4  Capital expenditure in R&D is expenditure incurred in acquiring non-current assets, such as setting up a new laboratory, procuring new equipment, etc. Current R&D expenditure is expenditure incurred on the day-to-day running of the business, for instance, the payment of salaries.
5  Except 2009–10, the year in which capital expenditure showed a decline.
6  In 2005–06, R&D capital and current expenditures at Ranbaxy were Rs 1,530 million and Rs 4,860 million, respectively. Thereafter, capital expenditure declined to Rs 980 million in 2006–07 and to Rs 170 million in 2011–12. Current R&D expenditure declined to Rs 3,860 million

in 2006–07, and thereafter remained at lower levels compared to the expenditure in 2005–06.

7  The possibility that takeover resulted in reduced R&D spending can be ruled out for the other three taken-over firms as well (Matrix, Dabur/ Fresenius Kabi Oncology and Shantha). The R&D intensity of Matrix increased from 8 per cent in 2005–06 to 12 per cent in 2006–07, and further to 14 per cent in 2009–10. Dabur/Fresenius Kabi Oncology did not report any R&D capital spending. Its R&D current spending declined from Rs 360 million in 2005–06 to Rs 260 million in 2006–07, a year before the takeover. After takeover, the current R&D spending of the firm increased to Rs 310 million in 2008–09 and to Rs 350 million in 2009–10. The R&D behaviour of Shantha shows a similar trend. The firm's total spending on R&D declined from Rs 120 million in 2006– 07 to Rs 110 million in 2007–08 and to Rs 100 million in 2008–09, the year of the takeover. In the next year, Shantha's R&D spending increased to Rs 170 million. These data are sourced from Prowess. For a more meaningful analysis of whether mergers and acquisitions lead to reduced R&D spending, trends would need to be examined over a longer period after takeover.

8  The decline in R&D spending by Dr. Reddy's in 2005–06 is not reflected in the overall R&D intensity of the industry. This is because the decline in R&D spending by Dr. Reddy's was well matched by the increase in R&D spending by Ranbaxy in 2005–06. The R&D intensity of the firm in 2011–12 was 9 per cent.

9  The current expenditure in R&D declined from Rs 2,520 million to Rs 2,330 million in 2005–06 and from Rs 4,210 million to Rs 4,020 mil- lion in 2009–10.

10  In its *Annual Report* (2004–05), the chairman's letter to the sharehold- ers states: 'our journey to becoming a discovery-led global pharmaceuti- cal player continues unabated'. See Dr. Reddy's (2005a).

11  'Clinical Trials', http://www.phrma.org/innovation/clinical-trials (accessed on 16 November 2014).

12  These PhRMA data are for the US in 1998. Quoted in Chaudhuri (2005a).

13  PDE4 is a protein that triggers off inflammation in various organs of the body. The development of the molecule was abandoned, though it completed phase II clinical trials.

14  The 771 version is an injectable, while 2349 is taken orally.

15  The PhRMA estimate is cited in Chaudhuri (2005a).

16  This figure is based on an unrepresentative sample and excludes the majority of new drugs which are extensions of existing drugs, and which have benefited from public funding. These estimates are also adjusted upwards to provide for the opportunity cost of capital. The actual out-of-pocket expenditure per drug estimated by DiMasi, Han- sen and Grabowski (2003) was only $403 million. When adjusted for opportunity costs, the estimate rose to $803 million. Other components included in R&D estimates are: (*a*) executive costs incurred in finding and negotiating with other firms for new products; (*b*) expenditure on medical writers and public relations efforts to develop stories and create

a market demand for products under trial as they progress; (*c*) support for scientific journals and supplementary issues in which the results of industry-supported research get published; (*d*) lectures and courses to inform physicians about current research; (*e*) legal fees devoted largely to patents and research-related issues; and (*f*) expenditure on land and buildings where research is done. Surely these are not the kind of 'investments' that should be considered for the statutory protection that the pharmaceutical industry is seeking. For a detailed discussion, see Dhar and Gopakumar (2008) and Chaudhuri (2005a).

17　The top 10 pharmaceutical R&D investors in India invested $3,172 million in the last 10 years, whereas Pfizer, the largest pharma firm in the world, invested $7,945 million in R&D in 2008. Estimates computed by the present author based on Prowess, Version 4.13, CMIE.

18　The 2009 estimate is provided in ICRA (2011).

19　More than 160 such plants existed in 2009. Italy, which has the second highest number of FDA-approved manufacturing units, has about 50 plants. For details, see *ibid*.

20　The Glenmark–Napo collaboration is discussed in further detail in a later section of this chapter.

21　Pre-clinical trials constitute 30 per cent of the business, and biology and chemistry research constitutes 18 per cent of the contract business. For details, see ICRA (2011).

22　'Chairman's Speech', March 2011, *Economic Times*, http://economic times.indiatimes.com/chairmanspeech.cms?companyid=8221& year=2011 (accessed on 31 October 2014).

23　Though the molecule entered phase III clinical trials, it is no longer part of the new drug pipeline of the company. See Glenmark, Drugs Discovery Overview, http://www.glenmarkpharma.com/UITemplate/Html Container.aspx?res=P_GLN_GDY_AOVR (accessed on 4 December 2010).

24　Piramal Life Sciences, 'NCE Research', http://www.piramal.com/ piramal-enterprises/piramal-lifesciences#ss1 (accessed on 4 December 2014).

25　Piramal Life Sciences, however, decided in August 2014 to exit from the drug discovery business. For details see Unnikrishnan (2014).

26　Diabetic dyslipidemia is a condition of high lipid and glucose levels in type-2 diabetic patients. It is reported that 80–90 per cent of diabetes patients suffer from this condition, which is managed through statins and other measures (Unnikrishnan 2013).

27　'Dr. Reddy's Laboratories', *Bloomberg Businessweek*, http://investing. businessweek.com/businessweek/research/stocks/people/person. asp?personId=2414261&ticker=DRRD:IN&previousCapId=881725& previousTitle=DR.%20REDDY'S%20LABORATORIES (accessed on 2 November 2014).

28　'Piramal Phytocare Ltd', *Bloomberg Businessweek*, http://investing. businessweek.com/businessweek/research/stocks/people/person.asp ?personId=13063514&ticker=41294361&previousCapId=32184&pr eviousTitle=Piramal%20Healthcare%20Ltd (accessed on 2 November 2014).

29 'New Chemical Entity: Adult Acute Infectious Diarrhea and Cholera', http://www.glenmarkpharma.com/UITemplate/HtmlContainer. aspx?res=P_GLN_GDY_BNCE_GTOS_CTOS_BIDC (accessed on 8 December 2014).

30 According to FDA reports, firms from India had 1735 DMF filings as of September 2008 (GoI 2010; Pandeya 2010). The top 10 Indian firms had 831 DMF filings as of March 2009.

31 Ranbaxy spent US$150 million as criminal fine and forfeiture, and US$350 million for settling civil claims. For details, see US Department of Justice (2013).

32 See Ranbaxy Research & Development, 'Touching Lives with Innovation', http://www.ranbaxy.com/researchndevelopment/overview.aspx (accessed on 3 November 2014).

33 Information on NMITLI available at www.csir.res.in/external/Heads/ NMITLI-info.doc (accessed on 3 November 2014).

34 Gatifloxacin is a fluoroquinolone and has broad spectrum antibiotic activity with the potential for shortening TB treatment duration. The clinical trial of this molecule was sponsored by the European Commission, OFLOTUB consortium, Institute de Recherche pour le Développement, and WHO TDR. Lupin also collaborated in the trials. The molecule completed phase III clinical trials in the last quarter of 2013. Though the molecule was found to be safe in the phase III trials, it failed to prove that it was not inferior to standard TB therapies. However, Lupin obtained USFDA approval for gatifloxacin for treating eye infections.

Moxifloxacin is also a fluoroquinolone having the potential of reducing TB treatment duration. This molecule is currently undergoing phase III trials sponsored by the Global Alliance for TB drug development, the US Centers for Disease Control and Prevention, University College London, Johns Hopkins University, and Bayer. The compound code-named PA-824 is a nitroimidazole, a new drug class for fighting TB. PA-824 is undergoing phase II trials sponsored by the TB Alliance. For details, see GoI (2006), Lessem (2013) and Lupin (2013).

35 The theme of the *World Investment Report 2011* was 'Non-equity Modes of International Production and Development'. See UNCTAD (2011).

36 Information for the four years beginning 2009–10 accessed at DST, Drugs and Pharmaceutical Research, Project List, http://dst.gov.in/ scientific-programme/td-drugs.htm (accessed on 9 December 2014). Information for 2013–14 accessed at DST (2014).

37 DPRP brochure, January 2008, http://dst.gov.in/scientific-programme/ td-drugs.htm (accessed on 4 November 2014).

38 Twelve were developed by CDRI, one each by the Regional Research Laboratory (RRL) Hyderabad, HAL Pune and the School of Tropical Medicine, Kolkata, and two by Ciba-Geigy.

39 This incident was revealed during a discussion between Sudip Chaudhuri and officials at Cipla and is reported in Chaudhuri (2005a).

40 OSDD Funding Policies, http://www.osdd.net/about-us/funding (accessed on 11 December 2014).

41 The OSDD has already received Rs 9.5 million of the Rs. 28.6 million grant.

42  Eight CSIR laboratories and 36 Indian universities and academic institutions have been selected as partnering institutions (Årdal and Røttingen 2012).

43  Leishmaniasis, sleeping sickness, chagas disease, and malaria are the principal focus areas of the DNDi programme. Recently, DNDi added two more diseases to its agenda – paediatric HIV and helminth infections. Information accessed from the DNDi website (DNDi 2011a).

44  The treatments include: two fixed-dose combinations for malaria, one co-administration drug for human African trypanosomiasis, one treatment for visceral leishmaniasis, and a paediatric dosage form of benznidazole for chagas disease.

45  The WHO in 2008 adopted the Global Strategy and Plan of Action on Public Health, Innovation and Intellectual Property (GSPA-PHI). The GSPA-PHI has eight elements, of which the seventh involved the establishment of an Expert Working Group on Research and Development: Coordination and Financing. The Expert Working Group submitted its report in 2010; however, the report was considered deficient in many respects. In the same year, the World Health Assembly passed a resolution to establish the CEWG on Research and Development: Financing and Coordination. The report of the CEWG was made public in April 2012. The report recommends the pooling of government funding to support R&D in a way that delinks the costs associated with R&D from the price of products paid by consumers. See WHO, http://www.who.int/phi/news/cewg_call_for_proposals.pdf (accessed on 4 November 2014).

46  The 90/10 gap refers to the fact that only 10 per cent of global pharmaceutical R&D is devoted to addressing diseases affecting 90 per cent of the global population.

47  Based on interactions with the employees of 31 pharmaceutical firms in India by Lanjouw and MacLeod (2005).

48  This was inferred from a comparison of the projects sanctioned by DPRP and the molecules that are currently at advanced stages of clinical trials.

49  The code names of molecules that have emerged from projects funded under the loan scheme are available from DST (2011). This information has been compared with the molecule pipeline data provided in the annual report of the different firms.

50  Based on statistics on projects aided by the DPRP, available at DPRP, Drugs and Pharmaceutical Research, Project List, http://dst.gov.in/scientific-programme/td-drugs.htm (accessed on 9 December 2014).

51  Taken-over Indian firms such as Ranbaxy, Matrix, etc., have not been included in the classification of MNC subsidiaries.

52  This judgement is analysed in Chapter 4.

# Chapter 4

# Intellectual property rights and access to medicines

A unique feature of the pharmaceutical industry is that price competition is less significant than other forms of competition. The demand for drugs is inelastic, and consumption is determined by the requirements imposed by the incidence of diseases. Hence, an increase in price as such will not drive consumers away from the market, nor will a reduction in price attract more buyers (Reekie 1975). Further, unlike other sectors, in medicine there is a disconnect between the source of decision making and the source of payment. The technical nature of drugs requires an expert – the doctor – to select the drug, while the patient makes the payment. This creates a perverted incentive among firms to invest more in promotional activities geared to doctors. This may explain why pharmaceutical firms tend to spend more on promotion than they spend on R&D. The consumer's lack of decision-making power results in huge variations among the prices of different brands containing the same active ingredients. For example, in the cetirizine market (cetirizine is a drug used to treat several allergy symptoms), the price difference between the least expensive and most expensive brands is more than 3,500 per cent.[1]

It was feared that the introduction of product patent rights in the country would lead to a rise in the prices of drugs. The monopoly conferred by patents would give patent holders the power to fix prices, under the pretext of rewarding R&D efforts. When patent rights are granted on a product, the chances are very high that the number of close substitutes is reduced to a minimum, or even zero, especially in new and emerging therapeutic areas. It has been the experience of all countries that have product patent rights in pharmaceuticals, as well as India's own experience prior to 1970, that drug prices rise irrespective of the ability of people to pay. Borrell (2007), based on a study covering 34 countries, finds that the price of antiretrovirals is higher wherever product patents are in force. Since most innovators are MNCs, they are likely to charge the same price for their patented drugs in developing country markets as they charge in developed country markets, irrespective of the capacity of people to pay.

Some authors (Danzon 2007; Danzon and Towse 2003; Scherer and Watal 2002) argue that the global pricing strategy that best combines equity with coverage of R&D costs is one in which prices are differentiated on the basis of the ability of consumers in different countries to pay. However, such differential pricing faces two challenges. First, it would be difficult for MNCs to offer lower prices, at least for essential drugs, because the lower price offered in a foreign country might be used as a reference price for regulating domestic drug prices (Aggrawal and Saibaba 2001; Danzon and Towse 2003). The second issue is parallel imports: lower-priced drugs may be exported to countries where they are priced at higher levels. These companies may also face political resistance in wealthy countries, where consumers may point out that the same product is available for substantially lower prices in other countries (Danzon and Towse 2003). Some other considerations have a significant and possibly overriding effect on differential pricing. Wong (2002) finds that prices are not affected by countries' per capita income, but rather by their income inequality, suggesting that companies are targeting well-off populations in developing countries.

Any increase in the prices of medicines in India would have deleterious consequences for the country's health sector. Unlike advanced countries, where private expenditure on health care is very low, out-of-pocket health expenditure accounted for 60 per cent of total health care expenditure in India in 2009.[2] As public health services and facilities are in decline, and the vast majority of the population is not covered by health insurance, people have no option but to seek health care services in the private sector at their own expense. In 2005, about 70 per cent of hospitals and 60–70 per cent of qualified doctors belonged to the private sector in India (Ma and Sood 2008). However, only 25 per cent of India's population is covered by any kind of health insurance (Reddy et al. 2011).[3]

The National Sample Survey (NSS) on consumer expenditure estimates that expenditure on medicines is the single largest component of health care spending. Expenditure on medicines constituted 66.4 per cent of out-of-pocket expenditure on health care in India in 2011–12; 68.6 per cent in rural areas and 62.9 per cent in urban areas.[4] As just described, 60 per cent of health care expenses in India are out-of-pocket expenses (WHO 2012). As a result, the cost of medicines can be a strong determinant of patients' access to health care facilities. Various rounds of the NSS covering morbidity and health care show that the number of cases of ailments that are not treated on account of financial constraints is on the rise in the country (Table 4.1).

The NSS data reveal that financial constraints are the most important factor preventing people with ailments from getting treated.[5] The percentage of sick people who do not avail of any treatment on account of financial constraints, especially in rural areas, is on the rise. Given the very high share of out-of-pocket expenditure on health care in the country, it is natural that the poor would find it difficult to seek health care services when they fall ill. The prices of drugs are a significant component of the cost of health care. Thus, any move to make drug prices more affordable would undoubtedly allow more patients to seek health care services. Conversely, any increase in the prices of medicines would prevent even more people from seeking care. It is

Table 4.1 Percentage of ailments not treated for various reasons, in different NSS rounds on morbidity and health care

| Reasons for not treating ailments | 2004 (60th round) | | 1995–96 (52nd round) | | 1986–87 (42nd round) | |
|---|---|---|---|---|---|---|
| | Rural | Urban | Rural | Urban | Rural | Urban |
| No medical facility available in the neighbourhood | 12 | 1 | 9 | 1 | 3 | 0 |
| Facility available, but lack of faith in health services provided by it | 3 | 2 | 4 | 5 | 2 | 2 |
| Long waiting period | 1 | 2 | 1 | 1 | 0 | 1 |
| Financial problems | 28 | 20 | 24 | 21 | 15 | 10 |
| Ailment not considered serious | 32 | 50 | 52 | 60 | 75 | 81 |
| Others (including not reported) | 24 | 25 | 10 | 12 | 5 | 6 |
| | 100 | 100 | 100 | 100 | 100 | 100 |

Source: Compiled by author from NSS data. Data from NSS 42nd and 52nd rounds have been accessed from NSSO (1998) and data from the 60th round from NSSO (2006).

worth noting in this context that, within one year of the launch of the free medicines scheme in the state of Rajasthan,[6] out-patient visits to public hospitals went up by more than 50 per cent,[7] and in-patient admissions rose by 30 per cent (Ebrahim 2012). The Rajasthan experience demonstrates the significance of drug prices in the public health care system in India.

The TRIPS Agreement contains certain flexibilities which member countries can exercise to protect their interests. For example, TRIPS requires only that 'patents shall be available for any inventions, whether products or processes, in all fields of technology',[8] but does not define what an invention is. It is up to the member country to define an invention. If a country wants to define an invention narrowly so as to enhance the standard of innovations, TRIPS allows for this. Articles 30 and 31 of the TRIPS Agreement provide for exceptions to the monopoly rights granted to a patent holder, and for the use of a patented invention without the authorisation of the patent holder. Member countries have flexibility in framing the grounds for exercising these exemptions within the TRIPS framework. The Doha WTO Ministerial 2001 Declaration on the TRIPS Agreement and Public Health (henceforth the Doha Declaration) underscored the right of member countries to use TRIPS flexibilities to protect public health. Paragraph 4 of the declaration states:

> We agree that the TRIPS Agreement does not and should not prevent members from taking measures to protect public health. Accordingly, while reiterating our commitment to the TRIPS Agreement, we affirm that the Agreement can and should be interpreted and implemented in a manner supportive of WTO members' right to protect public health and, in particular, to promote access to medicines for all.
>
> (WTO 2001a)

Similarly, Article 8 of the TRIPS Agreement makes clear that while amending their laws and regulations, member countries have the right to adopt measures necessary to protect public health and nutrition and to promote the public interest in any other sector of vital importance, provided that these measures are consistent with TRIPS provisions.[9]

The impact of the change in patent law on access to affordable medicines depends to a great extent on the use of the flexibilities built into the TRIPS Agreement. Therefore, it is important to see how India has made use of the TRIPS flexibilities.

## Introduction of product patents in pharmaceuticals in India

At the Ministerial Conference held at Marrakesh in 1994, the Government of India ratified the Final Act of the 1986–94 Uruguay Round of trade negotiations establishing the WTO. Thereafter, it became obligatory for India to implement the various agreements incorporated in the Final Act. The TRIPS Agreement, an important instrument of the WTO covering various forms of IPRs, had to be implemented by amending the existing IPR laws of the country. The IPR laws covered by TRIPS relate to:

1    Copyrights and related rights
2    Trademarks
3    Geographical indications
4    Industrial designs
5    Patents (also includes *sui generis* protection for plant varieties)
6    Layout designs of integrated circuits
7    Protection of undisclosed information

While members of the WTO are obliged to enforce the minimum standards of IPR protection prescribed by the agreement, they have leeway in framing the working of the IPR provisions, for instance, the scope of patentability and the exercise of compulsory licensing provisions. All the laws on IPRs in India, except those relating to patents, have been amended without much debate in Parliament or protests from the public. Amendment of the Patents Act, 1970, however, has been a crucial issue, especially for the general public and the pharmaceutical industry (NWGPL and PILS&RC 2003). It was feared that the Indian pharma industry, which has thrived under the process patent regime of the Patents Act, 1970, would no longer be able to continue with its *modus operandi* of reverse engineering and the production of cheap medicines. Thus, amending the Patents Act, 1970, was the most important hurdle in making the Indian IPR system TRIPS-compliant.

The TRIPS Agreement allowed some transitional arrangements in the case of developing country members. Though the provisions of the agreement were expected to be in force by 1 January 1996, developing countries were given an extension of four years, i.e. till 1 January 2000.[10] However, the agreement required these member countries to make provisions for receiving patent applications.[11] Those developing countries that were obliged to extend product patent protection in areas of technology not so protectable in their territories on the general date of application of the agreement, i.e. 1 January 1996, could delay the application of the provisions for an additional period of five years, i.e. till 1 January 2005.[12] India had no existing product patent regime in pharmaceuticals and agro-chemicals, and thus the country had time till 1 January 2005 to extend product patent rights in these sectors, though in other areas it had to meet its obligations by 1 January 2000.

India complied with its obligations under the TRIPS Agreement in three steps. The first step was the Patents (Amendment) Act, 1999, which provided for the receipt of patent applications (mailbox applications) and for exclusive marketing rights.[13] Next, the Patents (Amendment) Act, 2002, introduced comprehensive amendments to bring various provisions of the Patents Act, 1970, into conformity with the TRIPS Agreement.[14] The third and most important amendment aimed at introducing product patent rights along with already existing process patent rights in pharmaceuticals and agro-chemicals. Towards this end, a bill amending the Patents Act was introduced in 2003 by the National Democratic Alliance government led by the Bharatiya Janata Party. However, the bill lapsed owing to the change of union government and the consequent dissolution of the Lok Sabha.

The new, Congress-led UPA coalition government, which had come to power with the external support of the left parties, pushed the 2003 bill to amend the Patents Act so as to meet the TRIPS timeline of 1 January 2005 (Basheer 2005; Keayla 2008). But the UPA could not gather the necessary support, particularly owing to the left parties' disagreement with the provisions of the bill. Hence, the bill was passed as a presidential ordinance on 26 December 2004 in order to meet the deadline. The government had six months to codify this ordinance by obtaining the approval of Parliament. In March 2005, the government introduced a substantially revised bill, which was passed in Parliament and became the Patents (Amendment) Act, 2005 (hereafter the Patents Act). The modifications to the ordinance were not incorporated voluntarily by the government, but were the outcome of hard bargaining by civil society groups and left political parties. The final act incorporates a number of TRIPS flexibilities that are critical in ensuring affordable access to medicines in the country.

### Stringent criteria for patentability

There had been serious concerns that a broad definition of what is patentable would lead to the 'evergreening' of patents, that is, the continuation of patent rights beyond the stipulated 20 years by the acquisition of patents for small changes made to the original invention. The third amendment restricted the scope for evergreening through its definition of pharmaceutical substance, and by clarifying what is meant by an 'invention' and 'inventive step'. These are the most important criteria determining the patentability of any subject matter. The Patents Act offers the following definition of a new invention:

New invention means any invention or technology which has not been anticipated by publication in any document or used in the country or elsewhere in the world before the date of filing of patent application with complete specification, i.e. the subject matter has not fallen in public domain or that it does not form part of the state of the art.[15]

An inventive step was defined in the amended act as follows: 'inventive step means a feature of an invention that involves technical advance as compared to the existing knowledge or having economic significance or both and that makes the invention not obvious to a person skilled in the art'.[16]

The definitions of invention and inventive step in the final act, as compared to those given in the ordinance, are much narrower, thus elevating the standard of patentable inventions. This, in effect, reduces the number of patents that would otherwise have obtained approval in India. The ordinance had defined these terms as follows: 'invention means a new product or process involving an inventive step and capable of industrial application,'[17] and 'inventive step means a feature that makes the invention not obvious to a person skilled in the art.'[18]

The scope of patentability is also restricted by defining inventions that are not patentable. Section 3 of the Patents Act covers inventions not patentable. Section 3(d) is noteworthy. It states that inventions are not patentable if

the mere discovery of a new form of a known substance which does not result in the enhancement of the known efficacy of that substance or the mere discovery of any new property or new use for a known substance or of the mere use of a known process, machine or apparatus unless such known process results in a new product or employs at least one new reactant.

*Explanation.* – For the purposes of this clause, salts, esters, ethers, polymorphs, metabolites, pure form, particle size, isomers, mixtures of isomers, complexes, combinations and other derivatives of known substance shall be considered to be the same substance, unless they differ significantly in properties with regard to efficacy.[19]

This section has been a powerful instrument in preventing frivolous patents, often inviting the ire of pharma MNCs. The case of Novartis in India provides the best example of how effective this section has been in preventing frivolous patents.

The origin of the *Novartis AG vs Union of India and Others* dispute[20] may be traced to the decision of the Assistant Controller of Patents and Designs of India, Chennai, on 26 January 2006, rejecting Novartis's application for a patent on imatinib mesylate in beta crystalline form. The reasons for the rejection were: (*a*) the invention was not new; it had been anticipated by the patent on the derivatives of N-phenyl-2-pyrimidine-amine (hereafter the Zimmermann patent);[21] (*b*) the invention was obvious to a person skilled in the art in view of the disclosures made in the Zimmermann patent specifications; and (*c*) the invention did not meet the patentability criteria set out by Section 3(*d*) of the Patents Act, 1970, as amended in 2005.

Novartis appealed against the decision of the Assistant Controller in the Madras High Court, but the case was transferred to the Intellectual Property Appellate Board (IPAB) in April 2007.[22] Novartis, however, also challenged the constitutional validity of Section 3(*d*) of the Patents Act in the Madras High Court. It argued that Section 3(*d*) of the Patents Act was vague and ambiguous and therefore violated the equality provision under Article 14 of the Indian Constitution. Moreover, it was not in compliance with the TRIPS Agreement of the WTO. Therefore, Section 3(*d*) of the Patents Act should be declared unconstitutional. The Madras High Court upheld the validity of Section 3(*d*) and clarified that the patent applicant needed to show that the invention had resulted in the enhancement of the known efficacy of the substance. Efficacy in the context of pharmaceutical compounds is equated with therapeutic efficacy in the body. Regarding TRIPS compliance, the court held that it had no jurisdiction to decide such matters, as they related to a multilateral international treaty. The proper forum for adjudication would be the WTO Dispute Settlement Body. Novartis did not file any appeal against this decision.

Novartis, however, challenged the decision of the Assistant Controller with regard to novelty, non-obviousness and Section 3(*d*) before IPAB. The board overturned the decision of the Assistant Controller that the invention was not new and obvious, and held that Novartis's invention met the criteria of novelty and non-obviousness. However, IPAB upheld the decision of the Assistant Controller that the patent application did not meet the criteria established in Section 3($d$) of the Patents Act.

Novartis then filed a special leave petition (SLP) in the Supreme Court against the decision of IPAB that its invention did not satisfy the patentability criteria of Section 3($d$). Natco Pharma and the Cancer Patients Aid Association also filed SLPs challenging IPAB's findings in favour of Novartis.[23] Others also intervened, including Shamnad Basheer, a professor at the National University of Juridical Sciences, Kolkata. The Novartis case in the Supreme Court became a test case for the validity of patentability standards set out by the Patents Act – novelty, non-obviousness and Section 3($d$).

Novartis argued in the Supreme Court that the imatinib mesylate beta crystalline form involved two inventions, beginning with imatinib. The first invention used methanesulfonic acid to produce methanesulfonic acid addition salts of the free base imatinib. The second invention involved developing the beta crystalline form of methanesulfonic acid, which is suitable for administration in solid oral dosage form. Novartis held that these inventions were not obvious to a person skilled in the art: the Zimmermann patent did not suggest the use of methanesulfonic acid in the first invention, or the therapeutic application of the second invention. Novartis held that the Zimmermann patent only described how to manufacture imatinib free base, which had the anti-tumour properties of the BCR-ABL kinase. However, the conclusion that the beta crystalline form of imatinib mesylate was effective in the treatment of chronic myeloid leukaemia involved two inventions that were new and not obvious to a person skilled in the art (Supreme Court of India 2013).

The Supreme Court, after examining the Zimmermann patent application and an article on the anti-tumoural properties of imatinib mesylate published in the journal *Cancer Research*, concluded that the Novartis patent application did not contain anything new.[24] The court observed that the Zimmermann patent application explicitly stated that the application covered the salts of the compound: 'any reference to the free compounds should be understood as including the corresponding salts, where appropriate and expedient' (Supreme Court of India 2013: para. 109). The application had also highlighted the therapeutic application of the compound as an anti-tumoural drug. The article in *Cancer Research*, co-authored by Jurg Zimmermann himself, discussed in detail the anti-tumoural properties of imatinib and its methanesulfonate salt, i.e. imatinib mesylate, stating that 'the reported findings with CGP 57148 suggest that it may be a development candidate for use in the treatment of Philadelphia chromosome-positive leukemias' (*ibid.*: para. 129). The court concluded:

> in the face of the materials referred to above, we are unable to see how Imatinib Mesylate can be said to be a new product, having come into being through an invention that has a feature that involves technical advance over the existing knowledge and that would make the invention not obvious to a person skilled in the art.
> (*ibid.*: para. 131)

The most contentious issue among the patentability standards has been Section 3(*d*). Novartis argued that Section 3(*d*) applied only when the product was a new form of a known substance having known efficacy; since imatinib or imatinib mesylate did not have any known efficacy, the beta crystalline form of imatinib mesylate could not be considered an improvement over the efficacy of imatinib or imatinib mesylate. Therefore, Section 3(*d*) could not be applied to the beta crystalline form of imatinib mesylate. After examining the new drug application filed by Novartis with the USFDA for imatinib mesylate for the treatment of patients with chronic myeloid leukaemia, the Supreme Court held that imatinib mesylate, which was a known substance from the Zimmermann patent, had undergone pre-clinical, technical and clinical research.[25] Therefore, the beta crystalline form of imatinib mesylate was a new form of a known substance the efficacy of which was well known. Therefore, Section 3(*d*) would apply in this case.

Novartis also argued that the beta crystalline form of imatinib mesylate showed a definite and tangible enhancement of efficacy as compared to imatinib in free base form, as it was highly soluble and therefore very suitable for administration in human beings. The court held that the test of efficacy required under Section 3(*d*) in the context of medicines was nothing but 'therapeutic efficacy'. Different forms of compounds listed in the note of explanation under Section 3(*d*) had some properties inherent to that form; e.g. solubility to salt and hygroscopicity to polymorphs, and 'mere change in the form with properties inherent to that form would not qualify as enhancement of efficacy of a known substance' (Supreme Court of India 2013: para. 181).

The most important aspect of the judgement is that therapeutic efficacy is clearly differentiated from other forms of efficacy. In response to the evidence presented by Novartis that the beta crystalline form had better properties relating to production and storage (e.g. heat stability), the court clarified that these properties might be important from a storage point of view, but were not relevant to enhanced therapeutic efficacy (Abbott 2013). This judgement has established clear guidelines for pharmaceutical firms seeking patent protection in India, by holding that a pharmaceutical product, if it is an already known substance, will get patent protection only if it demonstrates enhanced therapeutic effects. The judgement also serves to underscore the rationale of Section 3(*d*), which seeks to strike a balance between providing incentives for genuine innovation (preventing evergreening), on the one hand, and the price of medicines, on the other, by including a review of the debates in Parliament in order to understand why policy makers had inserted this section in the Patents Act.

The impact of Section 3(*d*) on drug prices has been tremendous. Novartis had charged Rs 120,000 for a one-month course of the drug when the company had exclusive marketing rights in India (Supreme Court of India 2013). With the rejection of Novartis's patent application, Indian pharma companies made the drug available in the market at a cost of Rs 8,000–10,000 for a one-month course (Kannan 2013). Now there are at least 11 companies in India manufacturing drugs based on the imatinib molecule.[26]

## Opposition to grant of patents

The Patents Act provides for both pre-grant[27] and post-grant[28] opposition to the grant of patents. Any entity can register its opposition to a patent on 11 grounds, before or after the grant of the patent. The rejection of Gilead's patent application for tenofovir, an antiretroviral drug, is a very good example of how the pre-grant opposition provision is useful in preventing frivolous patents, especially from a public health perspective.

Tenofovir was patented by Gilead Sciences (patent valid till 2018) and licensed to Indian pharmaceutical companies for production and marketing. When Gilead sought to obtain a patent in India for the medicine, the move was met with large-scale opposition from activist groups and associations such as the Indian Network for People Living with HIV and the Delhi Network of Positive People, who filed pre-grant oppositions against Gilead's patent application. The major legal ground of opposition was that tenofovir was produced by the addition of a salt (fumaric acid) to an existing compound (tenofovir disoproxil); therefore, the drug did not meet the patentability requirement under Indian patent law. The granting of a patent would eliminate competitive products and escalate the cost of the drug in India. While tenofovir cost US$5,718 per patient per year in developed countries, Cipla sold the generic version of the drug at a cost of US$700 per person per year in India (Gentleman and Kumar 2006). The Patent Office of India rejected Gilead's patent application in 2009 on grounds of violation of Section 3(d).

### Compulsory licensing provisions

The Patents Act provides for compulsory licensing. There are three clauses under which a Compulsory Licence (CL) can be granted in India – Sections 84, 92 and 92.A. Section 84 of the Patents Act provides that anyone can apply for CL after the expiry of three years of the grant of a patent on any of the following grounds:

1   The reasonable requirement of the public with respect to the invention has not been met.
2   The patented invention is not available to the public at reasonably affordable prices.
3   The patented invention is not worked within the territory of India.

A CL under Section 84 requires that the applicant for a CL should have made an attempt to secure a licence from the patentee on reasonable terms and conditions.[29] The act restricts the period for the successful negotiation of licences to six months.

The Patent Office of India granted Natco the first CL in the country on 9 March 2012, for Bayer's patented cancer drug Nexavar. This CL was issued under Section 84 of the Patents Act. Nexavar is used in the treatment of kidney and liver cancer, and patients need to take the medication their entire lives. The cost of the drug was Rs 280,428 per month, and Bayer's supply met only 2 per cent of the total requirement of the drug in the country.[30] Bayer also chose to import the drug rather than manufacturing it in India.

The Controller of Patents found that all three grounds for issuing a CL obtained in the case of Nexavar. The reasonable requirement of the public with respect to the invention was not met, since only 2 per cent (8,842) of the total number of eligible patients were accessing the drug. The patented invention was not available to the public at a reasonable price; 98 per cent of the patients were not able to buy the medicine. Further, the patented invention was not worked in India, as the company did not have any manufacturing facility in the country.

Under the CL, Natco agreed to supply the drug at Rs 8,800 per month (a pack of 120 tablets), which is 3 per cent of the price of Bayer's drug. Natco also undertook to provide the drug at no cost to at least 600 patients every year. The order issuing the CL also stated that the licencee (Natco) would pay a royalty of 6 per cent of net sales to Bayer. Bayer's appeal to IPAB seeking a stay on the operation of the CL was rejected.

Section 92 of the Patents Act provides that the central government may grant CLs in the circumstances of a national emergency, extreme urgency, or for public non-commercial use. This clause requires that products manufactured under CLs 'shall be available to the public at lowest prices consistent with the patentees deriving a reasonable advantage from their patent rights'.[31]

Section 92A of the Patents Act provides for the export of medicines under CL to countries with an insufficient manufacturing capacity in pharmaceuticals:

> Compulsory licence shall be available for the production and export of patented products to any country having insufficient or no manufacturing capacity in the pharmaceutical sector . . . provided compulsory licence has been granted by such country or such country has, by notification or otherwise, allowed importation of the patented pharmaceutical products from India.[32]

Article 31(*f*) of the TRIPS Agreement originally stipulated that the CL provision was to be used predominantly for the supply of the domestic market of the member country authorising such a licence.[33] This required domestic manufacturing capacity as a pre-requisite for the exercise of the CL. A number of developing and least developed countries raised this matter at the WTO Ministerial at Doha. Paragraph 6 of the Doha Declaration recognised the difficulty such countries were facing, and instructed the Council of TRIPS to find a solution. The chair of the TRIPS Council proposed a solution in December 2002, known as Implementation of Paragraph 6 of the Doha Declaration on the TRIPS Agreement and Public Health.[34] The proposal was approved by the WTO General Council on 30 August 2003. This decision offered a temporary solution by waiving the Article 31(*f*) restriction, such that countries producing generic versions of patented products under CLs would be allowed to export these products to eligible importing countries. The waiver was originally proposed for a period of six months, the time required for amending the TRIPS Agreement. Until now, however, the amendment has not been introduced, and the waiver decision is still in force.

Imports of medicines produced under CLs in India have been of crucial significance for health activists and governments in developing countries. These countries have benefited from the import of cheap and good-quality medicines from India. Politicians, UN officials and international non-governmental organisations have called on Indian policy makers to take into account India's responsibility as a supplier of affordable medicines.[35] A *New York Times* editorial called upon the Indian Parliament to ensure that India could continue to play its role as leading supplier of low-cost medicines and to ensure that the amended patent law protected India's ability to make AIDS medicines available (*New York Times* 2005). This editorial received serious attention in India and was read out in Parliament in March 2005 during the debate on the bill amending the Patents Act, 1970 (Hoen 2009). Three applications have been filed so far for CLs under Section 92A of the Patents Act; however, these applications were withdrawn subsequently (DIPP 2010).

### Production of generic versions of 'mailbox' patented drugs

Possibly the biggest concern expressed after the promulgation of the ordinance amending the patents law related to the continued production of drugs for which applications were pending in the mailbox. It was apprehended that generic medicines that were already produced and marketed in India, for which patent application were pending in the mailbox, would go off the market once the patent was granted, leading to a quantum jump in drug prices. The Glivec case, involving the anti-cancer drug imatinib mesylate for which Novartis had obtained exclusive marketing rights in 2003, is the best indicator of the concerns regarding drug prices.

When Novartis introduced Glivec in India in 2001, it charged US$2,500 for a one-month course of the drug, whereas Indian generics companies were making the generic version available at 8 per cent of Novartis's price, i.e. US$200. In 2003, when Novartis obtained exclusive marketing rights for Glivec in India, nine companies were producing generic versions of the drug in India. Six of these nine companies were asked to stop producing the drug when Novartis obtained exclusive marketing rights (Menghaney 2012a). These generic drugs going off the market would mean that patients had little choice other than to buy highly expensive patented medicines, or else allow the disease to progress without medication. The third amendment to the Patents Act clarified that Indian companies that were already producing medicines for which applications had been filed in the mailbox, could continue to produce them even after a patent had been granted to the drug, after paying a royalty to the patent owner.

Section 11A.7 of the Patents Act provides for the continued manufacture of drugs for which patent applications had been filed through the mailbox. The mailbox system was an arrangement mandated by the TRIPS Agreement for countries that had availed of the transition period of 10 years. Applications in the mailbox were to be examined only after 1 January 2005. India incorporated the mailbox provision in its Patents Act through an amendment carried out in 1999. More than 6,000 applications had accrued in the mailbox at the time of the third amendment of the Patents Act, 1970 (March 2005) (Hoen 2009). Many Indian companies had started producing medicines for which applications had been filed in the mailbox, as it was legally permissible to do so. The act provides that, after a patent is granted to applications in the mailbox,

> the patent-holder shall only be entitled to receive reasonable royalty from such enterprises which have made significant investment and were producing and marketing the concerned product prior to the 1st day of January, 2005 and which continue to manufacture the product covered by the patent on the date of grant of the patent and no infringement proceedings shall be instituted against such enterprise.[36]

All these provisions in the Indian Patents Act have ensured that the potential number of pharmaceutical patents is reduced to a minimum. Gopakumar (2010) observes that only a few drugs would qualify for patents in India if the provisions of the patent law are strictly observed. He finds that of the 301 NMEs approved by the USFDA for marketing during the 10-year period from 1995 to 2005, only 26 have patent expiry dates in or after 2015. This indicates that only 26 NMEs were originally invented after 1995. The Orange Book,[37] however, does not list the earliest patent histories of 64 NMEs. When the patent histories of these 64 NMEs, as well as of the 26 NMEs identified by Gopakumar (2010), were further scrutinised using the Merck Index, the European Patent Office database and scientific journals, it was found that only 7 NMEs were invented in the post-1995 period. The TRIPS Agreement requires patents to be granted only to those inventions that emerged after 1 January 1995, when the WTO came into being. The seven NMEs are listed in Table 4.2.

*Table 4.2* NMEs invented between 1995 and 2004

| NME | Year of approval | Therapeutic use |
| --- | --- | --- |
| Oxcarbazepine | 2000 | Anti-epilepsy |
| Valdecoxib | 2001 | Osteoarthritis |
| Atomoxetine hydrochloride | 2002 | Hyperactivity disorder |
| Atazanavir | 2003 | HIV/AIDS |
| Vardenafil | 2003 | Erectile dysfunction |
| Erlotinib hydrochloride | 2004 | Cancer |
| Technetium 99m tc fanolesomab | 2004 | Imaging of appendicitis |

*Source:* Gopakumar (2010: 115).

Among these seven NMEs, three received marketing approval in India prior to 2005. Indian companies could continue to market these three drugs, subject to paying royalty to the patent holders. The remaining four NMEs could be the only drugs for which substitutes are not available in the country.

This view assumes that all NMEs, other than the seven listed in the table, are not eligible for patent rights in India, because they were all invented prior to 1995. However, these drugs could very well be patentable in India if the companies are able to demonstrate improvement in efficacy. Even if many of the NMEs are patentable in India, if Indian companies were manufacturing them prior to 2005, substitutes will continue to be available. Gopakumar (2010) analyses marketing approval data from the Central Drug Standard Control Organisation of India to see how many of the 301 NMEs are already being marketed in the country. He finds that of the 301 NMEs approved by the USFDA for marketing between 1995 and 2004, 161 are available in India. Of these 161 drugs, 128 were given permission for marketing prior to the introduction of product patents in 2005. This implies that Indian companies manufacturing these 128 NMEs can continue to manufacture them on payment of a reasonable royalty to the patent holder.

Though India has been legitimately exercising the TRIPS flexibilities to ensure access to affordable medicines for its citizens, pharma MNCs and some advanced countries are mounting pressure on India to step back from the use of such flexibilities. They fear that the example set by India might be followed by many other developing countries.

## Pressure from the US against the use of TRIPS flexibilities by India

The US has been very critical of the exercise of TRIPS flexibilities by India. The business lobby in the US has been pressurising its government to curtail the use of TRIPS flexibilities by India before other developing countries begin to imitate the Indian model. The Supreme Court of India's verdict on the Novartis case resulted in sharp criticisms from within the US. The US Trade Representative (USTR), in its *2013 Special 301 Report*, said that the US was concerned that the judgement would have the 'effect of limiting the patentability of potentially beneficial innovations. Such innovations would include drugs with fewer side effects, decreased toxicity, or improved delivery systems' (USTR 2013: 38). The US-India Business Council president Ron Somers stated that, without adequate IP protection, India would not be able to attract investment in this or in other highly complex sectors (USIBC 2013). Another US body, PhRMA, observed that the verdict reflected another example of the deteriorating innovation environment in India: 'In order to solve the real health challenges of India's patients, it is critically important that India promote a policy environment that supports continued research and development of new medicines for the health of patients in India and worldwide' (PhRMA 2013a). Criticism is also directed by PhRMA against Section 3(*d*) of the Patents Act of India, as being inconsistent with the TRIPS Agreement (PhRMA 2013b).

However, experts are of the view that India was right in incorporating Section 3(*d*) in its Patents Act. Frederick Abbott, Edward Ball Eminent Scholar Professor of International Law at the Florida State University College of Law, regularly serves as a panelist for the World Intellectual Property Organization Arbitration and Mediation Center. Abbott observes that the Supreme Court judgement supported the decision of the Indian Parliament that patients in India needed to pay for expensive, patented drugs only when those drugs contained genuine advancements over existing drugs. According to Abbott, the Supreme Court's decision 'affirmed that India has adopted a standard of pharmaceutical patenting that is stricter than that followed by the US or the EU' (Abbott 2013). But this standard, Abbott states, is not a new one. The US Patent Office had followed this approach until 1995, when the Court of Appeals for the Federal Circuit pronounced its decision in the *In re Brana* case.[38] Abbott believes that the Indian standard of pharmaceutical patenting will encourage genuine innovations:

'granting patents after researchers have demonstrated that drugs will accomplish something significant in terms of curative effect will encourage researchers to concentrate on achieving desirable end results, rather than winning marketing games' (*ibid.*).

There has also been criticism that India's CL provision violates the rules of the WTO. Deputy director of the US Patent and Trademark Office Teresa Stanek Rea is reported to have said that she was 'dismayed and surprised' when she heard about the Indian act. She characterised the CL as 'an egregious violation of WTO treaties'.[39] Similarly, PhRMA was of the view that compulsory licensing by India on grounds of affordability of medicines would not be in compliance with TRIPS provisions. In its Special 301 Submission 2012, PhRMA stated: 'At a minimum India should ensure that the CL provisions comply with TRIPS by clarifying that importation satisfies the "working" requirement . . .; and eliminating price as a trigger to CL' (PhRMA 2012: 35).

The United States International Trade Commission has already initiated an investigation against India on its trade, investment and industrial policies, especially with regard to protection of IPRs. The USTR has been asked by US industry associations such as PhRMA, the National Foreign Trade Council and the Biotechnology Industry Association to include India as a priority foreign country in the Special 301 Report for 2014 (South Centre 2014). Under the Special 301 provision of the US Trade Act of 1974, if a country is designated as a priority foreign country, that country will face unilateral trade sanctions by the US unless it engages in negotiations with the US or makes significant progress in areas of concern to the US. The US had earlier used Special 301 provisions to change IPR laws in countries such as Taiwan, Thailand and South Korea (Doane 1994).

India has responded sharply to this pressure from the US. The Indian ambassador to the US, S. Jaishankar, said during a speech at the Chicago Council of Global Affairs that 'affordable healthcare cannot be the prerogative of a few' (Embassy of India 2014: para. 13). Moreover, the Doha Declaration clearly states that TRIPS flexibilities can be used for public health purposes. So far, no member country has brought any dispute to the WTO challenging the legality of Section 3(*d*) of India's Patents Act, or the granting of a CL to Natco. The US trade bodies and pharma MNCs are probably aware of the futility of raising a dispute at the WTO, and are therefore resorting to arm-twisting tactics to restrain India from exercising TRIPS flexibilities. It should be noted that India is not the only country granting CLs; other countries, including the US, also issue CLs (Table 4.3).

Table 4.3 Details of CLs issued by various countries

| Country | Details of CL | Objective of CL |
|---|---|---|
| Thailand | 2006: a CL was issued to import from India the HIV/AIDS drug efavirenz, for which Merck held the patent | To protect public health |
| | 2007: two CLs were issued to the Government Pharmaceutical Organization of Thailand for the HIV/AIDS drug Kaletra and heart disease drug Plavix[40] | |
| Taiwan | 2005: a CL was issued to manufacture and sell the generic version of Tamiflu, for which Gilead Sciences held the patent. | To protect public health |
| Malaysia | 2003: a CL was issued to a local firm to import from India (Cipla) three drugs to treat HIV/AIDS[41] | To protect public health |
| Indonesia | Indonesia issued a CL (under government use, by presidential decree) three times: | To protect public health |
| | 2004: to manufacture and supply generic versions of two HIV/AIDS drugs (lamivudine and nevirapine) | |
| | 2007: to manufacture and supply the AIDS drug efavirenz, patented by Merck | |
| | 2012: to make, import and sell generic versions of seven patented drugs used in the treatment of HIV/AIDS and hepatitis B[42] | |
| Ghana | 2005: issued government use CL for the importation of generic HIV/AIDS drugs from India | To protect public health |
| Eritrea | 2005: issued a government use CL for the importation of HIV/AIDS drugs | To protect public health |
| Ecuador | 2010: CL issued to Eske Group, SA, for the HIV/AIDS drug ritonavir, patented by Abbott | To protect public health |
| Italy | 2006: the Italian Competition Authority AGCM granted a CL to Fabbrica Italiana Sintetici SpA (FIS) for Glaxo's sumatriptan succinate, an active ingredient used in the production of anti-migraine medicine. Glaxo had initially refused FIS's request to license the technology. Further, AGCM ordered Glaxo to grant a number of additional procedural licences to allow FIS to save the time otherwise required to research and test an efficient manufacturing process for sumatriptan succinate. | To facilitate licensing of technology; to compensate for the time lost by refusing to license a technology |

(Continued)

*Table 4.3* (Continued)

| Country | Details of CL | Objective of CL |
|---------|---------------|-----------------|
| US | 2001: the Secretary of the Department of Health and Human Services (DHHS), USA, threatened to exercise a CL (for government use[43]) to authorise imports of the generic ciprofloxacin for stockpiles against possible anthrax attack. The DHHS wanted to stockpile 1.2 billion pills. Bayer, which held the patent on ciprofloxacin, could not meet the demand in a timely fashion. | To protect public health |
| US | 2006: Johnson & Johnson was granted a CL on three patents held by Dr Jan Voda related to guiding catheters – medical devices used in performing angioplasty. This case was decided under the new US Supreme Court standard for granting injunctions on patents.[44] | To facilitate licensing of technology |
| US | 2007: the Federal Trade Commission found that Rambus had monopolised markets for four technologies in violation of Section 2 of the Sherman Act. The commission ordered Rambus to compulsorily license the four patented technologies to anyone interested in the technology. This CL was a remedial measure against illegal exercise of monopoly rights. | To remedy illegal monopoly created by a patent |
| US | 2005: the Federal Trade Commission issued a CL to Abbott for Guidant's patent on an RX delivery system for drug-eluting stents. This CL was granted while considering the anti-competitive effects of Boston Scientific's takeover of Guidant. | To avoid anti-competitive effects of mergers and acquisitions |

*Source:* Khor (2012), Love (2007), KEI (2014), and Correa (2013).

For developing countries like India, the price of medicines is an important factor influencing people's decision whether or not to seek health care services when they are ill. Hence, compulsory licensing on grounds of public health is very much justifiable. In advanced countries, out-of-pocket expenditure in health care is relatively low, and there is a well-established system to ensure that the burden of the cost of medicines is not passed on directly to patients. So, compulsory licensing on public health grounds is not very common in these countries. Rather, their concerns with respect to IP are related to the anti-competitive practices emerging out of monopoly rights; therefore, compulsory licensing in developed countries is resorted to mostly on grounds of competition.

Apart from the pressure on India to give up the use of TRIPS flexibilities, there is also pressure to introduce data exclusivity, which would delay the entry of generic drugs in the market.

## Data exclusivity

Data exclusivity refers to the protection of clinical trial and other test data. Pharmaceutical or agricultural and chemical companies are required to generate and submit these data to national drug or pesticide approval authorities to obtain marketing approval for a particular product in a country. Data exclusivity ensures that data submitted by an originator company for obtaining marketing approval are not relied upon by others for obtaining marketing approvals. In order to obtain marketing approval for generic drugs, an applicant is not required to reproduce the entire safety and efficacy data, but is required to prove that the drug is bioequivalent with the originator's drug.[45] Thus, when Cipla applied for marketing approval for its version of imatinib mesylate in India, it did not conduct the entire range of clinical trials, but only showed that its version was bioequivalent to Glivec, which had been approved in the US. Granting exclusive rights over test data would adversely impact the approval of generic drugs, and thus adversely affect the objective of making drugs affordable and accessible.

The US and the EU have been pressurising India to provide statutory protection to test data in the country. While 10–11 years of protection are granted in EU, five-year data exclusivity from the date of the FDA approval is granted to new drug products containing NCEs in the US.[46] The *2013 Special 301 Report* of the USTR urges India to 'provide an effective system for protecting against unfair commercial use, as well as unauthorized disclosure, of undisclosed test or other data generated to obtain marketing approval for pharmaceutical and agricultural chemical products' (USTR 2013: 39). In its Special 301 Submission to the USTR in 2013, PhRMA (2013b: 35–36) argues that the reliance of Indian regulatory authorities on test data submitted by originators to another country for marketing approval results in 'unfair commercial use prohibited by the TRIPS Agreement'. Data exclusivity was one of the major contentious issues in the proposed FTA between India and EU until 2013, when EU announced that it was no more seeking data exclusivity in India (*Hindu* 2013).

Apart from impacting the availability of generic drugs, data exclusivity can also affect the issuing of CLs if exclusive rights are granted to test data. In compulsory licensing, the licensee is required to obtain marketing authorisation for the drug. If data exclusivity is present, the authorities will not be able to certify the bioequivalence of the licensee's drug with the originator's drug.

Article 39.3 of the TRIPS Agreement forms the basis for the demand for data exclusivity. According to this article,

> Members, when requiring, as a condition of approving the marketing of pharmaceutical or of agricultural chemical products which utilize new chemical entities, the submission of undisclosed test or other data, the origination of which involves a considerable effort, shall protect such data against unfair commercial use. In addition, Members shall protect such data against disclosure, except where necessary to protect the public or unless steps are taken to ensure that the data are protected against unfair commercial use.[47]

There are two obligations under Article 39.3: to protect data submitted for marketing approval against unfair commercial use; and to protect the submitted data against disclosure by the authorities. To be eligible for protection, the product in question needs to consist of NCEs, and the generation of the data should involve considerable effort. However, disclosure is allowed in two circumstances: to protect the public, or when steps are taken to protect the data against unfair commercial use. Since the data are protected against unfair commercial use, the important question is whether reliance on the originator's data for subsequent marketing approval constitutes an unfair commercial use under Article 39.3 of TRIPS. While TRIPS does not define unfair commercial use, it makes a reference to 'unfair competition as provided in Article 10*bis* of the Paris Convention'.[48] Article 10*bis* of the Paris Convention defines unfair competition as 'any act of competition contrary to honest practices in industrial or commercial matters'.[49] The article also lists certain acts as prohibited, but it does not talk about any exclusive rights over undisclosed information. Neither does the Paris Convention define the parameters of unfair competition. Therefore, a member country can define the parameters of unfair commercial use to exclude data exclusivity.

India maintains the stance in the WTO that member countries have flexibility in implementing the obligation to protect test data, and that test data are not entitled to exclusive rights. In its submission to the TRIPS Council on 29 June 2001, India stated that

> Article 39.3 of the TRIPS Agreement leaves considerable room for Member countries to implement the obligation to protect test data

against unfair competition practices. The Agreement provides that 'undisclosed information' is regulated under the discipline of unfair competition, as contained in Article 10 bis of the Paris Convention. With this provision, the Agreement clearly avoids the treatment of undisclosed information as a 'property' and does not require granting 'exclusive' rights to the owner of the data.

(WTO 2001b: para. 39)

Further, India added that 'Article 39.3 does permit a national competent authority to rely on data in its possession to assess a second and further applications, relating to the same drug, since this would not imply any 'unfair commercial use' (*ibid.*: para. 40).

Reports from within the US government also suggest that the US position on data exclusivity is against the spirit of the Doha Declaration. The report of the US Government Accountability Office (USGAO) points out that the US trade strategy of extension and enforcement of the IP provision on data exclusivity has gone against the spirit of the Doha Declaration (USGAO 2007). The report says that data exclusivity can be used as a tool for extending exclusivity beyond the length of the patent term. More importantly, the report acknowledges that the

data exclusivity provision might prevent the marketing of generic drugs produced under a compulsory licence. For instance, if a compulsory licence is granted to a generic producer, but that producer is not able to rely on the data generated by the innovator company to obtain needed marketing approval, it will not be possible to distribute the drugs under a compulsory license.

(*ibid.*: 38)

Concerns have been raised by a section of legislators in the US over the impact of its trade policies in IP on access to medicines in developing countries. According to the USGAO report just cited,

certain members [of Congress] emphasized the need to better balance IP protection for pharmaceuticals with the promotion of access to affordable medicines, including through robust generic competition. These members expressed unease over the balance achieved in the FTAs negotiated by USTR to date – specifically the impact of the pharmaceutical-related IP provision in FTAs on developing countries. These members urged USTR to ensure that the FTA provisions do not restrict the availability of generic competition and put affordable health care at risk. In response to these concerns, in

May 2007, Members of the congressional leadership agreed on a bipartisan compromise with the administration to revise four of the recently negotiated FTAs, in order to alter provisions pertaining to a variety of areas, including IP provision and access to medicines.

(USGAO 2007: 41)

This renewed position of the US administration was manifested in the FTAs signed since the second half of the 2000s. Article 16.10.2 of the US–Peru FTA, which was signed on 12 April 2006, states:

(a) If a Party requires, as a condition for approving the marketing of a pharmaceutical product that utilizes a new chemical entity, the submission of undisclosed test or other data necessary to determine whether the use of such products is safe and effective, the Party shall protect against disclosure of the data of persons making such submissions, where the origination of such data involves considerable effort, except where the disclosure is necessary to protect the public or unless steps are taken to ensure that the data are protected against unfair commercial use. (b) Each Party shall provide that for data . . . submitted to the Party . . . , no person other than the person that submitted them may, without the latter's permission, rely on such data in support of an application for product approval during a reasonable period of time after their submission. For this purpose, a reasonable period shall normally mean five years from the date on which the Party granted approval to the person that produced the data for approval to market its product, taking account of the nature of the data and person's efforts and expenditures in producing them. . . . (c) Where a Party relies on a marketing approval granted by the other Party, and grants approval within six months of the filing of a complete application for marketing approval filed in the Party, the reasonable period of exclusive use of the data submitted in connection with obtaining the approval relied on shall begin with the date of the first marketing approval relied on.[50]

This needs to be contrasted with the provisions in the US–Jordan FTA, which was concluded much earlier.[51] Para. 22 of the US–Jordan FTA states:

It is understood that protection for new chemical entities shall also include protection for new uses for old chemical entities for a period of three years. . . . It is understood that, in situations where there is reliance on evidence of approval in another country, Jordan shall at a minimum protect such information against unfair commercial use for the same period of time the other country is protecting such information against unfair commercial use.[52]

The US–Jordan FTA includes TRIPS-plus language on registration data that requires Jordan to provide exclusivity for the same period as granted by the country where the data were filed, if they were filed outside of Jordan.[53] Thus, Jordan may be made to honour the US's terms of protection – or even the longer term of protection afforded in the EU, which is not a signatory to the US–Jordan FTA and requires a longer exclusivity period than the US, without specified exceptions. Though the US has relaxed its position on the degree of protection to be granted for test data, it is till pressurising India to implement data exclusivity.

Faced with this global pressure, the Government of India established an Inter-ministerial Committee, which included independent experts, to 'consider the steps to be taken by the Government in the context of the provisions of Article 39.3 of the TRIPS Agreement for the protection of undisclosed information' (GoI 2007b). The chairperson of the committee submitted a report on 31 May 2007. The report proposed three different regimes for agro-chemicals, herbal/traditional Indian medicines, and modern pharmaceutical products, respectively. In agro-chemicals, fixed-term data protection for three years from the date of registration in India was recommended. During this period, the regulator would not rely on the data submitted by the originator while granting market approval for the same products of second and subsequent applicants. In the case of herbal/traditional Indian medicines, the report recommended a fixed period of at least five years of protection.

In pharmaceuticals, the report adopted a cautious approach while recommending data protection. It recommended a transitional phase to be followed by fixed-term data protection for five years. During the transitional period, the drug regulator would continue with the existing practice of approving new drugs as per the Drugs and Cosmetics Act, 1940, and at the same time applications would be received for the protection of test data. Safeguards should be enacted to ensure that specified undisclosed data submitted for seeking marketing approval for pharmaceutical products are not disclosed to any third party during the transitional phase. In the second phase, the drug regulator would provide five-year data protection to proprietary test data[54] submitted by the originator for obtaining marketing approval for a new drug. While the data are protected, the drug regulator would not accord final approval to any subsequent applicant by relying on the data submitted by the originator.

The report also recommended that suitable safeguards should be set up in order to avoid any adverse effects arising out of data protection for pharmaceutical products with regard to the protection of public health interests. The safeguards suggested by the report include the following:

1   Protection would be for only undisclosed proprietary data, and not for data already published or publicly available through publication in journals, symposiums, promotional literatures, and information available on the websites of various drug approving authorities and other related websites.
2   In the case of data protection for patented drugs, the period of protection should not go beyond the 20-year period of patent protection in India.
3   The period of data protection may be counted from the date of first marketing approval anywhere in the world. The originator of the data must apply for marketing approval in India within 24 months of that date.
4   Marketing approval of a new drug would cease to be valid if the product was not marketed within six months of the grant of such approval and if not marketed for 12 consecutive months at any time thereafter.
5   Provisions for the grant of CLs should be introduced in the relevant laws, and these should override the provisions for data protection. In case a CL was issued for a patented drug, there would be automatic waiver of data protection.
6   The government would have the right to waive all or any provisions pertaining to data protection in case of a public health emergency. In such a situation, the drug regulator would be free to grant marketing approval to subsequent applicant(s) based on published data and limited test data generated in India.
7   Drugs for life-threatening diseases like HIV/AIDS may be exempted from the provisions of fixed-period data protection as mentioned previously, i.e. the drug regulator may rely on the data submitted by the first applicant in India/foreign country and grant market approval to subsequent applicants for same product in India.

*Prima facie*, the recommendations made by the Data Protection Committee do not seem to have major adverse implications for access to affordable medicines in the country. The safeguards recommended include exemptions to life-threatening diseases and the exercise of CLs, both of which are extremely relevant to ensuring access. Generics firms in any case will not be able to sell generics of patented drugs, and the data protection provision does not extend beyond the period of patent protection. One of the most relevant concerns in the wake of data protection has been the ability of firms obtaining CLs to manufacture the drug if the regulator is not able to rely on the data of the innovator. This issue has been addressed in the recommendations of the report. The data protection regime adopted by India, a regime that is yet to gain proper shape, must ensure that domestic firms that have developed similar products by investing in R&D are not denied permission to market the product in India (Dhar and Gopakumar 2008). This is important in the context of increasing R&D efforts by pharma firms in India.

## Trends in patent applications in India

The number of patents granted shows an increase during the initial years of the second half of the 2000s (Figure 4.1). The number came down steeply in 2009–10. Analysis of patent filings and patent grants shows that reforms in the patent regime in India have benefited foreign applicants more than Indian innovators. The share of foreign applicants in

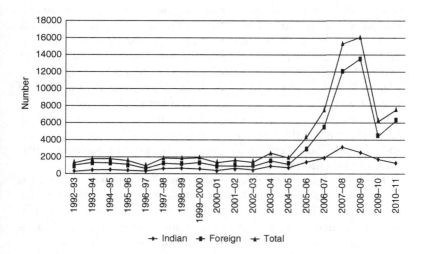

*Figure 4.1* Number of patents granted in India

Source: Indian Patent Office, *Annual Reports*, various years, http://www.ipindia.nic.in/ (accessed on 24 November 2014).

total patent filings increased from 74 to 79 per cent between 2000–01 and 2010–11.

In patent application filing, the largest number of applications were for computer/electronic innovations, followed by mechanical, chemical and drug innovations. In 2010–11, patent applications pertaining to drugs constituted 9 per cent of the total number of applications. The corresponding figure for 1999–2000 was 21 per cent. The leading Indian pharma firms in patent filing include Ranbaxy, Wockhardt, Cipla, and Hetero. The leading applicants from public sector laboratories and institutions of higher education include CSIR, Indian Institute of Technology (IIT), Amity University, Defence Research and Development Organisation (DRDO), Indian Council for Agricultural Research (ICAR), and Indian Institute of Science (IIS).[55]

In patent grants, the share of foreign applicants increased from 70 per cent to 83 per cent between 2000–01 and 2010–11. The share of patents pertaining to drugs, however, came down from 21 per cent in 2000–01 to 8 per cent in 200–10. In pharmaceuticals, 3,488 product patents were granted by the Indian Patent Office between 2005–06 and 2009–10. Of these, the bulk of patents were granted to foreign applicants – 3,079 (88 per cent).[56] Table 4.4 analyses the pharmaceutical product patents granted in India.

Table 4.4 is based on a list published in 2010 by the Indian Patent Office, titled *Product Patents in Pharmaceuticals Granted by Indian Patent Office during 2005–06 to 2009–10*. This list does not provide the nationality of the applicant. In order to find out the nationality status of the patentee, the data provided in this list were compared against data in another list published by the Indian Patent Office, titled *List of Granted Patents by Indian Patent Office to Foreign Applicants during 2007–08 to 2009–10*.[57] For names that did not figure in the latter list, a website search was done to ascertain their nationality (i.e. whether Indian or foreign). Based on this research, it was found that 382 Indian applicants and 27 unidentified applicants[58] were granted product patents in pharmaceuticals in this period.

Table 4.4 brings out three prominent observations: (*a*) R&D is skewed in favour of lifestyle diseases and preventive care; (*b*) public sector laboratories and institutions of higher education play an important role in research on neglected diseases; and (*c*) herbal-based R&D is becoming prominent. In the case of national diseases such as tuberculosis and malaria, public sector research laboratories and institutions of higher education play a much more crucial role than private sector initiatives. Out of the four patents granted on tuberculosis to Indian

Table 4.4 Product patents in pharmaceuticals granted by Indian Patent Office, 2005/06–2009/10

| | Indian | | | Foreign | Total | Indian |
| | Private Industry | Public sector laboratories/ institutions of higher education | Other | Industry/public sector laboratories/higher education/individuals | (Indian + Foreign) | (% of total) |
| --- | --- | --- | --- | --- | --- | --- |
| Cancer | 1 | 4 | | 37 | 42 | 12 |
| Diabetes | 2 | 1 | | 17 | 20 | 15 |
| Obesity | 1 | 0 | | 6 | 7 | 14 |
| Cardio/hypertension | 1 | 0 | | 5 | 6 | 17 |
| Tuberculosis | 1 | 3 | | 3 | 7 | 57 |
| Malaria | 0 | 2 | | 2 | 4 | 50 |
| Herbal | 11 | 12 | | 6 | 59* | 39 |
| Vaccine | 2 | 3 | | 53 | 58 | 9 |
| Total no. of patents | 166 | 75 | 168 | 3,079 | 3,488 | 11 |

Note: *30 patents held by individuals whose names sound Indian, but their nationality is not known.

Source: Computed by the author based on data from the Indian Patent Office.

applicants, only one is from the private sector – Lupin Laboratories. Similarly, of the three patents granted to foreigners for tuberculosis, only one is from the private sector – Syngenta. These conclusions are based on a search for key disease terms in the titles of patents granted. Such analysis has limitations, since the titles of patents do not necessarily indicate the therapeutic area in which the patented subject matter belongs. There may be new forms of molecules, such as salts and derivatives, and new combinations of existing compounds whose therapeutic application need not be mentioned in the title of the patent. Despite this limitation, the title search does give us some indication regarding the focus areas of pharmaceutical R&D.

## Notes

1 A comparison of drug prices in India is provided given in Table 5.1, Chapter 5.
2 Out-of-pocket expenditure as a proportion of total public health expenditure is 6 per cent in the Netherlands, 7 per cent in France, 10 per cent in the UK, and 12 per cent in the US. The global average is 15 per cent. For details, see WHO (2012: 41).
3 Insurance companies covered only 5 per cent of the population in 2010. Various central and state government schemes cover another 20 per cent of the population. However, none of the government insurance schemes, except the Employee State Insurance Scheme and the Central Government Health Scheme, provides cover for out-patient care.
4 Computed from unit level data of NSS 2011–12, Ministry of Statistics and Programme Implementation, Government of India, New Delhi. These figures have been computed and made available by Dr. Anup Karan, Associate Professor, Indian Institute of Public Health Gandhinagar, India.
5 'Ailment not considered serious' is not regarded as a constraint.
6 The free medicines scheme launched in October 2011 began with the supply of 200 generic medicines free of cost at public hospitals. The Rajasthan Medical Services Corporation is the nodal agency implementing this scheme. For more details, visit its website at www.rmsc.nic.in.
7 At the first anniversary of the launch of the scheme, the chief minister of Rajasthan reportedly offered this statistic regarding the increase in the number of patients visiting the out-patient departments of government hospitals. For details see *Hindu* (2012).
8 TRIPS Agreement, Article 27, http://www.wto.org/english/docs_e/legal_e/27-trips_04c_e.htm (accessed on 14 November 2014).
9 TRIPS Agreement, Article 8, http://www.wto.org/english/tratop_e/trips_e/t_agm2_e.htm (accessed on 14 November 2014).
10 TRIPS Agreement, Article 65.2, http://www.wto.org/english/docs_e/legal_e/27-trips.doc (accessed on 14 November 2014).

11  TRIPS Agreement, Article 70.8, http://www.wto.org/english/docs_e/ legal_e/27-trips.doc (accessed on 14 November 2014).
12  TRIPS Agreement, Article 65.4, http://www.wto.org/english/docs_e/ legal_e/27-trips.doc (accessed on 14 November 2014).
13  An ordinance was issued on 31 December 1994 amending the Patents Act, 1970, to introduce the mailbox provisions. But the amendment was not passed by Parliament. The US dragged India to the WTO's Dispute Settlement Body over India's failure to provide the mailbox facility. (See Dispute DS50, India: Patent Protection for Pharmaceutical and Agricultural Chemical Products, http://www.wto.org/english/tratop_e/dispu_e/cases_e/ ds50_e.htm [accessed on 19 November 2014].) The decision went against India. This necessitated amendments to the Patents Act, 1970, to provide for the mailbox facility and exclusive marketing rights. Exclusive marketing rights entail a five-year, patent-like monopoly for products covered by product patent applications filed under the mailbox system. A company securing an exclusive marketing right has the exclusive right to sell or distribute an article or substance covered by a patent application in the country.
14  The act introduced 64 amendments (Basheer 2005).
15  Patents Amendment Act, 2005, Section 2(*l*), http://ipindia.nic.in/ipr/ patent/patent_2005.pdf (accessed on 20 November 2014).
16  Patents Amendment Act, 2005, Section 2(*ja*), *ibid.*
17  Patents Act, 1970, Section 2(*j*), http://ipindia.nic.in/ipr/patent/pat ent_Act_1970_28012013_book.pdf (accessed on 27 December 2014). The ordinance did not incorporate any changes in this clause. See the Patents (Amendment) Ordinance, 2004, http://lawmin.nic.in/Patents%20 Amendment%20Ordinance%202004.pdf (accessed on 27 December 2014).
18  Patents Act, 1970, Section 2(*ja*), http://ipindia.nic.in/ipr/patent/ patent_Act_1970_28012013_book.pdf (accessed on 27 December 2014). The ordinance did not incorporate any changes in this clause. See the Patents (Amendment) Ordinance, 2004, http://lawmin.nic. in/Patents%20Amendment%20Ordinance%202004.pdf (accessed on 27 December 2014).
19  Patents Amendment Act, 2005, Section 3(*d*), http://ipindia.nic.in/ ipr/patent/patent_2005.pdf (accessed on 20 November 2014).
20  Civil Appeal Nos 2706–2716 of 2013 (*Novartis AG vs Union of India and Others*), Civil Appeal No. 2728 of 2013 (*Natco Pharma vs Union of India and Others*), and Civil Appeal Nos 2717–2727 of 2013 (*M/s Cancer Patients Aid Association vs Union of India and Others*). See Supreme Court of India (2013).
21  Jurg Zimmermann obtained a US patent on N-phenyl-2-pyrimidine-amine derivatives on 28 May 1996 (patent no. 5521184). These derivatives were also granted a European patent later (patent no. EP-A-0564409).
22  Originally, the appeal was filed in the Madras High Court. Later, when IPAB became functional, five writ petitions challenging five orders of the Assistant Controller were transferred to IPAB. Two writ petitions on the constitutional validity and TRIPS compliance of Section 3(*d*) were heard by the high court.

23  Natco Pharma and the Cancer Patients Aid Association were among the five parties who filed pre-grant oppositions at the Patents Office against Novartis's patent application.

24  The article 'Inhibition of the Abl Protein-Tyrosine Kinase in Vitro and in Vivo by a 2-Phenylaminopyrimidine Derivative' by Buchdunger *et al.* was published in the January issue of *Cancer Research* in 1996. See para. 127 of the Supreme Court Order.

25  Novartis had filed an investigational new drug application for Gleevec on 19 April 1998, and a new drug application for imatinib mesylate on 27 February 2001 at USFDA. Novartis sells the drug imatinib mesylate under the brand names Gleevec and Glivec.

26  Based on information available at http://www.medindia.net/drug-price/imatinib.htm and http://www.medindia.net/drug-price/imatinib-mesylate.htm (accessed on 27 December 2014).

27  Pre-grant: when an application for a patent has been published, but a patent has not yet been granted.

28  Post-grant: the period after the grant of a patent, but before the expiry of one year from the date of publication of the grant of the patent.

29  Patents Amendment Act, 2005, Section 84.6(iv), http://ipindia.nic.in/ipr/patent/patent_2005.pdf (accessed on 20 November 2014).

30  All information in this paragraph is sourced from the Compulsory Licence Order issued by the Controller of Patents on 9 March 2012 (GoI 2012d).

31  Patents Act, 1970, Section 92.1(ii), http://ipindia.nic.in/ipr/patent/patent_Act_1970_28012013_book.pdf (accessed on 21 November 2014).

32  Patents Act, 1970, Section 92A, *ibid.*

33  TRIPS Agreement, Article 31.f, http://www.wto.org/english/docs_e/legal_e/27-trips.doc (accessed on 14 November 2014).

34  WTO General Council, Implementation of Paragraph 6 of the Doha Declaration on the TRIPS Agreement and Public Health, WT/L/540 and Corr.1, 1 September 2003, http://www.wto.org/english/tratop_e/trips_e/implem_para6_e.htm (accessed on 21 November 2014).

35  This was discussed in greater detail in Chapter 1.

36  Patents Amendment Act, 2005, Section 11A.7, http://ipindia.nic.in/ipr/patent/patent_2005.pdf (accessed on 20 November 2014).

37  The USFDA publication *Approved Drug Products with Therapeutic Equivalence Evaluations* (commonly known as the Orange Book) identifies drug products approved on the basis of safety and effectiveness.

38  The US Patent and Trademark Office guidelines require patent applications to comply with utility requirements under 35 USC 101; 112.35 USC 101 calls for rejection of the patent application if it lacks utility, and 35 USC 112 calls for rejection of the patent application if the disclosure fails to teach how to use the invention. Brana *et al.* applied for a patent, on 30 June 1988, on 'non-symmetrically substituted 5-nitrobenzoisoquinoline-1, 3-dione compounds for use as antitumor substances'. The patent examiner rejected the application on the basis of 35 USC 101, on the grounds that the molecule did not prove utility as compared to existing ones to treat tumours in humans. When this issue was taken

up in court, the court held that superiority in utility proven even at the animal testing stage would be sufficient to grant a patent in the pharmaceuticals sector. Though the patent commissioner held that proven superiority at the animal testing stage is no guarantee that the molecule would have superior utility in humans, the court did not agree. For details, see 'Background and Summary of the Decision of the Court of Appeals for the Federal Circuit in *In re Brana* Concerning Practical Utility Requirements for Pharmaceutical Inventions and New USPTO Utility Examination Guidelines', http://www.sughrue.com/files/Publication/aee39f07-a979–4d6a-a945–597bf14a4d7f/Presentation/Publication Attachment/a980e399–5d44–4e34–80ac-612229c32783/back_summ. htm (accessed on 27 December 2014).

39 'US slams India for allowing generic version of cancer drug', 14 July 2012, http://www.domain-b.com/industry/Healthcare/20120714_cancer_drug.html (accessed on 22 November 2014).

40 Abbott holds the patent for Kaletra, and Sanofi Aventis for Plavix.

41 The three drugs are didanosine (patented by Bristol-Myers Squibb), zidovudine (GSK), and the lamivudine + zidovudine combination (GSK). This CL was for two years commencing 1 November 2003.

42 The seven drugs are: efavirenz, abacavir (patent held by Glaxo), didanosine (Bristol-Myers Squibb), lopinavir + ritonavir combination (Abbott), tenofovir (Gilead Sciences), tenofovir + emtricitabine combination (Gilead Sciences), and tenofovir + emtricitabine + efavirenz combination (Gilead Sciences). The 2012 CL will enable the supply of better first-line and second-line antiretroviral treatment (Khor 2012).

43 Section 1498 of Title 28 of the US Code provides for government authorisation to third parties for the manufacture or use of a product or IP without the permission of the rights holder. In such cases, the remedy shall be by action against the US in the US Claims Court for the recovery of compensation for such use.

44 In May 2006, the US Supreme Court issued an opinion in *eBay vs Merc-Exchange*, which set the standards which courts resort to when considering requests for injunctions to enforce patent owners' exclusive rights to authorise the use of a patented invention. The standards are: (*a*) that the plaintiff has suffered an irreparable injury; (*b*) that other possible legal remedies, including the payment of royalties, are inadequate to compensate for the injury; (*c*) that considering the balance of hardships between the plaintiff and defendant, a remedy in equity is warranted; and (*d*) that the public interest would not be disserved by a permanent injunction (Love 2007).

45 Bioequivalence is the property whereby two drugs with the same active ingredient possess similar bioavailability and effect the same action in the physiological area where the drug is expected to act.

46 The EU Pharmaceutical Legislation adopted in 2004 created a harmonised, eight-year data exclusivity provision, with an additional two-year market exclusivity provision. This effective 10-year market exclusivity can be extended by an additional year if the originator obtains an authorisation for new therapeutic indications with significant clinical benefit.

47  TRIPS Agreement, Article 39, http://www.wto.org/english/docs_e/legal_e/27-trips_04d_e.htm (accessed on 23 November 2014).

48  TRIPS Agreement, Article 39.1, *ibid.*

49  Paris Convention for the Protection of Industrial Property, http://www.wipo.int/treaties/en/text.jsp?file_id=288514#P213_35515 (accessed on 23 November 2014).

50  USTR, US–Peru Trade Promotion Agreement, Intellectual Property Rights, http://www.ustr.gov/webfm_send/1031 (accessed on 27 December 2014).

51  The US–Jordan FTA was signed on 24 October 2000.

52  Agreement between the United States of America and the Hashemite Kingdom of Jordan on the Establishment of a Free Trade Area, p. 7, http://www.ustr.gov/sites/default/files/Jordan%20FTA.pdf (accessed on 24 November 2014).

53  'TRIPS-plus' refers to IPR requirements in trade agreements that go beyond what is required by the TRIPS Agreement.

54  'Proprietary test data' are defined by the committee as data that are not published or known to the public at the time of or after their submission for marketing approval anywhere in the world. See GoI (2007b: 50).

55  In 2009–10, the number of patent filings was: CSIR: 162; IIT: 109; Amity: 81; DRDO: 80; ICAR: 55; and IIS: 45.

56  Eleven per cent to Indian applicants and 1 per cent to unidentified applicants. These calculations are based on Indian Patent Office, *Product Patents in Pharmaceuticals Granted by Indian Patent Office during 2005–06 to 2009–10*, http://www.ipindia.nic.in/iponew/Patent_PharmaProduct_2005_06_2009_10.pdf (accessed on 24 November 2014).

57  *List of Granted Patents by Indian Patent Office to Foreign Applicants during 2007–08 to 2009–10*, http://ipindia.nic.in/iponew/TotalPharma_Foreign_200708_200809.pdf (accessed on 24 November 2014).

58  The list published by the Indian Patent Office does not provide the names of the applicants in 10 cases. In 17 cases, the names are given, but the web search did not yield any results regarding their nationality.

# Chapter 5

# The drug price control system in India and access to medicines

The drug price control system in India has been a major factor contributing to the relatively low prices of medicines in the country as compared to many other countries. The policy changes which have taken place in the pharmaceuticals sector since the mid-1990s have had no direct impact on the drug price control mechanism in India. The introduction of product patent rights and economic liberalisation policies did not directly impact the ability of the drug price control system to regulate drug prices so as to enable more patients to access medicines. As patients' access to medicines at reasonable prices depends crucially on the drug price regulation mechanism, any analysis of the likely impact of reforms in the pharmaceuticals sector on access to medicines in India will have to examine the drug price control system in India.

Regulation of drug prices in independent India began in 1962 during the Indo-Chinese war. The government feared that the prices of medicines would rise as a result of the war. As a counter-measure, it promulgated the Drugs (Display of Prices) Order in 1962, and the Drugs (Control of Prices) Order in 1963, under the Defence of India Act, 1915. The prices of drugs were frozen as of 1 April 1963. Details of the drug price control mechanism in India since 1963 were discussed earlier in Chapter 1. Drug price control in India began with a wide coverage in its initial phases, narrowing down gradually in the course of time. The DPCO of 1979 brought 347 bulk drugs under its purview, covering 80–90 per cent of the pharmaceutical market in the country. However, subsequent DPCOs reduced the number of bulk drugs under their purview, and thereby their market coverage. The 1987 DPCO covered 142 bulk drugs, accounting for 60–70 per cent of the pharmaceutical market, while the 1995 DPCO covered only 74 bulk drugs constituting 25–30 per cent of the pharmaceutical market (Sengupta *et al.* 2008).

The current drug price control system in India is governed by NPPP 2012 (GoI 2012a) and DPCO 2013(GoI 2013b). The NPPP of 2012 adopts a new approach to the regulation of drug prices: a 'market-based' system of price regulation, which ensures the availability of essential medicines 'at reasonable prices', and at the same time provides 'sufficient opportunity for innovation and competition to support the growth of industry' (GoI 2012a: 6). It aims to strike a balance between the need to ensure reasonable prices of medicines and the need to promote innovation and competition in an economy that is largely market-driven.[1]

## Key features of NPPP 2012

The three key principles for regulation of drug prices in NPPP 2012 are: (*a*) the essentiality of medicines; i.e. the prices of all medicines listed in the NLEM are to be regulated; (*b*) the regulation of prices of only formulations; i.e. the prices of bulk drugs will not be regulated; and (*c*) a market-based approach to price regulation; i.e. the ceiling price will be determined on the basis of the average price of all brands of a medicine, each having a market share of at least 1 per cent. These features of NPPP 2012 mark a major departure from the previous drug price control system under the Modifications in Drug Policy, 1986, and DPCO 1995. The essentiality of medicines was not an issue of concern in the previous price regulation mechanism. A market-based approach was used to identify the drugs whose prices were to be controlled. Further, the previous mechanism sought to control the prices of both bulk drugs and formulations, and adopted two different approaches to their pricing. While the financial size and investments made by firms were taken into account in determining the sale price of bulk drugs, the actual cost of production determined the maximum sale price of formulations.[2]

### *Essentiality of medicines*

The drug price control regime in India has shown a tendency to move away from the principle of essentiality of medicines to a market-based system as the basis for identification of drugs for price regulation. Essentiality was the basis for categorising drugs into four groups in the 1979 DPCO, which included 347 bulk drugs under its purview. But in the 1995 DPCO, drugs were identified based not on their essentiality but on market principles. The number of drugs identified for price control would have declined further if the DP of 2002, which proposed a more liberal, market-oriented approach, had been notified. The essentiality principle has been brought back into the drug price regulation system in India largely due to the contribution of the judiciary. In 2003, the Supreme Court of India ordered the government to 'consider and formulate appropriate criteria for ensuring essential and life-saving drugs not to fall out of price control and further directed to review drugs which are essential and life-saving in nature till 2nd May, 2003' (GoI 2008b). Accordingly, all medicines (dosage forms) listed in the NLEM, as revised from time to time, were subjected to price regulation by NPPP 2012.[3] The NPPA, the government body responsible for implementing drug price regulation, has notified the ceiling prices of 440 formulations belonging to the NLEM as of 30 January 2014.

Since the operational aspect of the essentiality principle is linked to the NLEM, the latter plays a significant role in promoting access to medicines at reasonable prices in the country. But the NLEM of 2011[4] has had major drawbacks, resulting in suboptimal realisation of the potentials of the drug price control system. The 2011 NLEM does not contain many of the essential drugs required for the protection and promotion of public health. For example, it does not contain any drug for treating multidrug-resistant tuberculosis (MDR-TB), such as capreomycin or cycloserine, even though MDR-TB has become a major public health challenge in the country. These drugs are listed in the WHO's Model List of Essential Medicines as second-line drugs for the treatment of MDR-TB.[5] The WHO reports that there was a 42 per cent increase in detected cases of MDR-TB globally in 2012 and that India was one of three countries where the increase was greatest (WHO 2013). Similarly, a number of essential anti-diabetic drugs are also missing from the list, which contains only two tablets – metformin and glibenclamide. Glibenclamide has been declared unsuitable for patients above 60 years. A range of other anti-diabetic drugs, such as glimepiride, gliclazide and glitazone, are not included in the list (ISID-PHFI 2014). The absence of a number of essential drugs in the NLEM will lead to such drugs falling out of the purview of the drug price control system.

The NPPP of 2012 assigns great importance to the NLEM, since the list draws on the WHO's Model List of Essential Medicines, the essential drug lists of various states, the medicines used in various national health programmes, and emergency care drugs.[6] However, there appears to be a disconnect between the NLEM and other lists of essential medicines. The ferrous sulphate and folic acid combination used in the National Nutritional Anaemia Prophylaxis Programme is missing in NLEM 2011, despite the fact that iron deficiency and anaemia are widespread among adults and children in India (ISID-PHFI 2014). Health being a state subject, many states have prepared their own lists of essential medicines in view of their public health priorities. Some of these state-level lists vary considerably from the NLEM at the union level. States like Rajasthan, Tamil Nadu and Delhi have come up with their own lists of essential medicines. A comparison of these lists reveals that 50 per cent of the medicines in the essential medicines list of Rajasthan, and 43 per cent of the essential medicines list of Tamil Nadu, do not correspond with NLEM 2011 (*ibid.*). Lack of coordination between the NLEM, the state-level lists of essential medicines, and other lists of essential medicines, constitutes a serious problem undermining the spirit of reincorporation of the essentiality principle in the drug price regulation system in the country.

The NLEM of 2011 contains 348 drugs, of which 333 are plain formulations and 15 are combinations. One objective of the NLEM is to promote rational use of medicines taking cost, safety and efficacy into consideration; this has kept the number of combination drugs at a minimum.[7] The list also specifies the dosage forms of the 348 essential medicines. For example, the list covers only the 500 mg dosage form of paracetamol tablets; it does not include other dosage forms of paracetamol available in the market. Since the new drug price control system will be applicable only to the dosage forms listed in the NLEM, firms might find an escape route by selling, or encouraging doctors to prescribe, dosage forms which are not listed in the NLEM. For example, if a firm manages to sell paracetamol 650 mg tablets, a dosage form already available in the market, it would be able to escape the price regulation system. Plain formulations and combinations in NLEM constitute only 27 per cent and 5 per cent, respectively, of the total market for plain drugs and combination drugs. In the total pharmaceuticals market, the share of plain formulations and combinations are 53 per cent and 47 per cent, respectively (ISID-PHFI 2014). This would mean that only 17 per cent of the total pharmaceuticals market is covered by the current drug price control system. It is highly likely that firms will use their promotional activities to influence doctors to prescribe dosage forms not listed in the NLEM. We have already seen in Chapter 1 that pharmaceutical firms in India spend substantially on promotional activities.

Loopholes in the current drug price control system in India allow firms to find ways to escape the price control net. If the price control system is to cater effectively to the objective of ensuring access to medicines at reasonable prices for the people of India, it is necessary to ensure that firms do not rely on irrational dosage forms and combinations to escape price regulation. Since the objective of the NLEM is to promote the rational use of medicines, it is not appropriate to suggest that the NLEM should include all the dosage forms of essential medicines and all combinations including essential medicines. There has to be a policy requiring doctors to prescribe only those drugs which are listed in the NLEM, and marketing approval should be given only to drugs that are rational. If doctors are to prescribe only the drugs included in the NLEM, the latter should contain a comprehensive list of essential medicines rather than a representative list, as it does currently.

### Deregulation of bulk drug price control

The approach of NPPP 2012 has been to regulate only the prices of formulations, and not bulk drugs (or APIs). When a market-based approach is adopted, there is no point in regulating the prices of inputs. But the justification offered for the exclusion of bulk drugs raises serious questions. The NPPP of 2012 states that the regulation of bulk drug prices in the previous DPCOs resulted in production shifting away from the notified category. Out of the 74 notified bulk drugs under DPCO 1995, only 47 are now in production.[8] However, the linking of changes in bulk drug production to the regulation of the prices of these drugs requires careful analysis. If price regulation has caused changes in the production pattern, a similar change would have been visible in the production of formulations as well. The policy document, however, is silent on this, and we do not have any evidence from the recent past to suggest that there has been a systematic shift in the production pattern of formulations. Moreover, the NPPP does not clarify whether the manufacturers of scheduled bulk drugs have moved into the production of non-scheduled bulk drugs. The NPPP of 2012 does not provide details of the production of bulk drugs that are not under the purview of DPCO 1995. If manufacturers are discontinuing the production of bulk drugs irrespective of whether they are scheduled or non-scheduled, this may be an indication of something happening in the bulk drug industry as a whole, rather than an outcome of price control, and therefore merits serious enquiry.

Other factors may be more relevant than regulation of prices in influencing production decisions with regard to bulk drugs. As we have seen in previous chapters, there has been a clear shift among leading pharmaceutical firms away from the business of bulk drugs to the production of formulations. This is because of the greater scope for fetching premium prices in the formulations segment, which is characterised by brand image. Bulk drugs, on the other hand, are highly price competitive, and the chances of fetching premium prices are low. The emergence of a more competitive bulk drug industry in China, coupled with the liberalisation of imports in India, has resulted in cheaper imports replacing domestic production of bulk drugs. Moreover, SMEs in the pharma sector, which were major producers of bulk drugs in the country, have been facing difficulties, and a number of such units have been shut down since 2005. Bulk drug production is also affected by environmental regulations in the country.

## Market-based approach to price regulation

The NPPP of 2012 applies a market-based approach to the regulation of prices of formulations, as against the cost-based approach of the earlier regime. The average price of all brands of an NLEM drug having at least 1 per cent market share is the stipulated ceiling price of that drug. This methodology results in a reduction in the prices of a number of medicines. In the pharmaceutical market in India, the market leader is also the price leader, or their prices are among the highest in many cases (see Table 5.1).

Table 5.1 Comparison of drug prices in India (as of 2008)

| Name of drug | No. of manufacturers | Market leader Rs (company) | Most expensive Rs (company) | Least expensive Rs (company) |
|---|---|---|---|---|
| Human insulin (40 IU, pack size 1) | 10 | 128.1 (Abbott) | 147.8 (Eli Lilly) | 101.5 (Biocon) |
| Glibenclamide (5mg, pack size 10) | 11 | 7.1 (Sanofi Aventis) | 7.1 (Sanofi Aventis) | 3.7 (Lupin) |
| Atenolol (50 mg, pack size 14) | 46 | 26.3 (Zydus) | 31.3 (Torrent) | 4.0 (Unison) |
| Atorvastatin (10 mg, pack size 10) | 58 | 68.0 (Ranbaxy) | 68.0 (Ranbaxy) | 9.1 (Hetero) |
| Cefixime (200 mg, pack size 10) | 51 | 79.1 (FDC) | 305.7 (Admac) | 64.6 (Laborate) |
| Ciprofloxacin (500 mg, pack size 10) | 94 | 73.6 (Ranbaxy) | 163.4 (Ind-Swift) | 11.7 (Laborate) |
| Omeprazole (20 mg, pack size 10) | 79 | 39.7 (Zydus) | 75.2 (Dolphin) | 2.5 (Medley) |

(Continued)

*Table 5.1* (Continued)

| Name of drug | No. of manufacturers | Market leader Rs (company) | Most expensive Rs (company) | Least expensive Rs (company) |
|---|---|---|---|---|
| Ranitidine (150 mg, pack size 10) | 48 | 4.1 (GSK) | 25.5 (Ranbaxy) | 2.7 (Welcure) |
| Methylergometrine injection (0.200 pack size) | 22 | 22.8 (Novartis) | 22.8 (Novartis) | 1.72 (Zydus) |
| Iron syrup (pack size 1) | 113 | 47.9 (Franco Indian) | 262.2 (Glenmark) | 11.3 (GSK) |
| Paracetamol (500 mg, pack size 10) | 62 | 8.2 (GSK) | 12.2 (Hetero) | 1.9 (UK Generics) |
| Diclofenac (50 mg, pack size 10) | 53 | 20.0 (Novartis) | 39.7 (Dr. Reddy's) | 1.7 (Lark) |
| Salbutamol inhaler (100y, pack size 200) | 6 | 66.7 (Cipla) | 66.7 (Cipla) | 61.9 (German Remedies) |
| Cetirizine (10 mg, pack size 10) | 80 | 27.8 (GSK) | 35.8 (Bactolac) | 0.98 (Khandelwal) |
| Fluoxetine (20 mg, pack size 10) | 27 | 28.9 (Cadila) | 38.6 (Wockhardt) | 4.2 (Ind-Swift) |
| Sodium valproate (200 mg, pack size 10) | 19 | 33.8 (Sun) | 44.2 (Modi) | 11.9 (Ind-Swift) |

*Source*: Compiled by the author from Selvaraj and Farooqui (2012).

In the atorvastatin market, Ranbaxy is the market leader and the price leader despite the availability of much cheaper brands. Similar trends are seen in other therapeutic markets also. All brands and generics of all drugs in India are expected to ensure the same quality standards, and therefore the higher prices of some brands cannot be attributed to superior quality. Firms are able to maintain their market leadership position, even when their prices are the highest, primarily on account of their promotional activities. The new methodology for fixing the ceiling prices of drugs has forced price leaders, in a number of cases, to reduce prices substantially. Up to February 2014, 404 formulations exhibited a reduction in the highest price to retailer. Of these 404 formulations, 112 (28 per cent) displayed a reduction of above 40 per cent in the prices of price leaders, while 101 (25 per cent) displayed a reduction in prices of between 25 and 40 per cent. The prices of price leaders fell up to 25 per cent in the case of 191 formulations (47 per cent) (Rajya Sabha 2014). This is certain to benefit patients who pay for medicines from out of their pockets. A market-based approach, in its true sense, should favour efficient firms. Ideally, inefficient firms (those that charge high prices) should have been compelled to bring down their prices to the levels of efficient firms (those which offer the lowest prices for the same products). From this perspective, the approach of NPPP 2012 is at best a distorted market-based approach.

Though NPPP 2012 claims that 'under the market based pricing, the pricing would be based on widely available information in the public domain . . . which would result in more transparent and fair pricing',[9] the actual calculation of ceiling price is based on proprietary data, which is prohibitively expensive and not available in the public domain. Section 4(vi) of NPPP 2012 states:

> ceiling price will be fixed on the basis of readily monitorable market based data (MDB). To begin with, the basis for this readily monitorable market data would be the data available with the pharmaceuticals market data specializing company – IMS Health (IMS) (GoI 2012a: 12).

IMS Health is an MNC that was founded in 1954 in the US. It specialises in the compilation of market data in health and pharmaceuticals. Obtaining pharmaceutical market data for India from IMS Health for just one year would cost about Rs 1.8 million.[10] Most of the individual researchers and research institutes in India cannot afford to conduct research on the new pharmaceutical pricing system in India based on IMS Health data. The University Grants Commission (UGC), which is the umbrella organisation governing the university system in India, is a major provider of research grants in the country. The maximum grant amount available for major UGC research projects in the social sciences is Rs 1.5 million, which includes the salary of research assistants, travel expenses, and other expenses like the purchase of computers and books.[11] Even the entire grant of a UGC major research project would not be sufficient to buy a year's worth of pharmaceutical market data from IMS Health.

It comes as no surprise, therefore, that the discourse in India on the likely impact of NPPP 2012 and DPCO 2013 has been very limited, although a number of civil society organisations and academics are working in the area of the drug price control system in India. Empirical studies on NPPP 2012 and DPCO 2013 have come from only one organisation in India – the Public Health Foundation of India (PHFI).[12] The data that the NPPA relies upon to arrive at the ceiling price is not available to the public. Therefore, it is not possible to ascertain the transparency and fairness of the ceiling prices through independent studies by the public. The NPPA is bound by a legal agreement with IMS Health to maintain the confidentiality of the market data supplied to it. The Department of Pharmaceuticals, in an affidavit to the Supreme Court of India in 2013, is said to have admitted that it is 'under obligation not to share the data with third party as per memorandum with IMS Health' (ISID-PHFI 2014).

Some problems in the data of IMS Health have been pointed out from time to time. The study by ISID-PHFI (2014) finds that IMS Health's market data are generated using a sampling method. IMS Health collects data from a sample of 5,600 stockists, and these data are extrapolated to the total number of stockists (around 25,000) to generate the total sales audit database. However, the details of the methodology used and its limitations and biases are not known (*ibid.*). Since the IMS Health estimates are based on sampling, the market estimates might vary depending on the methodology and the sample size. A comparison of the market estimates of IMS Health and AIOCD AWACS (a pharmaceutical market research company established by All Indian Origin Chemists & Distributers in collaboration with Trikaal Mediinfotech) revealed that their annual sales estimates for 2012 for the top 300 selling brands were Rs 222,570 million and Rs 212,110 million, respectively. Differences were also observed in the sales value and ranking of brands. Lantus, marketed by Sanofi Aventis, was ranked 14 in the IMS Health data with annual sales of Rs 1,510 million, whereas the same brand was ranked 91 with annual sales of Rs 750 million by AIOCD AWACS.

The report of the Drug Price Control Review Committee (GoI 1999) points out a few other lacunae of the data generated by IMS Health. The report states:

> The ORG-MARG [IMS Health] study on trends in price index of pharmaceutical formulations (1995–1998) conducted in March, 1999 brings out that the pharma market during the said period increased by 9.3 per cent and the price index increased by 10.6 per cent. It implies that there was a decline in the quantity produced during this period which is not factually correct. While working out the index numbers for each year, the base year figures have been

substantially changed by ORG-MARG for which no satisfactory reasoning has been given. Clearly a statistical bias appears to have been introduced to keep the index depressed. For instance (i) in table 3.1.1 the value in 1994 is worked out by taking the quantity of 1995 and prices of 1994, resulting in to a lower value. And to work out the change in the price index, the value in each of the base year has been jacked up. Same is true of other tables/exercises given in the report. Appropriately, a common base figure (1994) should have [been] taken to arrive at a realistic assessment of the increase in prices in 1998. . . . Moreover, the prices given in the ORG report are the price at which drugs are sold to the wholesale chemist. The retail prices for the consumer are those which are printed on the pack and which normally are changed by the chemist after adding the local taxes etc. Therefore, the tendency of many of the manufacturers to retain the price for the whole seller static while increasing the consumer price will not reflect the real increase through the ORG study. In view of these weaknesses, the committee does not consider their assessment as reliable.

(quoted in Srinivasan and Anurag 2004: 32–33)

The ISID-PHFI (2014) study also finds discrepancies between IMS Health's market data and the conclusions arrived at by NPPA based on IMS Health's data. The study discovered that, in the cases of 33 NLEM formulations, only one manufacturer held at least 1 per cent of the market share. But the NPPA identified more than one manufacturer with over 1 per cent of the market share for the same formulations.

There are serious concerns about the transparency and fairness of the ceiling prices arrived at by NPPA using the IMS Health data. Lack of clarity in the critical parameters of IMS Health's data, which form the foundations of the market-based approach to the regulation of drug prices, is a major concern. Lack of access to this data by the public makes independent scrutiny impossible. The public is left with no option but to believe that the ceiling prices notified by the NPPA are fair and have been arrived at by a transparent methodology.

## DPCO 2013

Following NPPP 2012, the new DPCO was announced on 15 May 2013 under Section 3 of the Essential Commodities Act, 1955. While NPPP 2012 provided the broad approach of the new price control system, DPCO 2013 gives the precise details of the operationalisation of the new approach. The new DPCO (GoI 2013b: 6) provides the following formula for arriving at ceiling prices:

$$P(c) = P(s) \times (1 + (M/100))$$

where
P(c) is the ceiling price
P(s) is the average price to the retailer of all brands and generics of a medicine having at least a share of 1 per cent of the total market turnover, on the basis of the moving annual turnover of that medicine
M is the margin allowed to the retailer and its value is 16.

When the number of manufacturers having at least 1 per cent share of the total market turnover of a drug is more than five, the simple average is used to arrive at P(s). But in the case of drugs with fewer than five manufacturers holding more than 1 per cent market share, a different formula is used to arrive at the average price (*ibid.*: 7):

$$P(s) = Pm \{1 - (Pi1+Pi2+. . .) / (N*100)\}$$

where
Pm is the price to the retailer of the highest-priced scheduled formulation under consideration
Pi is the percentage reduction in the average price to the retailer of other strengths and dosage forms in the list of scheduled formulations with reference to the highest-priced formulation taken for calculating the average price to the retailer of such strengths and dosage forms
N is the number of such other strengths or dosage forms or both in the list of scheduled formulations.

Thereafter, the formula for arriving at the ceiling price P(c) is applied. Local taxes are applicable on the ceiling prices of drugs. Therefore, MRP = P(c) + local taxes as applicable.

The ceiling prices of scheduled drugs under the new DPCO were based at the outset on the market data in May 2012.[13] Revision in the ceiling price based on moving annual turnover is to be carried out five years from the date of fixing of ceiling prices, or as and when the NLEM is revised.[14] However, the ceiling prices will be revised every year to accommodate changes in the wholesale price index (WPI). The government will revise the ceiling prices based on the WPI of the previous year as declared by the Department of Industrial Promotion and Policy on

1 April every year. The DPCO of 2013 also provides that the prices of scheduled formulations specified in the first schedule of DPCO 1995, fixed and notified under the provisions of DPCO 1995 up to 31 May 2012 or after 31 May 2012, would remain effective for one year from the date of notification of such prices.[15]

A comparison of the ceiling prices fixed under DPCO 2013 and the MRP of the market leader (Table 5.2) shows that there will be a considerable reduction in the prices.

A comparison of the prices of these 10 drugs (Table 5.2) shows an overall reduction of about 20 per cent from the prices of market leaders. Of the 10 drugs we analysed, the price of only one drug increased. The downward movement of prices will benefit the majority of patients, since price leaders have also been the market leaders in many cases in the pharmaceuticals market in India. The fact that market leaders are also the price leaders, or their prices are among the highest for any particular drug, indicates that the majority of patients have been prescribed higher-priced medicines, although much cheaper alternatives have been available in the market.

In order to ensure the availability of scheduled drugs (price-controlled drugs), the new DPCO provides that the government will monitor their supply. Any manufacturer intending to discontinue the production of scheduled formulations is required to issue a public notice and inform the government at least six months in advance. The government may, in the interests of the public, direct the manufacturer to continue production for a maximum of one year.[16] Although only the prices of scheduled formulations will be fixed, DPCO 2013 provides for the monitoring of the prices of non-scheduled formulations by the government. The prices of non-scheduled formulations will not be allowed to increase by more than 10 per cent per year.

The new DPCO incorporates provisions to discourage firms from exploring escape routes, as we saw in the previous section, by regulating the introduction of dosage forms not listed in the NLEM. Any firm wanting to launch a new dosage form of an NLEM drug (other than the specified dosage form included in the NLEM) would have to obtain the prior approval of the government. Additionally, the prices of such formulations will be fixed by the government.[17] Given these hurdles, firms would not be interested in producing new dosage forms of essential drugs to escape price control. However, these regulations are not applicable to dosage forms of essential medicines not listed in the NLEM, which existed prior to the new DPCO. For example, a firm that was already marketing paracetamol 650 mg tablets can circumvent price

Table 5.2 Comparison of DCPO 2013 ceiling prices and MRPs of market leaders for selected drugs

| Drug | Therapeutic area | DPCO 2013 Ceiling price (Rs per tab./vial) | Brand leader | Market leader price (Rs per tab./vial) | % change as compared to brand leader's price |
|---|---|---|---|---|---|
| Paracetamol (500 mg) | Analgesic | 0.94 | Calpol | 1.65 | −43.0 |
| Sodium valproate (200 mg) | Anticonvulsant | 3.07 | Valprol | 2.44 | +25.8 |
| Azithromycin (50 mg) | Anti-infective | 19.86 | Azithral | 30.67 | −35.2 |
| Vancomycin hydrochloride (inj. 500 mg) | Anti-infective | 330.60 | Vansafe-CP | 355.00 | −6.9 |
| Ethambutol (800 mg) | Anti-tuberculosis | 3.74 | Combutol | 4.53 | −17.4 |
| Lamivudine (150 mg) + Nevirapine (200 mg) + Stavudine (930 mg) | Antiretroviral | 17.29 | Triomune | 22.10 | −21.8 |
| Imatinib (400 mg) | Cancer | 268.33 | Veenat | 352.00 | −23.8 |
| Atorvastatin (5 mg) | Blood cholesterol | 3.82 | Storvas | 5.20 | −26.5 |
| Metoclopramide (10 mg) | Antiemetic (used for treating nausea and vomiting) | 1.04 | Perinorm | 1.50 | −30.7 |
| Glibenclamide (2.5 mg) | Anti-diabetic | 0.48 | Daonil | 0.53 | −9.4 |

Source: NPPA notifications dated 14 June 2013 revising the prices of 151 drugs based on DPCO 2013, http://www.nppaindia.nic.in/wh-new-2013/wh-new-16-2013.html (accessed on 28 November 2014); for information on brand leaders and their prices: unpublished note circulated by Amit Sengupta, Jan Swasthya Abhiyan (People's Health Movement), comparing ceiling prices with MRPs.

regulation by focusing on this dosage form. The objective of DPCO 2013 is to ensure that firms should not shift their focus from the production of NLEM dosage forms to dosage forms of essential medicines not listed in the NLEM as a business strategy to escape price control. In the process, however, the DPCO gives undue advantage to non-NLEM dosage forms of essential medicines that pre-date the new price control order.

The DPCO of 2013 also discriminates against efficient producers (who sell drugs at lower prices). While firms are required to bring down their prices to the level of the ceiling price, firms selling at prices below the ceiling are not allowed to increase their prices to the ceiling level. Such firms are required to continue with their existing MRPs, and only the annual increase (or decrease) as per the WPI is allowed.[18] Though this provision appears to be well intentioned, it results in different ceiling prices for different producers. As in the case of NPPP 2012, the DPCO of 2013 also does not favour efficient firms; ideally, a market-based approach should reward efficient producers.

The role of doctors in the pharma market, combined with a cost-based pricing methodology, allowed firms to maintain a market leadership position along with price leadership. The cost-based price control methodology, by default, permitted firms that were able to show higher costs of production to maintain higher prices for scheduled drugs.[19] Assuming that prescription patterns remain the same, a downward movement of prices would benefit most patients. At the same time, however, the new approach would result in eroding the margins of market leaders. AIOCD AWACS estimates a loss of about Rs 5,300 million to the industry on account of implementation of the new DPCO. Pfizer alone will see a reduction of Rs 540 million (Krishnan 2013a). The pharma industry in India has had a mixed response to the new DPCO. While the industry is concerned about the decline in margins as a result of the new DPCO, it is appreciative of the steps to eliminate the cost-based pricing methodology.[20]

Though the analysis in Table 5.2 shows that the new market-based pricing methodology would benefit patients more in the immediate future compared to the cost-based pricing methodology, this may not be the case in the long run. In the cost-based approach of the earlier DPCO, upward movement in prices was allowed only when the cost of production went up. But in the new approach, prices increase in tune with the WPI irrespective of the cost of production. This would result in the prices of essential medicines going up every year. Sengupta *et al.* (2008) found that under DPCO 1995, there was no increase in the prices of scheduled drugs.[21] The results of that study are presented in Table 5.3.

Table 5.3  Price index for drugs under DPCO 1995

|  | 1996 | 2000 | 2004 | 2005 | 2006 |
|---|---|---|---|---|---|
| Paasche Index for 118 drugs | 100.0 | 110.3 | 134.8 | 139.3 | 139.9 |
| Drugs under price control (DPCO 1995) | 100.0 | 93.0 | 98.6 | 101.1 | 100.0 |
| Non-DPCO | 100.0 | 179.0 | 219.0 | 235.0 | 237.0 |

Source: Sengupta et al. (2008).

We see from the table that the price of the basket of drugs as a whole increased by 39.9 per cent between 1996 and 2006. The prices of drugs under DPCO did not show any increase. Thus, DPCO 1995 was effective in pegging down the retail prices of scheduled drugs, with no rise taking place in 10 years. Linking ceiling prices to WPI in DPCO 2013 will harm patients in the long run, while it would benefit firms.

In many respects, the new DPCO is an improvement upon the previous DPCO. In DPCO 2013, imported drugs are also subject to the ceiling prices notified by the government. In the earlier regime, importers were allowed a 50 per cent markup over the declared landed cost. No mechanism was in place to verify the cost of production in foreign countries; therefore, the declared cost was considered as the actual. This provided an opportunity for MNCs to import rather than produce drugs in India and use the transfer pricing loophole to evade the effects of the DPCO.

Despite the improvements that the new DPCO incorporates and its adoption of a market-based approach, NPPP 2012 has not done enough to unleash market forces. When market forces are at play, competition would determine prices. In a competitive market, the brand that sells at the lowest price would have the highest market share. But the opposite is the case in India's pharma market. The role of the specialist (the doctor) in decision making prevents the free play of market forces. In order to correct this situation, several committees appointed by the Government of India have recommended that doctors give prescriptions using only the generic names of drugs. This move would have brought competition into the pharmaceuticals market, which would have benefited patients greatly. The prices at which pharma firms in India supply drugs to the Tamil Nadu Medical Service Corporation (TNMSC) indicate that medicines can be priced at much lower levels than they are priced today. While ciprofloxacin (50 mg, 10 tablets) is supplied to TNMSC at Rs 9.82, Ranbaxy, the market leader, charges a price that is 10 times higher (Rs 98.6) (Selvaraj et al. 2012). Though it may be argued that TNMSC prices are lower, since firms sell in large quantities to TNMSC, this does not justify a 10-fold difference in price. Thus, great potential exists for price competition for the benefit of patients. Prescriptions made in generic terms would open the door to price competition in the pharmaceuticals market. Unfortunately, only half-hearted efforts have been made in this direction in India.

## Initiatives towards mandatory prescription in generic names

The Ministry of Health and Family Welfare has often been in the limelight for its efforts to make medicines more affordable for patients. In October 2012, the ministry issued a directive to the state drug licensing authorities under Section 33(P) of the Drugs and Cosmetics Act, 1940, to issue or renew licences only of drugs with generic names, and not drugs with brand names.[22] This move was expected to benefit patients by bringing down the prices of medicines considerably.

It appears, however, that there are many loose ends in the regulation that prevent the benefits of the new directive from being transferred to patients. The directive permitting only generic names in manufacturing and distribution has to be accompanied by another directive requiring practitioners to prescribe using only generic names. The initiatives taken in this direction by some state governments and the union Ministry of Health and Family Welfare target less than half of all prescriptions. The directive of the Delhi government is applicable only to practitioners in hospitals empanelled in the Delhi Government Employee Health Scheme (DGEHS).[23] The majority of private sector hospitals are not empanelled with DGEHS, and patients visiting non-DGEHS hospitals will not benefit from the directive regarding generic name prescriptions. Similarly, the directive from the union health ministry is also applicable only to hospitals under its control. With the private sector emerging as the major provider of health services in the country, directives on generic name prescriptions have to be made applicable to all practitioners in India irrespective of whether they practise in the private or the public sector.

The other problem with current guidelines on prescriptions is that they do not require prescriptions 'only in generic names'. A press note issued by the Karnataka Medical Council in August 2012 mentions that doctors registered with the Karnataka Medical Council are required to write their prescriptions 'legibly and readable by a pharmacist. . . . Trade name and within brackets the generic name'.[24] Such guidelines or practices will nullify the intended outcomes of the directive on generic name prescription.

As multiple agencies are involved in the regulation of health care, it is important to formulate standard treatment guidelines (STGs) to which all concerned agencies must adhere. Such guidelines need to state clearly that prescriptions of medicines should be made only in generic names. The report of the Steering Committee on Health for the 12th Five Year Plan has recommended the establishment of STGs incorporating generic prescriptions for drugs in the NLEM. The report states that '[STG] in the public and private sectors is a priority to address drug resistance, promote rational prescriptions and use of drugs, and contain health care costs' (GoI 2012b: 57).

Transmission of the benefits of doing away with brand names also calls for fixing responsibilities for chemists, the selling point of medicines. Medicines are a unique category of products where the consumer – the patient – does not make the selection. This situation would continue even with the shift to generic prescriptions. The chemist is not required to sell the lowest-priced generic drug. In the absence of a law requiring chemists to dispense the lowest-priced drug, doing away with brand names will only lead to a shift in the focus of the promotional activities of pharmaceutical companies from the doctor to the chemist. The move to generic names for medicines will benefit patients only if it becomes mandatory for chemists to sell the lowest-priced drug. This would result in prices moving downward, making medicines more affordable. Unfortunately, so far there are no regulations that would make the chemist sell the lowest-priced drugs.

The underlying assumption when moving to generic names and generic name prescription is that all drugs available in the market meet the prescribed quality parameters, and that hence it is safe for patients to shop around for the best prices irrespective of the manufacturer. In India, drugs are expected to meet the quality standards prescribed by the WHO. But discussions in the Parliament of India reveal that 4.7 per cent of the drugs in the Indian market are substandard, and 0.4 per cent are spurious. The shift to generic names may provide a perverse incentive to producers of substandard and spurious drugs (Lok Sabha 2012). It is highly important that our regulatory system maintains zero tolerance of medicines that are not up to the prescribed quality standards, that all manufacturing units conform to WHO quality standards, and that substandard and spurious drugs do not enter the supply chain and land up in chemists' shops. The state drug licensing authorities need to ensure that quality parameters are complied with in production facilities, and chemists need to ensure that they do not stock drugs that fail to comply with quality standards.

### Other shortcomings of DPCO 2013

Instances of rising prices of inputs call for revision in the ceiling prices. The DPCO of 2013 has a stringent provision for revision in such situations. It provides for revision only when

> the number of manufacturers of a scheduled formulation, having price of a scheduled formulation more than or equal to seventy five percent of the ceiling price fixed and notified by the Government, has decreased by twenty five percent or more than the number of manufacturers as existing on the reference date.[25]

This means that for a drug *x*, for which the ceiling price is Rs 10 per tablet and there are 20 manufacturers of which 12 sell the drug at more than Rs 7.50, the ceiling price would be revised only when the number of firms selling the drug at prices above Rs 7.50 has decreased at least by three. In other words, DPCO 2013 would revise prices only after evidence of a crisis in the industry has been manifested. With the exit clause in Section 21(2) of DPCO 2013, a 25 per cent decline in the number of firms would mean that the industry is in a severe crisis. This is not a desirable policy instrument, and the DPCO should have provisions for firms to approach the NPPA for revision of prices as and when required. However, DPCO 2013 provides that in extraordinary situations, government may allow increase or decrease in ceiling prices. But what constitutes an extraordinary situation is not specified.

The DPCO of 2013, like its predecessors, lacks the power to prosecute violations. The new DPCO states that any manufacturer selling a scheduled drug at prices above the ceiling price will be liable to deposit the overcharged amount along with the interest thereon. However, the DPCO does not have any provision for compounding of offences or imposing a fine for the offence. The NPPA has published statistics on overcharging and recovery thereof ever since its inception in August 1997. In January 2014, Rs 33,123.70 million was owed to the NPPA on account of overcharging, of which it managed to recover only Rs 2,741.2 million,[26] i.e. only about 8.3 per cent of what was owed to it. The biggest violator of the pricing norms, and the biggest defaulter in handing over the overcharged amount, has been Cipla. The amount overcharged by Cipla between August 1997 and January 2014 is Rs 20,965.5 million, which is 63.3 per cent of the total overcharged amount by more than 250 firms during the same period.[27] Cipla has not handed over any overcharged amount to the government; these dues account for 69 per cent of the amount to be recovered.

The State Drug Controllers who are in charge of enforcing the DPCO provisions have to resort to prosecution and arrest in cases of violation under the provisions of the Essential Commodity Act. There is no provision for compounding of offences. The lengthy procedure of prosecution sometimes deters state officials from taking action. Moreover, for such action, numerous agencies are involved, such as the State Drug Administrations, police authorities and the judiciary. The effect of enforcement of the DPCO is sometimes not achieved along the desired lines. Hence, the *Interim Report of the Committee to Examine the Span of Price Control for Medicines* (GoI 2004) recommends that it would be appropriate to examine whether provisions can be made in the Essential Commodities Act/DPCO for compounding of offences and for the levy of fines and penalties for violation of the provisions of the DPCO. The Drug Price Control Review Committee (GoI 1999) had also recommended providing greater powers to the Drugs Control Authorities to dispose of small and petty offences or contraventions by a provision for compounding such offences in the DPCO. This would obviate the necessity of launching prosecutions in minor cases. The Seventh Report of the Standing Committee on Chemicals and Fertilizers on *Availability and Price Management of Drugs and Pharmaceuticals* (GoI 2005b) observes that

> the stringent action of prosecution under the Essential Commodities Act sometimes does not lead to desired results. Since there are no provisions for compounding of offences and no provisions of fine or penalties for the violation of the DPCO in accordance with the Essential Commodities Act and the only provisions available are for prosecution and recovery of the overcharged amount, the State Governments find the process cumbersome for initiating any action.

The Pronab Sen Committee (GoI 2005a) had recommended that the DPCO, which is at present an order under the Essential Commodities Act, 1955, should be converted into a legislative enactment – the Drugs and Therapeutic (Regulation) Act.

## Conclusion

A market-based approach to the regulation of drug prices in India was adopted in the 1990s, in line with the philosophy of economic reforms introduced in the Indian economy. The principle of essentiality of medicines was done away with when the market-based approach was introduced. But the essentiality principle was brought back into the drug price control system through the intervention of the judiciary. The essentiality principle was incorporated in NPPP 2012 and DPCO 2013 along with the market-based approach in the drug price control mechanism. The essentiality principle is used to identify drugs for which prices are to be controlled, and the market-based approach is used to arrive at the ceiling prices.

The current drug price control system in India is an improvement upon the previous one in many respects. Our brief analysis shows that the prices of many widely prescribed medicines will decrease. Still, there are a few areas where the new system has serious deficiencies. The most important of these is the lack of transparency in the data used by NPPA to arrive at ceiling prices. The data are not available to the public, and, therefore, the transparency and fairness of the ceiling prices arrived at by the NPPA cannot be ascertained by independent scrutiny. Further, the new system does nothing to bring in price competition, which is strikingly absent in the Indian pharmaceuticals market. Even with the best intentions of making essential drugs available at reasonable prices, the new drug price control system will not ensure affordability of medicines for all. The 'reasonable price' may not be affordable for all. The DPCO alone cannot ensure affordability. Health being a state subject, the state governments also play an important role in ensuring access to medicines. The efforts of states like Rajasthan and Tamil Nadu to buy essential medicines in bulk and efficiently distribute them to patients through public sector hospitals are praiseworthy.

## Notes

1 Explaining the reasons for adopting a market-based approach to regulating drug prices, NPPP 2012 states that the Indian economy is market-driven, and that the prices of manufactured products are determined by market forces. See Section 3.3(iv) of NPPP 2012 (GoI 2012a: 10).
2 For further details, see Chapter 1.
3 See Section 3.1(i) of NPPP 2012 (GoI 2012a: 6–7).
4 National List of Essential Medicines of India, Department of Pharmaceuticals, Ministry of Chemicals and Fertilizers, Government of India, http://pharmaceuticals.gov.in/nlem.pdf (accessed on 24 December 2015).
5 WHO Model List of Essential Medicines, http://apps.who.int/iris/bitstream/10665/93142/1/EML_18_eng.pdf?ua=1 (accessed on 27 November 2014).
6 See Section 3.1(ii) of NPPP 2012 (GoI 2012a: 7).
7 For details, see National List of Essential Medicines of India, Preamble, pp. 4–5, http://pharmaceuticals.gov.in/nlem.pdf (accessed on 27 November 2014).

8   See Section 3.2(ii) of NPPP 2012 (GoI 2012a: 8).
9   Section 3.3(ii) of NPPP 2012 (*ibid.*: 9).
10  This was revealed during a discussion with Dr Sakthivel Selvaraj of the Public Health Foundation of India, which has purchased IMS Health data to evaluate the effectiveness of NPPP 2012 and DPCO 2013.
11  See *UGC Research Projects for Teachers: XII Plan Guidelines (2012–2017)*, http://www.ugc.ac.in/pdfnews/7716504_12th-plan-guidelines.pdf (accessed on 27 November 2014).
12  Researchers at PHFI have published three studies on NPPP 2012 and DPCO 2013: Selvaraj and Farooqui (2012), Selvaraj *et al.* (2012) and ISID-PHFI (2014).
13  Section 9.3 of DPCO 2013 (see GoI 2013b: 10).
14  Section 18(i) of DPCO 2013 (*ibid.*: 16).
15  There have been cases where the ceiling price was fixed on the basis of DPCO 1995 even after the notification of DPCO 2013. The NPPA notified the revised prices of 86 scheduled drugs on 10 June 2013 under DPCO 1995.
16  Section 21.2 of DPCO 2013 (GoI 2013b: 18).
17  For details, see Section 15 of DPCO 2013 (*ibid.*: 14–15).
18  For details, see Section 13 of DPCO 2013 (*ibid.*: 13).
19  The cost-based pricing methodology of DPCO 1995 is discussed in detail in Chapter 1.
20  Director General of the Organisation of Pharmaceutical Producers of India, Tapan Ray, is reported to have said that DPCO 2013 would cut into both the sales and the margins of companies substantially. At the same time, he appreciated the new system, as it was more transparent and prudent compared to the cost-based system. See *Economic Times* (2013).
21  The study by Sengupta *et al.* (2008) covered the retail prices of 118 drugs contributing 54 per cent of the retail market. Among the 118 drugs, drugs in the EDL represented 45 per cent of the market (24 per cent of the retail market); drugs under price control represented 22 per cent (12 per cent of the retail market); and drugs not in the EDL or under price control represented 33 per cent (18 per cent of the retail market). The retail prices of drugs were adjusted against the consumer price index. The data were then analysed using a Paasche Index to compute the changes in medicine prices over 10 years.
22  The circular was issued on 1 October 2012.
23  Office Order F.25(III)/DGEHS/243/DHS/2011–12/10865–96 dated 24 February 2012, DGEHS, Directorate of Health Services, Government of NCT of Delhi.
24  Press note No. 08/12 dated 24 August 2012 addressed to the editors of *Times of India, Deccan Herald, Hindu*, and *Indian Express*.
25  See Section 18(ii) of DPCO 2013, in GoI (2013b: 17).
26  'Year-wise Break-Up of Overcharged Amount from Inception (August 1997) of NPPA to 2013–14 (up to January 2014)' , http://www.nppaindia.nic.in/index1.html (accessed on 27 December 2014).
27  Computed by author based on data on overcharging and recovery available at *ibid.*

# Conclusion

The objective of this book has been to analyse the impact of policy reforms in the pharmaceuticals sector since 1994 on the important areas of exports and imports, R&D, and prices of medicines. These issues have been studied in detail in the preceding chapters. Chapter 1 reviewed the development of the Indian pharmaceutical industry since independence and discussed the policy changes that have taken place since the mid-1990s. We observed that under the liberalised policy regime, the pharmaceutical industry has thrived in terms of growth in production, sales, exports, and R&D investments. The market concentration (market share held by the top 5 and top 10 firms) showed an increase over the 15-year period between 1994–95 and 2011–12. The pharmaceutical industry continues to spend more on promotional activities than on R&D. The liberalisation of foreign investment has resulted in a spate of takeovers of major Indian firms by MNCs, which is seen as a way to cut short the time and effort involved in organic growth. This raises concerns about the long-term vibrancy of the Indian pharmaceutical sector.

Chapter 2 found that the Indian pharmaceutical industry underwent a structural change in its export orientation with the changes in the IPR regime. There are two aspects to this shift. First, the sector has become more export-oriented as a response to the threat of reduced domestic operability and in order to continue to remain in business. Second, of the two export categories of bulk drugs and formulations, the focus has shifted to formulations. The acceleration in formulations exports has been driven by the US and the African continent. The share of exports to Europe has shown a declining trend throughout the period. The share of exports to neighbouring countries (Asia) and to Latin America has also remained at relatively lower levels. Africa being a major source of growth for exports, the over-zealous drive for IPR enforcement under the aegis of anti-counterfeiting initiatives in the region, especially Eastern Africa, is a cause of concern for the Indian pharmaceutical industry.

The change in export orientation to the formulations segment has resulted in a change in the production structure. In order to maintain price competitiveness in the international market, firms had to look for options for reducing costs, a new compulsion which they did not face when they were focused mainly on the domestic market. The cost-based drug price control system, which covered a substantial part of the retail medicine market, assured a pre-defined rate of profits; hence, the incentive was not on reducing cost but on promoting the product. As a result, imports of bulk drugs, intermediates and other raw materials from cheaper sources began to increase, and domestic production from basic stages began to decline. Though there has been a decline in the growth of production in the bulk drugs category (which includes not only the final bulk drugs but also their intermediates), it should be noted that the industry is now focusing more on the production of bulk drugs at the higher end of the value chain. Until 1994, the DP required the production of bulk drugs within India from the penultimate stage. Now there is no such compulsion, and firms are free to import. Currently, about half of the imports of bulk drugs and other raw materials are sourced from China alone. Heavy dependence on a single country for raw materials puts the industry at risk.

Chapter 2 establishes that there is a positive relationship between export orientation and the import of raw materials. The abolition of the ratio parameter and reduction in import duties facilitated imports by large producers. On the other hand, the implementation of GMPs led to the closure of a number of bulk drug producers in the small-scale sector, affecting the production of bulk drugs. As the import of bulk drugs and other raw materials continues to grow, the industry faces a negative trade balance in the bulk drugs category. However, in formulations, the industry has a substantial surplus in trade which offsets the trade deficit of the bulk drugs segment; so overall, the industry has a trade surplus. In formulations, imports have not experienced any surge, since the Patents Act incorporates high patentability criteria which limit the number of patented drugs. It also includes a provision for the continued manufacture of those patented medicines for which Indian companies had obtained marketing approvals prior to January 2005. Import of formulations, though very limited, is undertaken mostly by MNCs. In the export of formulations, on the other hand, the leading players are all Indian firms.

Chapter 3 found that the policy reforms aimed at boosting pharmaceutical R&D include liberalisation of foreign investment and foreign technology collaborations, exemptions from tax obligations, exemptions from drug price regulation, and product patent rights for pharmaceutical innovations. The analysis of the R&D expenditure of pharmaceutical firms shows that there had been a growth in R&D intensity since 2000–01, but this stagnated after 2005–06. The breakdown of R&D expenditure into capital and current expenditures shows that change in the capital R&D investment does not explain the stagnation in the post 2005–06 period: one may expect firms to incur capital R&D investment to set up new R&D facilities or expand current R&D facilities, after which there is no need of capital expenditure in the next few years. The analysis of leading firms showed that the decline/stagnation has been primarily on account of the review of their R&D strategies by two leading firms – Ranbaxy and Dr. Reddy's. After their initial success in developing a few molecules in-house, they hiked their R&D spending considerably, reaching up to 18 per cent of sales turnover. But when they realised that the failure rate was quite high and that MNCs were not interested in developing the (out-licensed) molecules unless they fit into their business model, the direct outcome was the pruning back of R&D expenditure.

The R&D profile of the Indian pharmaceutical industry includes the development of generics, new drug delivery systems and new drug development. The data on patents granted to leading Indian pharmaceutical firms by the US Patent and Trademark Office show that patents on new products account for only 5 per cent of all patents; the rest involve new processes, new dosage forms and drug delivery systems. It appears that the growth in R&D intensity of Indian pharma firms has been the outcome of the fear of shrinking market opportunities – the fear that they would no longer be able to reverse-engineer and produce new drugs – rather than induced by the incentives of the new patent regime. Analysis of the new drug pipelines of leading Indian pharma firms shows that their R&D activities are increasingly concentrated on global lifestyle diseases and that they do not find a sufficient profit opportunity in local diseases such as TB and malaria.

The policy reforms, however, paved the way for the 'globalisation' of the Indian pharmaceutical industry – it has now become part of the global production and development network of MNCs. The participation of Indian firms in the global network of MNCs has come as more of an income generation opportunity than as a means of competence building. The liberalisation measures were indeed aimed at making foreign investment and technology collaborations increasingly important channels for competence building. In contract research, collaborative research projects, and out-licensing and in-licensing partnerships, Indian firms have been partners of subordinate status who perform piecemeal projects in drug research and are not exposed to the whole process of new drug development. In these collaborations, the scope for transfer of technology and joint ownership of technology is also very limited. The subordinate status of Indian firms in the long run may result in a dependency relationship with MNCs. This can have deleterious consequences for the country in many ways. Being trusted allies in the global strategy of MNCs, Indian companies may lose interest in therapeutic areas that do not have a global presence (for example, tropical country diseases). These allies might also withhold from exercising compulsory licensing provisions, the TRIPS instrument to counter abuse of patent monopoly as well as to address national health emergencies. On the positive side, some of the leading Indian pharmaceutical firms have been investing the money gained from alliances with MNCs in building up capacities in new drug development.

The lack of capacity of Indian firms to develop new drugs, both in terms of S&T skills and financial resources, leaves them with no other option but to collaborate with MNCs. In the earlier policy regime, public sector companies and laboratories had played a major role in augmenting the S&T skills of private sector industry. Under the new policy regime, public sector companies have been assigned an inferior status, and a few of them have already been closed down. The aversion to indigenous innovations at the regulatory approval stages and at the promotional stages also encourages Indian firms to develop new drugs in collaboration with MNCs.

Under the new policy regime, R&D for neglected diseases has become a major challenge. Despite PPPs, soft loans, grants, and other incentives for pharmaceutical R&D, firms are not coming forward to invest in developing new drugs for neglected diseases. The success of the OSDD programme of the CSIR will depend on the willingness of the industry to take the product to the market. Since private industry has stayed away from the neglected diseases market, the only way out is the revival of public sector companies which had played a leading role in the earlier policy regime.

The liberalisation measures, on the other hand, have attracted foreign investment in pharmaceutical R&D in India. A number of foreign R&D centres have been set up in the country. But it has been revealed that the bulk of foreign investment in R&D in the pharma sector has been in the clinical phase, especially in phase III trials, and not in biology and chemistry research for new drug development. Phase III requires a large number of human subjects in the trials. Multinationals are attracted to India because of its large and ethnically diverse population that suffers from various ailments. A significant number of English-speaking people and a well-developed communications network with information technology capabilities are also advantages that India offers in clinical trials. A 2005 amendment in Schedule Y of the Drugs and Cosmetics Rules,

1945, removed the restrictions imposed on foreign players in conducting clinical trials in India. The amended rules require that clinical studies should be conducted in accordance with the principles of the Declaration of Helsinki, the Indian Good Clinical Practice Guidelines, and the ICMR's Ethical Guidelines for Biomedical Research on Humans. Despite all these requirements, and the establishment of the Clinical Trial Registry of India, unauthorised trials involving a large number of human subjects are rampant in many parts of the country. There have been recent instances of trials being conducted on women without obtaining their informed consent.

Chapter 4 provides an analysis of IPRs and access to medicines in India. The patent law in the country has played an important role in keeping the prices of drugs under control. Patent law does not directly interfere in pricing, but patentability criteria and other important provisions have implications for prices. The stringent patentability criteria adopted in the Patents Act have reduced the number of potential patented drugs in the country. This provides room for the operation of generics firms. Section 3(d) of the Patents Act eliminates the scope for frivolous patents and the evergreening of patents by providing that mere change in forms will not make an invention eligible for patent protection. The Patents Act also provides for the unabated supply of generics of mailbox patented drugs, providing patients with cost-effective substitutes. All these provisions in Indian patent law have resulted in fewer patented drugs, on the one hand, and more substitutes for patented drugs on the other – positive steps in the direction of enabling access to affordable medicines. In March 2012, India granted the first CL in the country on the grounds of affordability and availability. This move will enable cancer patients in the country to access the drug at 3 per cent of the patent holder's price. The Novartis case in the Supreme Court of India, rejecting the patent for its drug Glivec, serves as the test case for the validity of Section 3(d) of the Patents Act. The Supreme Court upheld the validity of Section 3(d) in this case.

Increasing instances of the use of TRIPS flexibilities by India has resulted in intense lobbying by MNCs, especially in the US, against India. They want the USTR to place India on its list of 'Priority Foreign Countries' in its Special 301 Report, so that the US can impose trade sanctions against India on account of Indian IPR laws. There is also mounting international pressure on India to provide data exclusivity protection in pharmaceuticals. India has not taken a decision so far on providing data exclusivity in pharmaceuticals.

It was observed in Chapter 5 that the drug price control system in India plays an important role in ensuring access to medicines at reasonable prices. The new drug price control system implemented under NPPP 2012 and DPCO 2013 is in many ways an improvement upon the previous DPCO. The analysis based on 10 drugs shows that the prices of widely used drugs will decline in many cases. Market leaders, who are also the price leaders or their prices are among the highest in the market, will be forced to bring down their prices. The new mechanism aims to strike a balance between the need for providing medicines to patients at reasonable prices and the need for creating an environment conducive to innovation and competition.

Despite the good intentions of the new system, the transparency and fairness of ceiling prices arrived at by the NPPA is questionable. The market data relied upon by NPPA for calculating ceiling prices are the proprietary data of an MNC, and are not available publicly. Lack of access of the public to the data makes independent scrutiny impossible. The limited study by ISID-PHFI (2014) shows discrepancies between the proprietary data and the conclusions arrived at by NPPA with regard to ceiling prices. The new system also falls short in initiating efforts to bring in price competition in the pharmaceutical market, which would have benefited patients much more. Enabling price competition is critically contingent upon changing prescription practice to only the generic names of drugs. There is not even a mention of this requirement in NPPP 2012 or DPCO 2013. Efforts thus far at different levels to implement the prescription of medicines by their generic names have been half-hearted at best.

The lack of enforcement powers is another major limitation of DPCO 2013. There is no provision for compounding of offences in the DPCO; if the provisions of the DPCO are violated, remedial actions have to be initiated under the provisions of the Essential Commodities Act, and not the DPCO. The lengthy process of prosecution sometimes deters state officials from taking action. As a result, the NPPA has been able to recover only a minuscule portion of the dues that are owed to it by drug companies on account of overpricing.

## Policy implications

The Indian pharmaceutical industry stands at a crossroads today, and it requires strong policy interventions to facilitate its onward progress. The policy reforms so far have had both positive and negative outcomes, as observed in the course of this book. Immediate interventions are needed in at least five areas to promote the further growth of the industry.

First, the SME segment of the pharmaceutical industry, which produces the bulk of the bulk drugs manufactured in the country, is struggling for survival. The implementation of Schedule M and competition from China are some of the important factors adversely affecting the ability of this segment to survive. These enterprises are also discriminated against by different government agencies while procuring medicines in bulk. Agencies like the Railways, the Steel Authority of India Limited, RITES Limited, and some state governments have laid down norms for turnover limits and size of the company, which prevents SMEs from participating in the tender process. While SAIL requires that only the top 100 companies based on sales turnover can apply for tenders, the Railways stipulates that the turnover of the applicant must be a minimum of Rs 500 million for participating in tenders for drug procurement (Alexander 2011). The drug procurement policy issued by the Government of Uttar Pradesh in May 2011 raised the annual turnover requirement from Rs 10 million in two of the last five years, to Rs 1,000 million for the last three years for companies from outside the state and Rs 250 million for the past three years for companies from within the state (*Indian Express* 2011). The turnover requirements in the drug procurement process are so huge that the SME segment becomes ineligible for participating in the tender process. Many committees appointed by the Government of India have emphasised the importance of SMEs in the pharmaceutical industry. It is very important to make a concerted effort towards the revival of SMEs in the pharmaceutical industry. Providing them a foothold in the drug procurement process should be a priority in the revival package for SMEs.

Second, bulk drug production faces huge challenges in India. Apart from the competition from China, another major concern is the environmental impact of bulk drug manufacturing – it is a highly polluting industry. Bulk drug manufacturing processes use numerous raw materials including solvents which generate solid wastes, liquid effluents and air emissions. The wastewater generated contains a high proportion of total dissolved solids and chemical oxygen demand, and is nonbiodegradable or only partially biodegradable. The Central Pollution Control Board has identified 17 industries as highly polluting; 'basic drugs and pharmaceuticals' are one among them.[1] Technologies like 'biocatalysts' which cut short the steps involved in the chemical process not only reduce the quantum of pollution generated in the production processes but also reduce the cost of manufacturing. This technology is in wide use in the US and EU in food processing and environment management (GoI 2008a). Since the EU and the US have shifted their bulk drug manufacturing to countries like India and China (through outsourcing), developed countries are not keen to develop biocatalysts for bulk drug manufacturing. Development of technologies which would cut short the number of chemical processes involved in bulk drug manufacturing would be an important step in the direction of reviving the bulk drug industry in India. Public sector laboratories and universities should be encouraged to take up this task. Public–private partnerships or collaborative projects involving bulk drug manufacturers, and public sector laboratories and universities, can further the development of new technologies for bulk drug manufacturing.

Third, an inadequate financing mechanism is a major problem facing new drug development in the country. Private venture capital is hesitant to fund pharma R&D projects due to its high-risk nature. In this context, the move by the National Innovation Council to come up with an India Inclusive Innovation Fund of Rs 5,000 million, which is to be increased to Rs 50,000 million in the next two years, to support Indian entrepreneurs with risk capital funding is welcome (GoI 2013d). The fund proposes to raise capital from a range of sources: seed fund contributions from the government and its agencies; contributions from various Indian public sector enterprises, banks, private investors, corporate, investment firms, etc. Though the Rs 50,000 million is a big amount, it will not be sufficient to fund many new drug discovery projects. Moreover, the Rs 50,000 million fund is to be shared among other industries as well. Even at just one-fourth of the average global investment that is required for the successful development of a new drug, Cadila, the first Indian firm to successfully develop an NCE through 100 per cent indigenous R&D, spent about Rs 12,500 million (US$250 million). Given the risky nature of pharma R&D, dedicated risk capital funding for the pharma sector under the leadership of the Government of India is highly desirable.

Fourth, the current price control system requires improvements at least in two aspects. One, the market data relied upon by NPPA for arriving at ceiling prices has to be made available to researchers for facilitating independent studies on the drug price control system in India. The market data of IMS Health used by NPPA are prohibitively expensive, so much so that even the entire research grant provided by the UGC for a major research project in the social sciences is not sufficient to buy this market data even for a single year. An assistant professor working at a central university in India would have to spend 32 months' worth of his/her gross salary to buy IMS Health market data for just one year. Two, the new drug price control system, which aims at facilitating competition in the pharmaceuticals sector, must have a component to facilitate price competition in the pharmaceuticals market. Despite the existence of a number of players in each therapeutic market, the difference in prices is very high.

This indicates that competitive forces are not at work in the pharmaceutical therapeutic market. Various committees appointed by the Government of India have recommended moving away from brand name prescription to generic name prescription to pave the way for competitive forces to determine prices. Since all drug manufacturing units in India are mandatorily required to comply with GMP standards, doing away with brand name prescription makes good sense. Prescription of medicines only in generic names will open the door to price competition in the pharmaceuticals market, and this would be a logical step forward in ensuring reasonable prices within a market-based framework.

Fifth, the Government of India has various incentive schemes in place to encourage R&D in drugs for neglected diseases. But firms have not come forth to invest their resources in neglected diseases. They have also been found to be uninterested in taking the technologies developed by public sector institutes to the market. Given this lack of interest in neglected diseases on the part of the private sector, the viable alternative appears to be the revival of public sector firms. The pumping in of money is important. Equally important is a transformation in the mind set of public sector firms, which need to become more performance-oriented and thus better competitors to private sector firms. The PPP strategies also need to be explored for incentivising R&D for neglected diseases. The revival of public sector firms also becomes significant for the exercise of policy instruments such as CLs to counter patent monopoly. Access to medicines in India is in such a bad situation that CLs are a vital policy instrument in public health. Unfortunately, private firms are not interested in exercising CLs, since they find better opportunities in collaborating with MNCs. In this context, revival of public sector firms has become an essential component of the strategy to promote public health.

The policy reforms have resulted in mixed outcomes in the pharmaceutical industry and health. The Indian pharmaceutical industry now stands at a crossroads, and it requires strong policy support for it to move forward in the desired directions.

## Note

1 *Annual Report 2008–09* of the Central Pollution Control Board.

# Bibliography

Abbott, Frederick M. 2013. 'Inside Views: The Judgment in Novartis v. India – What the Supreme Court of India Said', *Intellectual Property Watch*, 4 April, http://www.ip-watch.org/2013/04/04/the-judgment-in-novartis-v-india-what-the-supreme-court-of-india-said/ (accessed on 21 November 2014).

Abrol, Dinesh, and C. Jayaraj. 1988. 'Indian Patent Law 1970 and Changing Global Economic and Technology Environment', *Conquest by Patent: On Patent Law and Policy*, New Delhi: National Working Group on Patent Laws.

Abrol, Dinesh, Pramod Prajapathi and Nidhi Singh. 2011. 'Globalization of Indian Pharmaceutical Industry: Implications for Innovation', *International Journal of Institutions and Economics*, 3(2): 327–65.

Aggrawal, Pradeep, and P. Saibaba. 2001. 'TRIPS and Indian Pharmaceutical Industry', *Economic and Political Weekly*, 36(39): 3787–90.

Alexander, Joseph. 2011. 'DoP Plans to Convene Meeting of All Stakeholders to Discuss Drug Procurement Issue', Pharmabiz.com, 21 July, http://www.pharmabiz.com/NewsDetails.aspx?aid=64055&sid=1 (accessed on 3 March 2015).

Anand, Nitya. 1988. 'Drug Research and CSIR', Drugs and Pharmaceuticals: Industry Highlights', CSIR, Lucknow.

Aoki, R., K. Kubo and H. Yamane. 2006. 'Patent Policy and Public Health in Developing Countries: Lessons from Japan', *Bulletin of the World Health Organization*, 84(5): 417–19.

Årdal, Christine, and John-Arne Røttingen. 2012. 'Open Source Drug Discovery in Practice: A Case Study', *PLOS Neglected Tropical Diseases*, 20 September, http://www.plosntds.org/article/info%3Adoi%2F10.1371%2Fjournal.pntd.0001827 (accessed on 4 November 2014).

Athreye, Suma, and Dinar Kale. 2006. 'Experimentation with Strategy in the Indian Pharmaceutical Sector'. Working Paper 16, The Open University Research Centre on Innovation, Knowledge and Development, Milton Keynes.

Attaran, Amir, and White Gillespie. 2001. 'Do Patents for Antiretroviral Drugs Constrain Access to AIDS Treatment in Africa?', *Journal of the American Medical Association*, 268(15): 1886–92.

Bagath, M. 1982. 'Aspects of Drug Industry in India, Centre for Education and Documentation', in Kannamma S. Raman (ed.), *The Government's Policy towards Drug Companies*, vol. 1, University of Bombay, Department of Civics and Politics.

Ballance, R., J. Pogany and H. Forstner. 1992. *The World's Pharmaceutical Industries: An International Comparative Study*. Aldershot: Edward Elgar.

Basheer, Shamnad. 2005. 'India's Tryst with TRIPS: The Patents (Amendment) Act 2005', *Indian Journal of Law and Technology*, 1: 15–46.

BioSpectrum. 2013. 'Zydus Cadila Launches Indigenous Diabetes Drug', 20 September, http://www.biospectrumasia.com/biospectrum/news/196060/cadila-s-indigenously-developed-diabetes-drug-launched (accessed on 13 December 2014).

Bisserbe, Noemie. 2010. 'Death of a Dream', *Business World*, 8 February, http://www.businessworld.in/news/business/pharma/death-of-a-dream/460435/page-1.html (accessed on 3 November 2014).

Borkar, S. K. 1983. 'Indian Drug Industry: A Retrospect', *IDMA Bulletin*, 14(4): 61.

Borrell, J. R. 2007. 'Pricing and Patents of HIV/AIDS Drugs in Developing Countries', *Applied Economics*, 39(4): 505–18.

*Business Line*. 2009. 'Jubilant in R&D Deal with AstraZeneca', 6 May, http://www.thehindubusinessline.com/todays-paper/tp-corporate/jubilant-in-rd-deal-with-astrazeneca/article1050973.ece (accessed on 31 October 2014).

*Business Standard*. 2007. 'Dabur Launches New Anti-cancer Drug System', 4 January, http://www.business-standard.com/article/companies/dabur-launches-new-anti-cancer-drug-system-107010400030_1.html (accessed on 3 November 2014).

———. 2009. 'USFDA Door Wide Open for Indian Pharma Cos', 6 March, http://www.business-standard.com/article/companies/usfda-door-wide-open-for-indian-pharma-cos-109030600052_1.html (accessed on 17 October 2014).

*Business World*. 2006. 'India Learns How to Discover Drugs', http://www.businessworld.in/index.php/India-Learns-How-to-Discover-Drugs.html (accessed on 16 November 2011).

Chang, Ha-Joon. 2003. 'Kicking Away the Ladder: The Real History of Free Trade', *Foreign Policy in Focus* Special Report, 30 December, http://fpif.org/kicking_away_the_ladder_the_real_history_of_free_trade/ (accessed on 3 March 2015).

Chaudhuri, Sudip. 2005a. 'R&D for Development of New Drugs for Neglected Diseases: How Can India Contribute?' Study prepared for WHO Commission on Intellectual Property Rights, Innovation and

Public Health, http://www.who.int/intellectualproperty/studies/S.%20 Chaudhuri.pdf (accessed on 4 October 2014).

———. 2005b. *The WTO and India's Pharmaceuticals Industry*. New Delhi: Oxford University Press.

———. 2007. 'Is Product Patent Protection Necessary in Developing Countries for Innovation? R&D by Indian Pharmaceutical Companies after TRIPS'. Working Paper 614, Indian Institute of Management, Kolkata.

———. 2010. 'R&D for Development of New Drugs for Neglected Diseases in India', *International Journal of Technology and Development*, 5(1): 61–75.

Chimni, B.S. 2010. 'Mapping Indian Foreign Economic Policy', *International Studies*, 47(163): 163–85.

CIPR (Commission on Intellectual Property Rights). 2002. *Integrating Intellectual Property Rights and Development Policy*. London: CIPR.

Correa, Carlos M. 2013. 'The Use of Compulsory License in Latin America', *South Views*, no. 60, South Centre, Geneva.

CSIR (Council of Scientific and Industrial Research). 2014. *OSDD, Annual Report 2013–14*, https://drive.google.com/viewerng/viewer?a=v&pid=sites&srcid=b3NkZC5uZXR8b3NkZG5ld3Zlcmlzb258Z3g6MTdiNTFFkNDI5ZTdhZmQ2Yw (accessed on 11 December 2014).

Danzon, P. 2007. 'At What Price?', *Nature*, 449(7159): 176–9.

Danzon, P. and A. Towse. 2003. 'Differential Pricing for Pharmaceuticals: Reconciling Access, R&D and Patents', *International Journal of Health Care Finance and Economics*, 3(3): 183–205.

DGCI&S (Directorate General of Commercial Intelligence and Statistics). 2012. Indian Trade Classification (Harmonised System), 2012, Section VI, Chapter 30: Pharmaceutical Products, Ministry of Commerce and Industry, Government of India, http://www.dgciskol.nic.in/itchs2012/pdfs/CHP_30.pdf (accessed on 4 November 2014).

Dhar, Biswajit. 2011. *Improving the Share of Manufacturing Sector in India: Some Key Considerations*, Discussion Note for internal discussion, Research and Information System for Developing Countries, New Delhi.

Dhar, Biswajit, and K.M. Gopakumar. 2003. 'Effect of Product Patents on the Indian Pharmaceutical Industry', http://wtocentre.iift.ac.in/Papers/3.pdf (accessed on 15 April 2014).

———. 2008. 'Effect of Product Patents on Indian Pharmaceutical Industry', http://wtocentre.iift.ac.in/Papers/3.pdf (accessed on 2 May 2011).

Dhar, Biswajit, and Niranjan C. Rao. 1993. 'Patent System and Pharmaceutical Sector', *Economic and Political Weekly*, 28(4): 2167–8.

Dhavan, Rajeev. 1988. 'A Monopoly by Any Other Name: An Introduction', *Conquest by Patent: On Patent Law and Policy*. New Delhi: National Working Group on Patent Laws.

DiMasi, Joseph, Ronald Hansen and Henry Grabowski. 2003. 'The Price of Innovation: New Estimates of Drug Development Costs', *Journal of Health Economics*, 22(2): 325–30.

DIPP (Department of Industrial Promotion and Policy). 2010. 'Compulsory Licensing'. Discussion Paper, 24 August, Government of India, New Delhi.

DNDi. 2011a. 'DNDi Launches New Drug Development Programme to Address Treatment Needs of Children with HIV/AIDS', 18 July, http://www.dndi.org/media-centre/press-releases/press-releases-2011/354-media-centre/press-releases/928-paediatric-hiv.html (accessed on 4 November 2014).

———. 2011b. 'Financing & Incentives for Neglected Disease R&D: Opportunities and Challenges', *DNDi Outlook*, no. 3, June, http://www.dndi.org/images/stories/pdf_outlooks/Outlook2_financing-and-incentives_july2011_low.pdf (accessed on 4 November 2014).

Doane, Michael L. 1994. 'Trips and International Intellectual Property Protection in an Age of Advancing Technology', *American University International Law Review*, 9(2): 465–97.

Dr. Reddy's. 2002a. 'Ragaglitazar (DRF 2725) clinical development suspended', media release, 22 July, http://www.drreddys.com/media/popups/jul22_2002.htm (accessed on 11 December 2014).

———. 2002b. *Annual Report 2001–02*, http://www.drreddys.com/investors/pdf/annualreport2002.pdf (accessed on 11 December 2014).

———. 2004. 'Novo Nordisk Terminates Further Clinical Development of Balaglitazone (DRF 2593) Out-Licensed by Dr. Reddy's', media release, 27 October, http://www.drreddys.com/media/popups/oct27_2004.htm (accessed on 11 December 2014).

———. 2005a. *Annual Report 2004–05*, http://www.drreddys.com/investors/pdf/annualreport2005.pdf (accessed on 28 November 2014).

———. 2005b. 'Dr. Reddy's Announces India's First Major Drug Co-development and Commercialization Deal', press release, 29 September, http://www.drreddys.com/media/popups/sept29_2005.htm (accessed on 4 December 2014).

———. 2009. *Annual Report 2008–09*, http://www.drreddys.com/investors/pdf/annualreport2009.pdf (accessed on 29 October 2014).

———. 2011. 'Teva and Dr. Reddy's Announce Launch of Generic Zyprexa® in the United States', press release, 25 October, http://www.drreddys.com/media/popups/oct25_2011_teva.html (accessed on 20 November 2014).

DSIR-IIFT (Department of Scientific and Industrial Research and Indian Institute of Foreign Trade). 2005. *Study on Foreign R&D Centres in India*, DSIR-IIFT, New Delhi.

DST (Department of Science and Technology). 2011. *Annual Report 2010–11*, Ministry of Science and Technology, Government of India, New Delhi, http://dst.gov.in/about_us/ar10–11/PDF/DST%20Annual%20Report%202010–11.pdf (accessed on 12 November 2014).

———. 2014. *Annual Report 2013–14*, Ministry of Science and Technology, Government of India, New Delhi, http://www.dst.gov.in/about_us/ar13–14/annual-report-2013–14.pdf (accessed on 9 December 2014).

Ebrahim, Zofeen. 2012. 'India Poised to Supply Free Drugs to 1.2 Billion People', IPS News Agency, 8 November, http://www.ipsnews.net/2012/11/india-poised-to-supply-free-drugs-to-1-2-billion-people/ (accessed on 14 November 2014).

*Economic Times.* 2002. 'Ranbaxy in Pact with Schwarz', 27 June, http://articles.economictimes.indiatimes.com/2002-06-27/news/27343173_1_treatment-of-benign-prostate-licensing-deal-ranbaxy-laboratories (accessed on 31 October 2014).

———. 2007. 'Alembic Signs Licensing Agreement with UCB', 23 May, http://articles.economictimes.indiatimes.com/2007-05-23/news/28449690_1_ndds-ucb-novel-drug-delivery-system (accessed on 3 November 2014).

———. 2008. 'Sick Bulk Drug Cos May Get Life Support', 15 August, http://articles.economictimes.indiatimes.com/2008-08-15/news/27735905_1_bulk-drug-prices-of-such-drugs-raw-material (accessed on 20 October 2014).

———. 2009. 'Piramal Life Lines up Rs 200 Cr for New Drug Research', 14 October, http://articles.economictimes.indiatimes.com/2009-10-14/news/28407499_1_cancer-drugs-piramal-lifesciences-drug-research (accessed on 31 October 2014).

———. 2010a. 'Ranbaxy Drug Gets US Nod', 22 September, http://articles.economictimes.indiatimes.com/2010-09-22/news/27604144_1_ranbaxy-drug-donepezil-ranbaxy-spokesman (accessed on 17 October 2014).

———. 2010b. 'Aurobindo, AstraZeneca Ink Supply Pact', 7 September, http://articles.economictimes.indiatimes.com/2010-09-07/news/27620685_1_generic-drugs-formulations-player-aurobindo-pharma (accessed on 20 October 2014).

———. 2013. 'New Drug Policy to Negatively Impact Pharma Sector: Industry', 17 May, http://articles.economictimes.indiatimes.com/2013-05-17/news/39336622_1_price-control-dpco-drug-policy (accessed on 28 November 2014).

EMA (European Medicines Agency). 2005. 'Note for Guidance on Data Elements and Standards for Drug Dictionaries', Document No. EMEA/CHM)/ICH/168535/2005, EMA, London.

Embassy of India. 2014. 'Speech by Ambassador Dr. S. Jaishankar at the Chicago Council on Global Affairs, Chicago on February 28, 2014', Embassy of India, Washington, D.C., https://www.indianembassy.org/press_detail.php?nid=2014 (accessed on 22 November 2014).

Erman, Michael, and Sumeet Chatterjee. 2010. 'Reckitt Benckiser to Buy Paras Pharma for $726 Million', *LiveMint*, Mumbai, 13 December, http://www.livemint.com/Companies/sjoE3rittsiPOXjmkwWT1N/Reckitt-Benckiser-to-buy-Paras-Pharma-for-726-million.html (accessed on 1 March 2011).

FICCI (Federation of Indian Chambers of Commerce and Industry). 2005. 'Competitiveness of the Indian Pharmaceutical Industry in the New Product Patent Regime', FICCI Report for National Manufacturing

Competitiveness Council (NMCC), New Delhi, March, http://pharmain diaweb.tripod.com/sitebuildercontent/sitebuilderfiles/pharma.pdf (accessed on 30 October 2014).

*Financial Times*. 2010. 'Drugs Groups Diversify Away from Patents', 21 October, http://www.ft.com/cms/s/0/d6fb3f60-dc9d-11df-84f5–00144feabdc 0.html#axzz3GC6kG0QC (accessed on 21 October 2014).

Frost & Sullivan. 2007. 'Frost & Sullivan Study Reveals the CRAMS Market in India to Be Valued at US $895 Million in 2006 and Expected to Reach to Close to US $6.6 Billion by 2013', 23 April, http://www.frost.com/prod/ servlet/summits-details-inthenews.pag?as=attend&eventid=96073131 (accessed on 13 December 2014).

Gentleman, Amelia, and Hari Kumar. 2006. 'AIDS Groups in India Sue to Halt Patent for U.S. Drug', *New York Times*, 12 May, http://www. nytimes.com/2006/05/12/world/asia/12aids.html?_r=0 (accessed on 21 November 2014).

Ghosh, Arun, and B. K. Keayla. 1998. 'Submission by Dr. Arun Ghosh and Mr. B K Keayla before the People's Commission', *Report of People's Commission on Intellectual Property Rights*. New Delhi: National Working Group on Patent Laws.

Glenmark. 2005. 'Glenmark Pharmaceuticals Ltd and Napo Pharmaceuticals Inc Announce Collaboration Agreement on Napo's Novel Anti-diarrheal Product Crofelemer', Mumbai, 7 July, http://www.glenmarkpharma. com/GLN_NWS/pdf/Napo_GlenmarkCollaboration_07Jul05.pdf (accessed on 2 November 2014).

———. 2008. 'Glenmark Pharmaceuticals to Get Back the Global Rights to Melogliptin, GRC 8200 from Merck Serono', press release, 1 February, http://glenmarkpharma.com/GLN_NWS/PDF/Glenmark_Gets_global_ rights_back_for_GRC8200_Feb0108.pdf (accessed on 4 December 2014).

———. 2008–09. *Annual Report 2008–09*, http://www.glenmarkpharma. com/Common/pdf/annual_report08_09.pdf (accessed on 4 November 2014).

———. 2009. 'Glenmark's Novel Molecule for Diabetes, Melogliptin to Enter Phase III Trials', press release, 24 June, http://www.glenmarkpharma.com/ gln_nws/pdf/Glenmarks_novel_molecule_for_Diabetes_Melogliptin_ phase_IIItrail.pdf (accessed on 4 December 2014).

———. 2012–13. *Annual Report 2012–13*, http://www.glenmarkpharma. com/Common/pdf/Glenmark_AR_FY13.pdf (accessed on 2 November 2014).

GoI (Government of India). 1948. *Industrial Policy Resolution*, 6 April, Government of India, New Delhi.

———. 1954. *Report of the Pharmaceutical Enquiry Committee* (Bhatia Committee Report), Ministry of Commerce and Industry, Government of India, New Delhi.

———. 1959. *Report on the Revision of the Patents Law* (Ayyangar Committee Report), Ministry of Commerce and Industry, Government of India, New Delhi.

———. 1975. *Report of the Committee in Drugs and Pharmaceutical Industry* (Hathi Committee Report), Ministry of Petroleum and Chemicals, Government of India, New Delhi.

———. 1991. 'Statement on Industrial Policy'. Ministry of Industry, New Delhi, 24 July, http://dipp.nic.in/English/Policies/Industrial_policy_statement.pdf (accessed on 28 October 2014).

———. 1999. *Report of the Drug Price Control Review Committee, Government of India*, Ministry of Chemicals and Fertilizers, Government of India, New Delhi.

———. 2000. Press note no. 2 (2000 series), Department of Industrial Promotion and Policy, Ministry of Commerce and Industry, 11 February, http://dipp.nic.in/English/policy/changes/press2_00.htm (accessed on 27 October 2014).

———. 2004. *Interim Report of the Committee to Examine the Span of Price Control (including the Trade Margin) for Medicines*, Ministry of Chemicals and Fertilizers, Government of India, New Delhi.

———. 2005a. *Report of the Task Force to Explore Options Other Than Price Control for Achieving the Objective of Making Available Life-Saving Drugs at Reasonable Prices*, Department of Chemicals and Petrochemicals, Government of India, New Delhi.

———. 2005b. *Availability and Price Management of Drugs and Pharmaceuticals*, Seventh Report of the Standing Committee on Chemicals and Fertilizers, Ministry of Chemicals and Fertilizers, Department of Chemicals and Petrochemicals, Government of India, New Delhi.

———. 2005c. *Draft National Pharmaceuticals Policy 2006*, Department of Chemicals and Pterochemicals, Government of India, New Delhi, 28 December, http://pib.nic.in/archieve/others/2005/documents-2005dec/documents2005dec_chemfert.pdf (accessed on 12 November 2014).

———. 2006. *Report of the Working Group on Drugs and Pharmaceuticals for the Eleventh Five-Year Plan (2007–12)*, Planning Commission, Government of India, New Delhi, http://planningcommission.nic.in/aboutus/committee/wrkgrp11/wg11_pharma.pdf (accessed on 31 October 2014).

———. 2007a. *Annual Report 2006–07*, Department of Chemicals and Petrochemicals, Ministry of Chemicals, Government of India, New Delhi.

———. 2007b. *Report on Steps to Be Taken by Government of India in the Context of Data Protection Provisions of Article 39.3 of TRIPS Agreement*, Department of Chemicals and Petrochemicals, Ministry of Chemicals and Fertilizers, Government of India, New Delhi, 31 May, http://chemicals.nic.in/DPBooklet.pdf (accessed on 24 November 2014).

———. 2008a. *Strategy for Increasing Exports of Pharmaceutical Products*, Ministry of Commerce and Industry, Government of India, New Delhi.

———. 2008b. 'Price Control of Essential Drugs', Ministry of Chemicals and Fertilizers, Government of India, New Delhi, 23 October, http://pib.nic.in/newsite/erelease.aspx?relid=44134 (accessed on 27 November 2014).

——. 2008–09. *Annual Report 2008–09*, Department of Pharmaceuticals, Government of India, New Delhi, http://pharmaceuticals.gov.in/annual report0809.pdf (accessed on 21 October 2014).

——. 2010. *Annual Report 2009–10*, Department of Pharmaceuticals, Ministry of Chemicals and Fertilizers, Government of India, New Delhi.

——. 2011a. *Draft National Pharmaceutical Pricing Policy 2011*, http://pharmaceuticals.gov.in/mshT2810/FTY2.pdf (accessed on 14 April 2014).

——. 2011b. *High Level Expert Group Report on Universal Health Coverage for India*, Planning Commission of India, New Delhi, November, http://planningcommission.nic.in/reports/genrep/rep_uhc0812.pdf (accessed on 4 November 2014).

——. 2012a. *National Pharmaceutical Pricing Policy 2012*, http://pharmaceuticals.gov.in/NPPP2012.pdf (accessed on 14 April 2014).

——. 2012b. *Report of the Steering Committee on Health for the 12th Five Year Plan*, Health Division, Planning Commission, Government of India, New Delhi.

——. 2012c. *Annual Report 2011–12*, Department of Pharmaceuticals, Ministry of Chemicals and Fertilizers, Government of India, New Delhi.

——. 2012d. Application for Compulsory Licence under Section 84(*1*) of the Patents Act, 1970, in respect of Patent No. 215758, C.L.A. no. 1 of 2011, Controller General of Patents Designs and Trademarks, Department of Industrial Policy and Promotion, Ministry of Commerce and Industry, Mumbai, 9 March, http://www.ipindia.nic.in/iponew/compulsory_license_12032012.pdf (accessed on 21 November 2014).

——. 2013a. 'Consolidated FDI Policy', Circular 1 of 2013, Department of Industrial Policy and Promotion, Ministry of Commerce and Industry, Government of India, New Delhi, http://dipp.nic.in/English/Policies/FDI_Circular_01_2013.pdf (accessed on 14 February 2015).

——. 2013b. *Drug (Prices Control) Order, 2013*, Department of Pharmaceuticals, Ministry of Chemicals and Fertilizers, Government of India, New Delhi, 15 May, http://www.nppaindia.nic.in/DPCO2013.pdf (accessed on 26 November 2014).

——. 2013c. *Annual Report 2012–13*, Department of Pharmaceuticals, Ministry of Chemicals and Fertilizers, Government of India, New Delhi, http://www.pharmaceuticals.gov.in/AReport201213.pdf (accessed on 20 November 2014).

——. 2013d. 'India Inclusive Innovation Fund', release by Press Information Bureau of India, release ID: 95159, 26 April, http://pib.nic.in/newsite/erelease.aspx?relid=95159 (accessed on 15 May 2013).

——. n.d. 'India's Industrial Policies from 1948 to 1991', Development Commissioner (MSME), Ministry of Micro, Small and Medium Enterprises, Government of India, New Delhi, http://www.dcmsme.gov.in/policies/iip.htm (accessed on 28 October 2014).

Gopakumar, K. M. 2010. 'The Landscape of Pharmaceutical Patent Applications in India: Implications for Access to Medicines', in Sudip Chaudhuri,

Chan Park and K. M. Gopakumar (eds), *Five Years into the Product Patent Regime: India's Response*, December, pp. 105–20. New York: United Nations Development Programme.

Government of Kenya. 2008. The Anti-Counterfeit Act No. 13 of 2008, *Kenya Gazette Supplement no. 97*, Government of Kenya, Nairobi, http://www.aca.go.ke/index.php?option=com_docman&task=doc_download&gid=28&Itemid=471 (accessed 18 October 2014)

Grace, Chery. 2004. *The Effect of Changing Intellectual Property on Pharmaeutical Industry Prospects in India and China*. London: DFID Health Systems Resources Centre.

Greene, William. 2007. 'The Emergence of India's Pharmaceutical Industry and Implications for U.S. Generic Drug Market'. Office of Economics Working Paper No. 2007–05-A, U.S. International Trade Commission, Washington, D.C.

GSK (GlaxoSmithKline). 2005. 'GSK India's Clinical Data Management and Analysis Centre, Bangalore', press release, 12 April, https://www.gsk-india.com/docs/PressReleases2005/GSK%20India%20Clinical%20Data%20Management%20Analysis%20Centre%20Blore.pdf (accessed on 31 October 2014).

———. 2009. 'GSK Announces a Strategic Alliance with Dr. Reddy's to Further Accelerate Sales Growth in Emerging Markets', press release, 15 June, http://us.gsk.com/en-us/media/press-releases/2009/gsk-announces-a-strategic-alliance-with-dr-reddyandrsquos-to-further-accelerate-sales-growth-in-emerging-markets/ (accessed on 30 October 2014).

Hamied, Y. K. 1988. 'The Indian Patents Act 1970 and the Pharmaceutical Industry', *Conquest by Patent: On Patent Law and Policy*. New Delhi: National Working Group on Patent Laws.

*Hindu.* 2012. 'After Generic Medicine Supply, Rajasthan May Go for Free Diagnostic Tests', 3 October, http://www.thehindu.com/news/national/other-states/after-generic-medicine-supply-rajasthan-may-go-for-free-diagnostic-tests/article3958927.ece (accessed on 14 November 2014).

———. 2013. 'Not Insisting on Patent Extension, Says EU', 13 April, http://www.thehindu.com/business/Economy/not-insisting-on-patent-extension-says-eu/article4610892.ece (accessed on 23 November 2014).

Hoen, Ellen F. M. 2009. *The Global Politics of Pharmaceutical Monopoly Power: Drug Patents, Access, Innovation and the Application of the WTO Doha Declaration on TRIPS and Public Health*. Diemen: AMB Publishers.

IBEF (India Brand Equity Foundation). 2011. *Pharmaceuticals*, http://ukrexport.gov.ua/i/imgsupload/file/Pharma_sectoral.pdf (accessed on 30 October 2014).

ICRA. 2011. *CRAMS India: Overlook and Outlook*, http://www.icra.in/Files/Articles/CRAMS%20Note,%20Overview%20and%20Outlook.pdf (accessed on 4 October 2011).

IDMA (Indian Drug Manufacturers' Association). 2004. *Indian Pharmaceutical Industry Going Global*, 42nd Annual Publication. Mumbai: IDMA.

——. 2014. *Indian Pharmaceuticals for Global Health*, 52nd Annual Publication. Mumbai: IDMA.

*India Today*. 2011. 'Hyderabad: DCGI Suspends Illegal Human Trial of Anti-cancer Drug', 25 June, http://indiatoday.intoday.in/story/hyderabad-illegal-human-trial-of-anti-cancer-drug-suspended/1/142692.html (accessed on 31 October 2014).

*Indian Express*. 2011. 'New Policy Makes Bidding Hard for Small Pharma Firms', 19 May.

IRI (Economics of Industrial Research and Innovation). n.d. 'The 2010 EU Industrial R&D Investment Scoreboard', http://iri.jrc.ec.europa.eu/research/scoreboard_2010.htm (accessed on 28 October 2014).

ISID-PHFI (Institute for Studies in Industrial Development and Public Health Foundation of India). 2014. 'An Independent Assessment of the National Pharmaceutical Pricing Policy 2012 and Drug Price Control Order 2013'. Unpublished report of ISID-PHFI Collaborative Research Programme, New Delhi.

James, T. C. 2009. *Patent Protection and Innovation: Section 3(d) of the Patents Act and Indian Pharmaceutical Industry*. Mumbai: Indian Pharmaceutical Alliance.

Jha, Ravinder. 2007. 'Indian Pharmaceutical Industry: Growth, Innovation and Prices'. Unpublished Ph.D dissertation, Jawaharlal Nehru University, New Delhi.

Joseph, Jaimon. 2011. 'A Facebook for Labcoats', IBN Live Blogs, 23 September, http://m.ibnlive.com/blogs/jaimonjoseph/326/62731/a-facebook-for-labcoats.html (accessed on 4 November 2014).

Joseph, Reji K. 2008. 'The Ranbaxy Model and Consolidation in Pharma Sector', *Economic Times*, New Delhi, June 24.

——. 2012. 'Policy Reforms in Indian Pharmaceutical Sector since 1994: Impact on Exports and Imports', *Economic and Political Weekly*, 47(18): 62–72.

Joshi, Bhubaneshwar. 1977. 'Economics of Transfer of Technology in Public Sector: A Study of Indian Drugs and Pharmaceuticals Limited', Unpublished PhD dissertation, Lucknow University.

Jubilant LifeSciences. 2009a. 'Jubilant and Lilly Extend Drug Discovery Collaboration on Successful Delivery of Pre-clinical Candidates', press release, 1 December, http://www.jubl.com/media-press-details.aspx?mpgid=73&pgid=74&pressid=49 (accessed on 31 October 2014).

——. 2009b. 'Duke University and Jubilant Organosys Intent to Enter Global Research and Drug Development Partnership', press release, 10 November, http://www.jubl.com/media-press-details.aspx?mpgid=73&pgid=74&pressid=53 (accessed on 31 October 2014).

Kannan, Ramya. 2013. 'Shot in the Arm for Generics, Say Oncologists', *Hindu*, 2 April, http://www.thehindu.com/news/national/shot-in-the-arm-for-generics-say-oncologists/article4570798.ece (accessed on 21 November 2014).

Keayla, B.K. 1994. 'Patent Protection and Pharmaceutical Industry', in K.R.G. Nair and Ashok Kumar (eds), *Intellectual Property Rights*. New Delhi: Allied Publishers.

———. 2008. 'Brief History of National Working Group on Patent Laws: Activities during Past 20 Years'. Unpublished report by Convener of NWGPL, New Delhi.

KEI (Knowledge Ecology International). 2000. 'Submission of the Pharmaceutical Research and Manufacturers of America (PhRMA), for the National Trade Estimate Report on Foreign Trade Barriers (NTE) 2000, December 3, 1999', India, http://www.cptech.org/ip/health/phrma/nte-99/india.html (accessed on 10 October 2014).

———. 2014. 'KEI Research Note: Recent European Union Compulsory Licenses', http://keionline.org/sites/default/files/Annex_B_European_Union_Compulsory_Licenses_1Mar2014_8_5x11_0.pdf (accessed on 27 December 2014).

Kettler, Hannah E., Karen White and Scott Jordan. 2003. 'Valuing Industry Contributions to Public-Private Partnerships for Health Product Development', Initiative on Public-Private Partnerships for Health, Geneva.

Khor, Martin. 2012. 'Asian Countries Act to Get Cheap Drugs', *South Views*, no. 37, South Centre.

Kimani, Dagi. 2009. 'Indian Drug Makers Say Kenya's Counterfeit Law Will Wipe Out Their Market', http://www.eac.int/customs/index.php?option=com_content&view=article&id=56:indian-drug-makers-say-kenyas-counterfeit-law-law-will-wipe-out-their-mar&catid=1:latest-news&Itemid=163 (accessed on 18 October 2014).

KPMG. 2006. *The Indian Pharmaceuticals Industry: Collaboration for Growth*. Zurich: KPMG International.

Krishnan, Vidya. 2013a. 'Drug Makers May Lose Rs. 530 Cr Revenue under New Pricing Regime', *LiveMint*, 20 June , http://www.livemint.com/Politics/rm9AcQY2wrxo7tRdcUg9jO/Drug-makers-may-lose-530-cr-revenue-under-new-pricing-regim.html (accessed on 28 November 2014).

———. 2013b. 'Novartis Won't Invest on R&D in India', *LiveMint*, 2 April, http://www.livemint.com/Companies/zMEjKd25zZf4oI5aOaS15H/Novartis-wont-invest-on-RD-in-India.html (accessed on 13 November 2014).

Kumar, Nagesh, and Pradhan Jayaprakash. 2007. 'Knowledge Based Exports from India: Recent Trends, Patterns and Implications', in Nagesh Kumar and K.J. Joseph (eds.), *International Competitiveness and Knowledge Based Industries in India*. New Delhi: Oxford University Press.

Lakshmi, Mahala B.V. 2009. 'Libya Third African Country to Ban Indian Drugs', *Financial Express*, 2 July.

Lalitha, N. 2002. 'Indian Pharmaceutical Industry in WTO Regime: A SWTO Analysis', *Economic and Political Weekly*, 37(34): 3452–555.

Lanjouw, Jean O. 1998. 'Introduction of Pharmaceutical Product Patents in India: "Heartless Exploitation of the Poor and Suffering"?' NBER

Working Paper No 6366, National Bureau of Economic Research, Cambridge, MA.

Lanjouw, Jean O., and Margaret MacLeod. 2005. *Statistical Trends in Pharmaceutical Research for Poor Countries*, http://www.esocialsciences. com/data/articles/Document126112009170.5472528.pdf (accessed on 15 May 2011).

Lessem, Erica. 2013. 'The Tuberculosis Treatment Pipeline', *Pipeline Report*, June, http://www.pipelinereport.org/2013/tb-treatment (accessed on 8 December 2014).

Levin, R. C., A. K. Klevorick, R. R. Nelson, and S. G. Winter. 1987. 'Appropriating the Returns from Industrial R&D', *Brooking Papers in Economic Activity*, 3: 783–820.

Linton, Katherine Connor, and Corrado Nicholas. 2007. 'A Calibrated Approach: Pharmaceutical FDI and the Evolution of Indian Patent Law', *Journal of International Commerce and Economics*, US International Trade Commission.

*LiveMint*. 2009. 'Suven Life Sciences Plans to Raise Funds for Clinical Trials', 17 November.

———. 2010a. 'Innovation Has Helped Drug Firms Take On Big Pharma', 8 September, http://www.livemint.com/Companies/F3PmB9BomMUl pjS3l4Fo7M/Innovation-has-helped-drug-firms-take-on-Big-Pharma. html (accessed on 17 October 2014).

———. 2010b. 'Piramal May Reabsorb R&D Spin-Off, 4 October, http:// www.livemint.com/Home-Page/VLTHQaeWDqMcCcpNL74R0K/ Piramal-may-reabsorb-RampD-spinoff.html (accessed on 20 October 2014).

Lok Sabha. 2012. 'Spurious and Substandard Drugs', unstarred question no. 2140, answered on 24 August.

Love, James. 2007. 'Recent Examples of the Use of Compulsory Licenses on Patents', *KEI Research Note* 2007:2, http://www.keionline.org/ misc-docs/recent_cls.pdf (accessed on 3 March 2015).

Lupin. 2013. 'Lupin Launches Generic ZYMAXID™ Ophthalmic Solution in the US', 3 October, http://www.lupinpharmaceuticals.com/3oct13. htm (accessed on 8 December 2014).

Ma, Sai, and Neeraj Sood. 2008. 'A Comparison of the Health Systems in China and India'. Occasional Paper, RAND Centre for Asia and Pacific Policy.

Mansfield, Edwin. 1986. 'Patents and Innovation: An Empirical Study', *Management Science*, 32(2): 173–81.

Maskus, Keith E., and Penubarti Mohan. 1995. 'How Trade-Related Are Intellectual Property Rights?', *Journal of International Economics*, 39: 227–48.

Mathew, Joe C. 2007. 'Ranbaxy Eyes Partners for Malaria Drug R&D', 5 November, http://www.business-standard.com/article/companies/ ranbaxy-eyes-partners-for-malaria-drug-r-d-107110501049_1.html (accessed on 3 November 2014).

——. 2014. 'Why Ranbaxy Won't Be the Last Co to Come under USFDA Scanner', *Businessworld*, 28 January, http://www.businessworld.in/news/economy/why-ranbaxy-won-t-be-the-last-co-to-come-under-usfda-scanner/1232832/page-1.html (accessed on 14 April 2014).

Menghaney, Leena. 2012a. 'Oppositions Made Simple: How to Start?' Paper presented during the 19th International AIDS Conference, 22–27 July, Washington, D.C.

——. 2012b. 'R&D for Neglected Diseases'. Presentation at the consultation on Health Impact Fund Research and Information System for Developing Countries, New Delhi, 20 July.

Mishra, Pallavi. 2010. 'Political Economy of Trade Related Intellectual Property Rights (TRIPS) and Public Health in Developing Countries'. Unpublished MPhil dissertation, Jawaharlal Nehru University, New Delhi.

Nandakumar, Namrata. 2012. '2 Generics Give Pharma Sector $400 Mn Boost', *LiveMint*, 4 March.

Narayana, P.L. 1984. *The Indian Pharmaceutical Industry: Problems and Prospects*. New Delhi: NCAER.

*New York Times*. 2005. 'AIDS Drugs Threatened', editorial, 5 March, http://www.nytimes.com/2005/03/05/opinion/05sat3.html (accessed on 21 November 2014).

NSSO (National Sample Survey Office). 1998. *Morbidity and Treatment of Ailments*, NSS 52nd Round, Report No. 441 (52/25.0/1), NSSO, Department of Statistics, Government of India, New Delhi, http://mospi.nic.in/rept%20_%20pubn/441_final.pdf (accessed on 14 November 2014).

——. 2006. *Morbidity, Health Care and the Condition of the Aged*, NSS 60th Round, January–June 2004, Report No. 507 (60/25.0/1), NSSO, Ministry of Statistics and Programme Implementation, Government of India, http://mospi.nic.in/rept%20_%20pubn/507_final.pdf (accessed on 14 November 2014).

NWGPL (National Working Group on Patent Laws). 2004. *Report of the Fourth Peoples' Commission on Review of Legislations Amending Patents Act 1970*, http://www.who.int/entity/intellectualproperty/documents/Report4thCommission.pdf (accessed on 14 April 2014).

NWGPL (National Working Group on Patent Laws) and PILS&RC (Public Interest legal Support & Research Centre). 2003. *Report of Peoples' Commission on Patent Laws for India*, New Delhi.

Pandeya, Radhieka. 2010. 'Innovation Has Helped Drug Firms Take On Big Pharma', *LiveMint*, 8 September, http://www.livemint.com/Companies/F3PmB9BomMUlpjS3l4Fo7M/Innovation-has-helped-drug-firms-take-on-Big-Pharma.html (accessed on 11 December 2014).

Panikar, P.G.K., Mohanan P. Pillai and T.K. Sundari. 1992. *International Environment, Multinational Corporations and Drug Policy*. Thiruvananthapuram: Centre for Development Studies.

Parthasarathi, Ashok. 2007. *Technology at the Core: Science and Technology with Indira Gandhi*. New Delhi: Pearson and Longman.

Pharmabiz. 2009. 'Empower SMEs while Embracing GMP', Bureau Report, Chronicle Specials, 5 November.

Pharmexcil (Pharmaceuticals Export Promotion Council of India). 2012. List of WHOGMP/USFDA/MHRA/EDQM Approved Indian Companies/ Products, Document Reference no. PXL/H.O./CIR-111/2012–13, 4 December.

PhRMA. 2007. *Drug Discovery and Development: Understanding the R&D Process*, February, http://www.phrma.org/sites/default/files/pdf/rd_brochure_022307.pdf (accessed on 28 November 2014).

——. 2012. PhRMA Special 301 Submission 2012, http://www.phrma. org/sites/default/files/pdf/phrmaspecial301submission2012.pdf (accessed on 22 November 2014).

——. 2013a. 'PhRMA Statement on India Supreme Court Decision on Glivec', 1 April, http://phrma.org/media/releases/phrma-statement-india-supreme-court-decision-glivec (accessed on 21 November 2014).

——. 2013b. PhRMA Special 301 Submission 2013, http://www.phrma. org/sites/default/files/pdf/PhRMA%20Special%20301%20Submission %202013.pdf (accessed on 21 November 2014).

Pilla, Viswanath. 2012. 'Dr Reddy's Profit Rises 88% on Schizophrenia Drug Sales', *LiveMint*, 4 February.

Pillai, Mohanan P. 1984. *Multinationals and Indian Pharmaceutical Industry*. Thiruvananthapuram: Kerala Sastra Sahitya Parishad.

Prakash, Pranesh. 2009, 'Does India Need Its Own Bayh-Dole?' Centre for Internet and Society, 24 April, http://cis-india.org/news/does-india-need-its-own-bayh-dole (accessed on 12 November 2014).

Prasad, Ashok Chandra H. 1999. *WTO Negotiations: Some Important Issues and Strategies for India*. New Delhi: Commonwealth Publishers.

Prasad, Ashok Chandra, and Shripad Bhat. 1993. 'Strengthening India's Patent System: Implications for Pharmaceutical Sector', *Economic and Political Weekly*, 28(21): 1037–58.

Ragavan, Srividhya. 2006. 'Of the Inequals of the Uruguay Round', *Marquette Intellectual Property Law Review*, 10(2): 272–304.

Rajya Sabha. 2005. 'Economically Unviable Units in Pharmaceutical Sector', unstarred question no. 3389, answered on 23 December 2005, Ministry of Chemicals and Fertilizers, Government of India.

——. 2010. 'Applications for Global Clinical Trials', unstarred question no. 874, answered on 16 November 2010, Ministry of Health and Family Welfare, Government of India.

——. 2013. 'Clinical Trials in the Country', unstarred question no. 250, answered on 26 February 2013, Ministry of Health and Family Welfare, Government of India.

——. 2014. 'Accessibility and Affordability of Medicines', unstarred question no. 3003, answered on 21 February 2014, Ministry of Health and Family Welfare, Government of India.

Raman, Kannamma S. 1989. 'The Indian Government's Policy towards Drug Companies', unpublished PhD dissertation, vols 1–2, Department of Civics and Politics, University of Bombay.

Ranbaxy. 2002. 'Ranbaxy and Schwarz Pharma Sign a Deal to Develop New Drug to Treat Benign Prostate Hyperplasia', Archives, 27 june, http://www.ranbaxy.com/ranbaxy-and-schwarz-pharma-sign-a-deal-to-develop-new-drug-to-treat-benign-prostate-hyperplasia/ (accessed on 11 December 2014).

———. 2009. *Annual Report 2009*, http://www.ranbaxy.com/media/2009/Annual-Report-2009.pdf (accessed on 4 November 2014).

Rao, O. R. S. 2007. 'Pharmaceutical Industry in India', presentation at CPhI, Shanghai, 20 June, http://www.scribd.com/doc/60180196/PPT-at-CPhI-Shanghai-by-ORS-Rao-Cygnus-India (accessed on 31 October 2014).

RBI (Reserve Bank of India). 2003. Foreign Exchange Management (Transfer or Issue of Security by a Person Resident outside India) (Second Amendment) Regulations, 2003, Notification No. FEMA 94/2003-RB, 18 June, http://rbi.org.in/Scripts/BS_FemaNotifications.aspx?Id=1437 (accessed on 27 October 2014).

Reddy, Srinath K., Sakthivel Selvaraj, Krishna Rao, Maulik Chokshi, Preeti Kumar, and Isheeta Ganguly. 2011. 'A Critical Assessment of the Existing Health Insurance Models in India', Research study submitted by the Public Health Foundation of India to the Planning Commission of India.

Rediff.com. 2009. 'India May Move WTO to Protest Drug Seizures', http://www.rediff.com/money/2009/aug/04wto-india-may-move-wto-to-protest-drug-seizures.htm (accessed on 8 November 2014).

Reekie, W. D. 1975. *The Economics of the Pharmaceutical Industry*. Chennai: Macmillan Press Ltd.

Sampath, Patmashree G. 2008. *India's Pharmaceutical Sector in 2008: Emerging Strategies and Global and Local Implications for Access to Medicines*, Report Commissioned by the Department for International Development, http://www.dfid.gov.uk/Documents/publications/indiapatentreport.pdf (accessed on 5 May 2009).

Scherer, F. M., and Jayasree Watal. 2001. 'Post-TRIPS Options for Access to Patented Medicines in Developing Countries'. Working paper No. 62, ICRIER, New Delhi.

———. 2002. 'Post-TRIPS Options for Access to Patented Medicines in Developing Nations', *Journal of International Economic Law*, 5(4): 913–39.

Selvaraj, Sakthivel. 2001. 'An Analysis of Policies relating to the Pharmaceutical Industry and Its Impact on the Health Sector in India since 1970'. Unpublished PhD dissertation, Jawaharlal Nehru University, New Delhi.

———. 2013. 'Patent Justice', *Hindu*, 7 April, http://www.thehindu.com/news/national/patent-justice/article4588895.ece (accessed on 13 nber 2014).

Selvaraj, Sakthivel, and Habib Hasan Farooqui. 2012. 'The Draft National Pharmaceutical Pricing Policy, 2011: Legitimising Unaffordable Medicines Prices?', *Economic and Political Weekly*, 47(46): 13–17.

Selvaraj, Sakthivel, Habib Hasan, Maulik Choski, Amit Sengupta, Amitava Guha, Mira Shiva, S. Srinivasan, Anand Phadke, K. M. Gopakumar, M. R. Santhosh, Leena Menghaney, and Kajal Bhardwai. 2012. 'Pharmaceutical Pricing Policy: A Critique', *Economic and Political Weekly*, 47(4): 20–3.

Sengupta, Amit. 1998. 'Indian Pharmaceutical Industry: Effect of Proposed Product Patent Regime', *Social Action*, 48: 406–31.

Sengupta, Amit Sen, Reji K. Joseph, Silpa Modi, and Nirmalya Syam. 2008. *Economic Constraints to Access to Essential Medicines in India*. Society for Economic and Social Studies, New Delhi, and Centre for Trade and Development, New Delhi, in collaboration with WHO Country Office India.

Singh, Parvinder. 1988. 'Intellectual Property Rights and the Pharmaceutical Industry', *Conquest by Patent: On Patent Law and Policy*, New Delhi: National Working Group on Patent Laws.

Singh, Satminder. 1985. *Multinational Corporations and Indian Drug Industry*. New Delhi: Criterion Publications.

Smith, Pamela J. 1999. 'Are Weak Patent Rights a Barrier to US Exports?', *Journal of International Economics*, 48: 151–77.

Smith, Sean Eric. 2000. *Opening Up to the World: India's Pharmaceutical Companies Prepare for 2005*, Asia-Pacfic Research Centre, Institute for International Studies, Stanford University, Stanford.

South Centre. 2014. 'Unilateral US Actions Targeting India's Intellectual Property Laws Undermines the Legitimacy of the WTO', South Centre, press release, 4 March 2014, http://www.southcentre.int/wp-content/uploads/2014/03/PRESS-RELEASE_20140304_EN.pdf (accessed on 22 November 2014).

Srinivasan, S., and Anurag Bhargava. 2004. *Impoverishing the Poor: Pharmaceuticals and Drug Pricing in India*. Vadodara: LOCOST/JSS.

Srinivasan, Sandhya, and Sachin Nikarge. 2009. *Ethical Concerns in Clinical Trials in India: An Investigation*. Mumbai: Centre for Studies in Ethics and Rights.

Sukumar, C. R. 2009. 'Suven Life Sciences Plans to Raise Funds for Clinical Trials', *LiveMint*, 17 November, http://www.livemint.com/Companies/h3ehJlloVr2CqbWbsn860O/Suven-Life-Sciences-plans-to-raise-funds-for-clinical-trials.html (accessed on 31 October 2014).

Supreme Court of India. 2013. *Judgement on Novartis AG vs Union of India and Others*, New Delhi, http://supremecourtofindia.nic.in/outtoday/patent.pdf (accessed on 7 October 2014).

Suven Life Sciences. 2014. *Annual Report 2013–14*, http://www.suven.com/Pdf/AnnualReport%202013–14.pdf (accessed on 4 December 2014).

Thakar, V. J. 2010. 'Historical Development of Basic Concepts of Ayurveda from *Veda* up to *Samhita*', *Ayu*, 31(4): 400–402, http://www.ncbi.nlm.nih.gov/pmc/articles/PMC3202268/ (accessed on 31 October 2014).

Thomas, Zakir. 2012. 'Open Source Drug Discovery', presentation at the Consultation on Access to Essential Medicines: Opportunities for

Cooperation among the BRICS and Global South, Research and Information System for Developing Countries and United Nations Development Programme, New Delhi, 21–22 March.

*Times of India*. 2006. '70 Pharma Firms Shut Shop', 24 January, http://timesofindia.indiatimes.com/city/hyderabad/70-pharma-firms-shut-shop/articleshow/1383834.cms (accessed on 17 October 2014).

*Times of Oman*. 2013. 'India: A Pharmaceutical Giant', 15 August, http://www.timesofoman.com/News/Article-20968.aspx (accessed on 11 January 2015).

Tufts CSDD (Center for the Study of Drug Development). 2014. 'Cost to Develop and Win Marketing Approval for a New Drug is $2.6 Billion', 18 November, http://csdd.tufts.edu/news/complete_story/pr_tufts_csdd_2014_cost_study (accessed on 30 December 2014).

Tyabji, Nasir. 2004. 'Gaining Technical Know-How in an Unequal World: Penicillin Manufacture in Nehru's India', *Technology and Culture*, 45(2): 331–49.

UNCTAD (United Nations Conference on Trade and Development). 2011. *World Investment Report 2011: Non-equity Modes of International Production and Development*. Geneva: United Nations.

UNDP (United Nations Development Programme). 2012. 'Anti-counterfeit Laws and Public Health: What to Look Out For'. Discussion Paper, 27 July, http://www.undp.org/content/dam/undp/library/hivaids/English/UNDP%20Discussion%20Paper%20-%20%28revised%29.pdf (accessed on 25 November 2014).

Unnikrishnan, C. H. 2007. 'Blow to Ranbaxy Drug Research Plans', *LiveMint*, 21 September, http://www.livemint.com/Companies/MxfKuYDBf474LLpEnamgMK/Blow-to-Ranbaxy-drugresearchplans.html (accessed on 3 November 2014).

———. 2013. 'Cadila Gets Approval for Diabetic Dyslipidemia Drug', *LiveMint*, 6 June, http://www.livemint.com/Companies/naOLKPOfw5mNnQt76hodiN/Cadila-Healthcare-gets-approval-to-market-diabetes-drug-in-I.html (accessed on 31 October 2014).

———. 2014. 'Piramal to Exit Drug Discovery Business', *LiveMint*, 27 August, http://www.livemint.com/Companies/7weGbimcrdp7lrKH0YaSnL/Piramal-to-exit-drug-discovery-business.html (accessed on 4 December 2014).

Unnikrishnan, C. H., and Ravi Ananthanarayanan. 2014. 'Sanofi Junks Glenmark's Painkiller Molecule', *LiveMint*, 15 May, http://www.livemint.com/Companies/RdthRWQs9wY8NC8h2jVMAP/Sanofi-junks-Glenmarks-painkiller-molecule.html (accessed on 4 December, 2014).

US Department of Justice. 2013. 'Generic Drug Manufacturer Ranbaxy Pleads Guilty and Agrees to Pay $500 Million to Resolve False Claims Allegations, cGMP Violations and False Statements to the FDA', 13 May, Department of Justice, Office of Public Affairs, http://www.justice.gov/

opa/pr/generic-drug-manufacturer-ranbaxy-pleads-guilty-and-agrees-pay-500-million-resolve-false (accessed on 3 November 2014).

USFDA (United States Food and Drug Administration). 2001. Guidance for Industry: Q7A Good Manufacturing Practice Guidance for Active Pharmaceutical Ingredients. Centre for Drug Evaluation and Research and Centre for Biologics Evaluation and Research.

USGAO (United States Government Accountability Office). 2007. 'Intellectual Property: US Trade Policy Guidance on WTO Declaration on Access to Medicines May Need Clarification'. GAO-07-1198, September, http://www.gao.gov/new.items/d071198.pdf (accessed on 24 November 2014).

USIBC (US-India Business Council). 2013. 'The U.S.-India Business Council Expresses Unease over Supreme Court of India's Ruling on Novartis Glivec Case: Seeks Reassurance for Investors', USIBC press release, 2 April, http://www.usibc.com/press-release/us-india-business-council-expresses-unease-over-supreme-court-indias-ruling-novartis (accessed on 21 November 2014).

US Senate. 1961. *Administered Prices, Drugs: Report of the Committee on the Judiciary, United States Senate, Made by Its Subcommittee on Antitrust and Monopoly.* Report No. 448, 87th Congress, 1st Session, Washington, DC.

USTR (United States Trade Representative). 2013. *2013 Special 301 Report*, Executive Office of the President of United States, Washington, DC., http://www.ustr.gov/sites/default/files/05012013%202013%20Special%20301%20Report.pdf (accessed on 21 November 2014).

Watal, Jayasree. 2000. 'Pharmaceutical Patents, Prices and Welfare Losses: A Simulation Study of Policy Options for India under WTO TRIPS Agreement', *World Economy*, 23(5): 733–52.

WHO (World Health Organization). 2012. *World Health Statistics 2012.* Geneva: WHO, http://www.who.int/gho/publications/world_health_statistics/EN_WHS2012_Full.pdf (accessed on 14 November 2014).

——. 2013. *Global Tuberculosis Report 2013.* Geneva: WHO, http://apps.who.int/iris/bitstream/10665/91355/1/9789241564656_eng.pdf (accessed on 27 nber 2014).

Wong, E. V. 2002. 'Inequality and Pharmaceutical Drug Prices: An Empirical Exercise'. Working Paper No. 02–19, University of Colorado at Boulder.

WTO (World Trade Organization). 1994. Uruguay Round Agreement, Marrakesh Declaration, Morroco, 15 April, http://www.wto.org/english/docs_e/legal_e/marrakesh_decl_e.htm (accessed on 1 October 2014).

——. 2001a. Declaration on the Trips Agreement and Public Health, Doha WTO Ministerial Conference, Fourth Session, Doha, 9–14 November, http://www.wto.org/english/thewto_e/minist_e/min01_e/mindecl_trips_e.htm (accessed on 14 November 2014).

——. 2001b. *TRIPS and Public Health*, Submission by the African Group, Barbados, Bolivia, Brazil, Cuba, Dominican Republic, Ecuador, Honduras, India, Indonesia, Jamaica, Pakistan, Paraguay, Philippines, Peru, Sri Lanka,

Thailand and Venezuela, TRIPS Council, Document No. IP/C/W/296, 29 June.

——. 2009. *International Trade Statistics 2009*, http://www.wto.org/english/res_e/statis_e/its2009_e/its2009_e.pdf (accessed on 21 October 2014).

——. 2010. *International Trade Statistics 2010*, http://www.wto.org/english/res_e/statis_e/its2010_e/its10_toc_e.htm (accessed on 14 February 2015).

——. 2012. *International Trade Statistics 2012*, http://www.wto.org/english/res_e/statis_e/its2013_e/its13_toc_e.htm (accessed on 14 February 2015).

——. 2013. *International Trade Statistics 2013*, http://www.wto.org/english/res_e/statis_e/its2013_e/its13_toc_e.htm (accessed on 14 February 2015).

——. 2014. *International Trade Statistics 2014*, http://www.wto.org/english/res_e/statis_e/its2014_e/its14_toc_e.htm (accessed on 14 February 2015).

Zhe, Li, and Guo Lifeng. 2011. 'Development of Biotechnology in China: Key Policies and Priorities', *Asian Biotechnology and Development Review*, 13(1): 1–16.

Zydus Cadila. 2013. 'Zydus Pioneers a Breakthrough with Lipaglyn, India's First NCE to Reach the Market', 5 June, http://www.zyduscadila.com/press/PressNote05–06–13.pdf (accessed on 30 December 2014).

# Index

Printed in the United States
by Baker & Taylor Publisher Services

Printed in the United States
by Baker & Taylor Publisher Services